The Late John Marquand

Books by Stephen Birmingham

THE LATE JOHN MARQUAND
THE GRANDEES
HEART TROUBLES
THE RIGHT PEOPLE
"OUR CROWD"
FAST START, FAST FINISH
THOSE HARPER WOMEN
THE TOWERS OF LOVE
BARBARA GREER
YOUNG MR. KEEFE

The Late John Marquand

A Biography

by

Stephen Birmingham

J. B. LIPPINCOTT COMPANY

Philadelphia and New York

U.S. Library of Congress Cataloging in Publication Data

Birmingham, Stephen.
    The late John Marquand.

    "A John P. Marquand check list": p.
    1. Marquand, John Phillips, 1893–1960. I. Title.
PS3525.A6695Z59   818'.5'209 [B]   76–39182
ISBN–0–397–00886–4

For Jean-Luc Dubois

*C*ontents

*A sixteen-page section of photographs
follows page 178.*

*I*ntroduction

I FIRST MET John P. Marquand in the summer of 1957. He was sixty-three, and I was in my twenties. I had published a handful of articles and short stories in magazines, and he was one of the most successful and celebrated novelists in America, the winner of a Pulitzer Prize in fiction, the author of what were considered some of the best novels of social comedy and social politics in the country, a twentieth-century Thackeray.

Our coming together was quite accidental. I had just completed the manuscript of my first novel and had delivered it, on a Friday morning, to the office of Carl Brandt, who was my literary agent, and who also represented Marquand and a number of other authors. I had not realized that, a few days earlier, Brandt had been taken to a hospital and was seriously ill.

What happened, as I learned later, was that my manuscript was picked up by Carl's wife, Carol, and taken home to their apartment, where John Marquand, down from Newburyport to see the Brandts, was staying. My manuscript was placed in a pile with other unread material. The next day, after a worried night and a visit to the hospital, Marquand said to

Carol Brandt, "Look, there's nothing we can accomplish just sitting around here worrying. Let's get to work. Give me something to read." Carol handed him the manuscript of my first novel. I am told that after reading the first thirty pages, he put the script down and said, "This is very bad," but that he picked up the script again, read another thirty pages, and said, "You know, this is pretty good." On Sunday, Carol telephoned me at my home to say, "I've had an unpaid reader reading your manuscript this week end. His name is John Marquand, and he'd like to talk to you."

I shall never forget the next afternoon in the Brandts' apartment when we met. We sat in the library over gin and tonics, and John offered me suggestions to remedy the trouble in the first thirty pages—mostly a matter of heavy blue-penciling. His other comments were remarkably vivid. He felt, for example, that when I shifted from one period of fictional time to another, my transitions were too abrupt. "Ease the reader into these time changes by adding a sentence or two," he told me. My chapter openings tended, by contrast, to be too leisurely, and he recommended that I cut sentences in these. I also had, he pointed out, the beginning writer's habit of being overly adverbial, particularly in my dialogue, and in this connection he suddenly stood up and launched into one of his famous—though I had never heard of them—verbal parodies. Pacing about the room, glass in hand, screwing his face into appropriate grimaces and flinging his free hand about in exaggerated gestures, he was "writing" a nonsense novel in which every line of dialogue was accompanied by a descriptive adverb:

> "Have you fed the baby?" she inquired mincingly.
> "No," replied Leopold, chortling cynically.
> "Why not?" she expostulated judiciously, lifting her face to his haltingly.

And so it went. It was a performance such as I had never seen or heard before, and it had me choking with laughter. If John Marquand had been unable to make a living as a novelist—an unlikely possibility at that point—he could have done so as a night club stand-up comic. At the same time, I have seldom since put an adverb on paper without thinking about that afternoon. "If your dialogue is good enough, it will stand on its own feet," he said. "You don't have to explain the tone of voice to the reader. All the reader needs to know is who said it, with 'he said,' or 'she said.' " It was all good and welcome advice. But the best thing he said that afternoon was, "I'd like, if you'll let me, to take this novel to my publisher."

He did, and it was published the following spring. He generously also produced a blurb for the book's jacket, a thing he hardly ever did—indeed, a thing he disapproved of authors' doing. It was even he who selected the title of the book, *Young Mr. Keefe.* ("Keep your titles simple; don't use words readers won't know how to pronounce. People are interested in people, and so names are good to use in titles.")

That afternoon at the Brandt apartment continued until dinnertime, and I was asked to remain for dinner. The evening lasted, in fact, until it was time to walk the dog. I saw John often after that, both socially and in a working sense. I do not wish to imply that I was in any way a protégé of John P. Marquand, but he served me as an informal editor and adviser on two novels and was waiting to read a third which I had not finished when he died. As John knew from his own experience, a young writer needs all the help he can get, and he was that help to me. I was therefore especially pleased when I was asked to write his biography.

As I researched this book, talking to as many men and women who knew Marquand as I could uncover, I inevitably encountered incidents and anecdotes that required, in order to relate them, direct quotation of John Marquand's spoken words. Since memory is, at best, a faulty instrument, it is impossible for me, or for anyone else, to say with any certainty that these quoted words represent exactly what Marquand said on this or that occasion. And so in every case I have put down what people recall his having said to the best of their recollections. In some cases, his words are to the best of my own recollections. He had a vivid speaking style. Not to attempt to capture it would be to evade an important aspect of his personality. If I have failed to capture it, I alone am at fault.

There are a number of people who have been helpful, and

exceptionally so. I would like to thank Mr. Robert Beverly Hale and Mr. Thomas Shaw Hale, both of New York, who are John's cousins, for their recollections of the Hale-Marquand family compound, Curzon's Mill, in Newburyport. I would like to thank Mr. and Mrs. Charles A. Lindbergh of Darien; John's old friend Mr. Edward Streeter of New York; Mr. Herbert R. Mayes of London, one of John's favorite editors; Mr. King Vidor of Los Angeles, with whom John worked on the film version of *H. M. Pulham, Esquire.*

Words of appreciation must also go to Mr. Philip Hamburger of New York, whose brilliant parody profile of "J. P. Marquand, Esquire" appeared in *The New Yorker* in 1952, and Miss Lillian Hellman of New York, who, though she did not know the subject well, retained impressions of two meetings with him. Mr. John J. Gross's book, *John P. Marquand,* was another helpful source. I am grateful too to Mr. E. Dickenson Griffenberg of Wilmington for letting me consult his scholarly thesis; to Mr. Melvin Johnson of the *Boston Globe* for supplying clips and files; to Mr. George Merck, Jr., of Far Hills, New Jersey, whose father was another close friend of John Marquand's; to John's friends Meredith and Helen Wood of Scarsdale, and to Mr. Meredith Wood, Jr., of the same city, who captured several of John's celebrated verbal performances on tape. Professor William H. White of Wayne State University was helpful with his thorough bibliography of Marquand's works.

I am also indebted to Mrs. Anne Kaufman Schneider of New York for her memories of the happy collaboration between Marquand and her father, George S. Kaufman, on the stage version of *The Late George Apley.* I am grateful to two of John Marquand's former editors at Little, Brown, Mr. Stanley Salmen of New York and Mr. Alexander Williams of Boston, for their insights and recollections. Thanks are due too to Messrs. Carl D. Brandt, the late Ewen MacVeagh, Warren Lynch, Leonard Lyons, and Evan W. Thomas III of New York; Mr. Brooks Potter and Miss Anne Ford of Boston, Mr. R. Minturn Sedgwick of Dedham, Mr. William Otis and Professor Roy Lamson of Cambridge, Massachusetts. John's publisher, the late Arthur Thornhill senior of Boston, was both encouraging and helpful. In Pinehurst, North Carolina, where John spent many winter months, a number of his friends, golfing companions, and former employees were helpful with reminiscences, including Mr. and Mrs. John Ostrom, Mr. George Shearwood, Mrs. Donald Parson, Mrs. Curtis Gary, Miss Mary Evalyn de Nisoff, Mr. Floyd Ray, and Mr. Robert ("Hard Rock") Robinson. Each of these people has been helpful with anecdotes, insights, memories, opinions.

It goes without saying that I am overwhelmingly grateful to John's friend and literary agent, Carol Brandt, who, happily, has been my friend and agent also, and who has been pivotal to this book.

As she has done with three previous books of mine, Miss Genevieve Young of Lippincott has edited this book, using her exceptionally fine mind and customary fine-toothed comb.

I would also like to thank my three children, Mark, Harriet, and Carey, for considerably lowering the volume of their collective six stereo speakers when they hear the sounds of my typewriter, and last of all my wife, Nan, who types, reads, queries with an instinctive good sense, and has otherwise lived through the book all the way.

S. B.

PART ONE

Some Beginnings

Chapter One

They stood in the empty entrance hall of an enormous post-Victorian monstrosity of a house and roared with laughter, these three old and good friends who had shared so much, professionally as well as emotionally, over the years. The three were the author John Marquand, then at the height of his career, holder of a Pulitzer Prize for fiction; his literary agent, Carl Brandt; and Brandt's wife, Carol. Of that merry threesome, only one, Carol Brandt, is living now.

It was an afternoon of high hilarity. After all, what was one to make of such a house? To laugh at it was the kindest way to treat it. Outside, it had pillars, a porte-cochere, everything but a flying buttress; inside, a huge dark-paneled living room the size of a ballroom. It was overpoweringly ugly. And it was almost inherent in the house—part of the whole ludicrous joke —that it should have been another exploit, another ridiculous enterprise, of Adelaide Marquand, John's second wife.

"Poor Adelaide," as people had begun to say. Of course one could not call Adelaide Ferry Hooker Marquand poor, exactly. Her father had been president and principal owner of the Hooker Electrochemical Company, and, on her mother's side, she was an heiress to the Ferry Seed Company money. Seeds and chemicals—these always struck John Marquand as a droll combination of products to have made his wife a rich woman. Whenever he ridiculed her, which was often these days, he enjoyed bringing up the fact that she had "seed money."

Furthermore, not only was Adelaide rich but she was surrounded by relations who were even richer. One of her three sisters, Blanchette, was Mrs. John D. Rockefeller III, another fact that John Marquand liked to point out when anyone displayed anything that bordered on pity for "poor Adelaide." But Adelaide had done a number of brash and aberrant things in recent months, and this was by far the most peculiar. Why would a wife buy, without consulting her husband—without even hinting that this was her intention—a new house for them to live in, particularly a house of this one's grotesque pretentiousness? Could she possibly have expected her husband to be pleased? On the contrary, when he learned of his wife's purchase, John Marquand, as any male might be, was furious. It was the early autumn of 1953, and Marquand, at sixty, was still recuperating from a heart attack, itself a fairly sobering experience, and one for which he indirectly blamed his wife and the trials she had been putting him through.

Since the attack he had purposely avoided seeing her, securing himself in his house at Kent's Island, in Newburyport, with Anna, an ancient and deaf retainer of the Hookers who had a year to work before she qualified for Social Security; with a nurse, Miss Malquinn; and with his younger daughter, Ferry. Those had been peaceful days during that early recovery period, with three pairs of feminine hands to tend him, but all that peace disappeared from Kent's Island when Adelaide informed him that she had bought a new house in Cambridge and had entered the children at the Shady Hill School. To Carl Brandt, Marquand had commented tersely that he doubted he would join the little group for many months—if ever.

Actually, for some time before the heart attack Marquand had been thinking of buying a house in Boston and had been talking, a trifle wistfully, of returning to his "roots" there. His roots were technically not in Boston—he had been born elsewhere—but over the years he had come to think of himself as a Bostonian, by rights as well as by nature. He had tried to establish his home in many places—New York, Hobe Sound, Aspen, Nassau—but to no purpose; he always came back to Boston. Most recently he had been shuttling back and forth between a New York apartment and Kent's Island. But he was weary of the New York pace, and Kent's Island was inconvenient in the heavy winter. One could be snowed in there for days. So he had been dreaming of owning one of the old bow-front brick houses in the quiet of Beacon Hill, houses whose purpled leaded-glass windows address the slope of the Common and the pools of the Public Garden, or perhaps a house on elegant, gaslit Louisburg Square, the setting of what is perhaps Marquand's most famous novel, *The Late George Apley,* all within walking distance of his beloved Somerset Club—in *Apley* he called it the Province Club. The provincialism of Old World Boston was something that both amused and comforted him.

But this preposterous house of Adelaide's was light years away from Beacon Hill. It was across the Charles River in unhilly Cambridge, at 1 Reservoir Street—even the address was offensive—in a bustling town where Harvard and M.I.T. students were underfoot wherever one went and nights were noisy with beer-hall laughter and dormitory record players. As for the house itself, nothing could have seemer farther from the Bulfinchian understatement Marquand had in mind than this architectural product of the Taft Administration. Number One Reservoir Street, Marquand commented slyly, gave one a good idea of what the reservoir was filled with.

Adelaide, of course, had doubtless just been trying—once more, after so many attempts—to show her husband that she loved him. She had bought this house (later, she would turn the vast living room into a kind of Marquand museum, with a bust of her husband, portraits, and copies of all his books, to record his literary fame and achievement) as a gift of love, a gift expressed, to be sure, in her own curiously heavy-handed and unfeeling terms.

In many ways, this was a typical Adelaide purchase, undertaken apparently without thought or reason, like the tweed deerstalker's cap she had bought him as a birthday present.

"My Sherlock Holmes hat," he would say, displaying it to friends. How could she have expected Marquand, whose taste in clothes ran to Boston-banker conservative, ever to put on such a hat? Whenever Adelaide wanted to buy something for herself, she might or she might not mention it to her husband beforehand. If she did, John—who possessed the Yankee sense of thrift to an extreme degree—would frequently insist that they could not afford whatever it was. Adelaide would then say airily, "Well, then *I'll* pay for it, John," and off she would go to buy it. She could never seem to understand why this sort of behavior would hurt and anger him. In recent years, since her mother's "seed" money had come down to her, her spending had escalated sharply. She bought compulsively, incessantly. John had given up on her.

Adelaide's acquisitiveness and stubbornness had also, a few years earlier, been responsible for an embarrassing lawsuit between Marquand and his first cousins, the Hales of Newburyport. John had lost the case and, as a result of the bitterness it stirred up, the Hale cousins, once his good friends as well, no longer spoke to him.

And now, on this autumn day in 1953, the Marquands' marriage had deteriorated to such a state that there was barely any communication between them. A few weeks earlier, Marquand had written to the Brandts in New York suggesting that he meet them in Boston for the week end, as soon as his doctor gave him permission. They would make a party of it, a kind of celebration of John's release from doctors' care. They would all stay at the Ritz-Carlton, and the high point of the reunion would be when the three friends drove over to Cambridge to inspect the house that his wife had bought. Naturally they would pick a time when Adelaide and the children were far away in Aspen. Now, in September, the moment was at hand. Carol Brandt came up on a Friday evening train, and Carl Brandt joined them on Saturday.

From the outset, the week end had been gloriously mirthful. Marquand and the Brandts set themselves up in an adjoining pair of the Ritz's famous suites, all of which contain—in addition to other amenities that have long since disappeared from American hotel-keeping elsewhere—wood-burning fireplaces in the sitting rooms. The three had thrown open the connecting doors so that the partying could be general, back and forth, and Marquand, after the slow weeks of recovery, was in top form. It was he who set the tone of the gathering, which was one of mockery mixed with spite. "Adelaide," he said, "*Adelaide*"—thrusting a sneer into the very pronunciation of her name—"it seems that *Adelaide* has purchased another *house*."

He struck a characteristic pose. Standing, drink in hand, he hunched forward, scowling darkly with beetled brows and pursed lips, and clapped his other hand to the back of his neck, gripping it as though he feared his head might be about to fly from its perch between his shoulders. In this pose, he paced the floor, back and forth—fireplace to window, window to fireplace. "A *house*. Which. We. Are. About. To. See!" A footfall accompanied each word and, as his nasal New Englander's voice spat out each syllable, his voice rose in pitch until the final syllable came out almost as falsetto, while the pink color came in his cheeks.

It was a stage performance, of course. Whenever he had an audience, particularly an audience of friends, he loved to perform these oral concertos. He had taught himself this exaggerated, theatrical delivery, and he did it well. He had become famous for the way he could hold a roomful of people as he told a story or delivered an anecdote, celebrated for the way he could build himself into a tower of mock rage over an apparent trifle. His imitations of people, particularly of the styles of other authors (he could do Hawthorne, Melville, James Fenimore Cooper, as well as any number of three-named lady writers), were incisive, cruel, and hilarious. But this afternoon in Boston, the fact that the target of his wit and venom was his own wife made his performance a particularly telling one. Though Carl and Carol Brandt were, at this point, no fonder of Adelaide than John was, it was hard to know, watching his dreadful parody of the woman, whether to laugh or weep.

In the car going over to Cambridge, he continued his verbal assaults on, and imitations of, Adelaide—Adelaide who was now drinking more than she should, who had allowed herself to become much too fat, who could never seem to get herself anywhere on time, though John was a stickler for punctuality;

Adelaide who dressed all wrong for her size, who got herself up in Indian costumes and peasant skirts with ruffled gypsy blouses, puffed sleeves, and little lace-up vests coming apart at the seams; Adelaide who had never been exactly pretty to begin with, and whose wild mass of ash-blonde hair now never seemed to be properly arranged. "Listening to John attack Adelaide that afternoon was like watching a woman being buried alive," Carol Brandt said later.

All over again, because he didn't mind repeating himself, John told the Brandts his story about Adelaide in New York at the Colony Club. It seemed that John and Adelaide had arrived at the Colony Club for some function, and Adelaide, who had made them late as usual, had dismounted from the taxi and, as was her habit, marched imperiously toward the front door without waiting for her husband to offer her his arm. The doorman had stepped quickly toward Mrs. John P. Marquand, wife of one of America's foremost novelists, sister-in-law of John D. Rockefeller III, daughter of a multimillionaire industrialist and a direct descendant of Thomas Hooker, seventeenth-century founder of Hartford, Connecticut, and said to her, "Sorry, lady, the service entrance is on the side." It was one of John Marquand's favorite stories about his wife.

Now the three friends were all in the front hall of 1 Reservoir Street, Cambridge, and Marquand had already seen enough. He wanted no more. The physical ugliness of the house repelled him. How could Adelaide possibly have found such a place remotely attractive? Because of his heart attack, he announced, he didn't want to climb the stairs to see the rooms above. Carl Brandt, who suffered from emphysema, also said that he didn't care enough to go up to the upper floors. And so Carol Brandt, who decided that John ought at least to know what the rest of the house was like, started up the stairs alone.

"There was a great curving staircase that went up from the center of the hall," Carol Brandt recalled later, "and on each floor there were balconies and overhangs. The upstairs rooms were all arranged around this central stair well. As I went up and around and into the various rooms, I would come back to the stair well and call down to the men below, trying to describe, as a journalist would, what was up there." Carol Brandt, a tall, striking woman then in her forties, is a woman of precision and efficiency. She is also a woman of extraordinary effectiveness. For a number of years, she herself was a literary agent with a distinguished list of clients and, following that, she was the highly paid East Coast story editor for Metro-Goldwyn-Mayer and the then studio head, Louis B. Mayer. Mutual friends of Marquand and Carol Brandt have long insisted that she was the real-life model for the beautiful and well-organized advertising lady, Marvin Myles, in Marquand's novel *H. M. Pulham, Esquire*—at which assertion Carol has always smiled and said, "John took many of his characters from the people he knew."

Of the Cambridge house that afternoon she has said, "The house was so grotesque that even though I tried to be very accurate about what I found in each room, the two men downstairs simply wouldn't believe that what I was telling them was the truth. There was a gun room on the third floor, for instance, and though the house was enormous there was a curious shortage of bathrooms. As I recall, there were only three. One of these had an enormous sunken marble tub that one had to climb down three steps to get into. And as I described each of these rooms and features of the house, John and Carl below kept calling back, 'No! You're joking! There *couldn't* be a sunken bathtub.' I couldn't convince them that I was absolutely serious."

All the way back to Boston, John Marquand kept muttering about the absurd house, absurd Adelaide, and the whole absurdity their marriage had become. The previous winter he had gone off alone to his island retreat in the Bahamas, just to be away from her, and now she had bought this hideous piece of real estate as some sort of gesture of conciliation. For some reason, of all the details of the house the sunken bathtub struck him as the worst, the most atrocious example of her tastelessness, of her pretentiousness, of his wife in one of her triumphs of mischief-making and of making him look ridiculous. "There *couldn't* be a sunken bathtub," he kept repeating. "Carol, promise me you were teasing about the sunken bathtub."

Back in the cool elegance of the Ritz-Carlton, drinks were

quickly poured. John Marquand liked to drink. So did the
Brandts. All three loved the Ritz, and John had often marveled
over the Ritz's charming eccentricities, such as the curiously
worded sign over the main entrance to the hotel which read, in
large crimson letters, "NOT AN ACCREDITED EGRESS
DOOR." This particular week end an awed assistant manager
had explained to John Marquand that the suite he was occu-
pying had recently been used by Mrs. Frances Parkinson
Keyes; she had lived there while working on one of her bosomy
best sellers, and the hotel manager proudly showed John a
plaque that had been placed within the suite attesting to this
signal honor. Mrs. Keyes, not one of his favorite authors, was
among the three-named lady novelists whose styles John could
parody. Could anyone imagine, he wanted to know, a more
incongruous juxtaposition than Frances Parkinson Keyes and
the Boston Ritz-Carlton Hotel?

John Marquand had a characteristic gesture. He would seize
his drink, curve his fist around it, and then begin swinging the
glass in rapid, determined circles in front of him as he spoke.
Talking now, swinging his glass, taking the center of the stage
once more—as, of course, he rather liked to do—he was back on
the subject of the Cambridge house all over again, doing a
parody of Carol's description of the rooms. Soon everyone was
convulsed with laughter. Suddenly John paused dramatically,
as he was very good at doing, and announced to the little
group, "I will—never—never—ever—*ever* live in that house,
so help me God." And he flung his hand heavenward.

But of course he did live in the house—though never for
very long, and never very happily. His marriage to Adelaide
would survive another five stormy years. Life is full of failed
promises and the need to compromise, as characters in Marquand's novels are repeatedly discovering. One must, as Marquand heroes are forever reminding themselves, learn to adapt
and adjust to circumstances, and in most cases such adjust-
ments are solitary ones, and solutions are second-best. In John
Marquand's last and most autobiographical novel, *Women and
Thomas Harrow*, the title character makes, in a final scene, an
abortive, half-unconscious, half-intentional attempt to commit
suicide by driving his automobile—a Cadillac—off the road

and over a high cliff above the sea. Tom Harrow does no more than crush a front fender against a fence post. While quietly congratulating himself, just as Marquand might have done, on the value of driving an expensive car, Harrow confronts a state trooper who witnessed the accident. The trooper asks Harrow if he can drive home alone. Harrow answers that he can, thinking wistfully, "In the end, no matter how many were in the car, you always drove alone."

But having to agree to live, after all, in the house of his wife's folly must have seemed to the late John Marquand a form of surrender, much like other situations and moments in his life when the very things he wanted the most (Adelaide, for one, to say nothing of his first wife, the beautiful Christina Sedgwick) had a way, once he attained them (his great financial success, his popularity, the Pulitzer Prize) of rising up against him, and mocking him, and defeating him.

Chapter Two

*T*hroughout his life, John Marquand liked to make the point that much of his childhood and young manhood had been hard and poor. A young man's struggle, against overwhelming odds, to achieve social and career success is a recurring theme in his books. Marquand was an exceptionally frugal, even tightfisted, man who counted pennies and appeared to hate to spend money, which was odd since he had an obvious taste for luxury and the trappings of wealth. New Englanders are traditionally thrifty, but Marquand's preoccupation with thrift and spending was almost neurotic—if, of course, one was to take him seriously. He blamed his attitudes on early poverty. "My father's greatest talent seemed to be a talent for losing money," he would remind his friends. "When he finally lost it all, there was no more money for anything."

Outwardly, at least, money obsessed Marquand. He claimed to disapprove of tipping and, when he was required to tip, he did so in miserly fashion. He once had a violent scene with a woman he loved over an air-mail stamp. To keep himself from spending money he adopted the practice, like that of royalty, of carrying no money on his person. As a result, he was a slight annoyance to his friends, who were forever having to make him small loans.

He would arrive from New York for a visit with the Gardiner H. Fiskes of Boston, and he would then have to borrow money from Gardi Fiske for the train fare home. He was forever having to mail the tiny sums back to Gardi—once it was a dollar that Gardi had advanced him for a guppy aquarium that had caught his eye. One evening during those years which he liked to refer to as "The Adelaide Period," and those were years when both Marquands had plenty of money, he and Adelaide were returning from a costume party on Long Island where they had gone dressed as Bedouins, and neither of them had enough money to pay the toll at the Triborough Bridge. It took some persuasion to get the Bedouins through the gate without paying.

When Marquand traveled, he tried to arrange, wherever possible, to stay with friends, thus avoiding hotel bills. When forced to stay in hotels, he indulged in a variety of petty economies. He would go down in the morning to the hotel newsstand to buy a newspaper because, he pointed out, it cost a dime more to have it delivered to the room.

At the same time, he was able to laugh at the excesses of Yankee stinginess that he observed around him. He liked to tell the story of the Back Bay couple he had watched splitting a stick of chewing gum, the wife saying to her husband, "Save the wrapper. We might find a use for it." Yet he himself could behave in a way that was every bit as penurious. For several years he and Adelaide owned a winter house at Hobe Sound in Florida, and one chilly afternoon his house guests—the Cedric Gibbonses and Philip Barry—suggested that a fire in the fireplace might be in order. Marquand muttered that firewood was "too expensive" and said that a perfectly acceptable fire could be built using coconuts picked up on the beach. An appropriate number of coconuts was gathered, the fire was lit, and a few minutes later coconuts were exploding noisily and messily all around the room.

Marquand's divorce settlement with Christina, his first wife, had been acrimonious and ungenerous, and still he complained that Christina had "milked" much more out of him than was

her due. After the divorce, when Marquand had moved down
to New York to live, he suspected Christina of "shouting
around Boston" that he had ill-used her financially. In all, he
explained, Christina had extracted from him some $8,400 for
alimony and support; at the same time, his father had come to
him for another $1,000 to cover the latter's gambling debts. He
felt, he told the Fiskes, almost as poor as when he had first
embarked on his writing career.

It was the mid-Depression year of 1936, and he had actually
earned over $57,000. The year before he had earned $45,000,
and the year before that $49,000. Still, in 1936, he complained
of having paid out $15,000 altogether for the two children.
That year he also bought and started to remodel a cozy farmhouse at the edge of a salt marsh on Kent's Island outside Newburyport, even though he bemoaned the fact that the remodeling seemed to be costing him more than twice the amount of
the highest estimate. He would smite his forehead and shake
his head in mock fury and dismay at the duplicity of women,
the extravagances of children, and the cupidity of carpenters,
all of whom had helped create what he claimed was his financial plight.

Marquand could work himself up into rages in his mind, just
as he could on his feet in the center of a room with an audience
of friends. You could tell when one of his explosions was building up inside him because he would sit very still, staring pur-
posefully into space, his lower jaw working slightly and his
face reddening. It was always a surprise when he got to the
point of blurting out what was angering him, but as often as
not the subject had something to do with money. Philip Hamburger, who profiled John Marquand for *The New Yorker*,
spent many hours observing and interviewing him and learned
to recognize when one of these inner volcanoes was building
up to the point of eruption. Still, Hamburger was completely
taken off guard one afternoon in Newburyport when, riding
with Marquand in his car, the author abruptly slammed on his
brakes, drew the car to a jolting halt in the middle of a country
road, and, banging his fist against the steering wheel, cried out,
*"And God damn it! My wife's sister is Mrs. John D. Rockefeller
the Third!"*

John Marquand would perhaps have preferred to have been born John D. Rockefeller III, or so he suggested, and it was the sole fault of his "papa" that he was not—or, again, so he said. Marquand, after all, was a writer of fiction who could view himself as a character in his own fiction. To say that he lied about his past would be unfair, since when has truth had all that much to do with fiction? But, just as he did with his present circumstances and the people around him, he created for himself a semifictive past, turning it into drama, into the stuff of art and dreams and the imagination, removing it in the process from the stuff of life. And in the story as he told it, the villain was most often his father, Philip Marquand.

Chapter Three

*P*hilip Marquand, whom everyone called Phil, was a small, trim, athletic man—he had been featherweight boxing champion of the Class of 1889 at Harvard—who cut quite a dashing figure as he walked about town swinging a gold-tipped walking stick. In his prime, Phil Marquand had been a great favorite with the ladies, but he also had an intellectual side and a serious bent for scholarship. At Harvard, he had been a splendid student and had been elected to Phi Beta Kappa. He was, to every outward appearance, the perfect Victorian gentleman, cultivated, correct, respectably affluent.

In terms of breeding and pedigree, which matter greatly to men like Phil Marquand, his credentials were faultless. There had been Marquands in New England, Phil would remind his only son, since 1732, when Daniel Marquand had arrived in the seaport town of Newburyport from the Isle of Guernsey. Daniel Marquand had prospered. So had his son, Joseph Marquand, who developed a large and successful fleet of privateer vessels that plied the Atlantic in the years before, during, and after the American Revolution. It was said that Joseph Marquand became so rich that his wealth became an embarrassment to his Puritan nature. He would pray, "Lord, stay Thine hand, Thy servant hath enough." Perhaps as a result of this entreaty his prayers were answered, and he lost his entire fortune.

The Marquand family affairs had taken a turn for the better by Phil's father's generation. John Phillips Marquand, John Marquand's grandfather, after whom he was named, was a prosperous New York stockbroker and investment banker. One of the stories in the family was that Grandpa Marquand was a man who placed such a high price on dignity and grandeur that, when he realized that his death was at hand, he summoned his valet and requested that he be dressed in evening clothes, saying that he did not intend to meet his Maker in anything less than formal attire.

This elegant gentleman married Margaret Curzon—the Curzons were a family of New England Brahmins and intellectuals—and there were six Marquand children: Joseph, Mary—whom everyone called "Aunt Mollie"—Elizabeth ("Aunt Bessie"), Phil, Russell, and Margaret. After John Phillips Marquand had been presented, properly attired, to the Almighty, and his will was read, it was discovered that he had left an estate amounting to about half a million dollars, which in the year 1900, before income or inheritance taxes had even been thought of, was a princely sum. The six Marquand children each received equal bequests, but the deceased's will directed that the boys were to get their inheritance outright, while the girls were to receive theirs in a trust that has remained unbroken to this day. Phil Marquand took his money and headed immediately for Wall Street, where he purchased a seat on the New York Stock Exchange. Within a year, he had lost both—the seat and most of his inheritance. John Marquand was a boy of eight.

Phil's problem was that he was a gambler. Gambling had come to possess him the way drink can possess the alcoholic. Why Phil's father had never noticed the self-destructive trait in his son's character, and had not tied a few precautionary strings to his son's inheritance, is a mystery. There had certainly been enough warning signals. For a while before his death Phil's father had tried to set his son up in the bond busi-

ness, where Phil displayed a steady losing streak. He would
lose because, whenever he won, he would pool his winnings
into one big speculative venture, and then the winnings would
be gone. Phil Marquand seemed aware of his unfortunate habit
and would shrug off his losses philosophically enough—and
then immediately embark on another get-rich-quick scheme.

Phil Marquand must indeed have been a trial, but he was
blessed in at least one regard. He had a wife who was strong-
willed, tough-minded, devoted to him, and above all loyal. She
was the former Margaret Fuller, named after her aunt, the
celebrated feminist and Transcendentalist who later became
the Marchioness Ossoli. New England's Fuller family is ancient
and eminent. For generations, the Fullers have provided Massachusetts with scholars, statesmen, and scientists (including
R. Buckminster Fuller, the engineer who created the geodesic
dome), and have decorated the New Hampshire coastal resort
of Little Boar's Head with their stately summer homes and the
beautiful Fuller Gardens, a public park. From the social standpoint, which mattered so much, the Fullers were even better
connected than the Marquands. Margaret Fuller Marquand
was a woman with an enormous intellectual drive, a capacity
to endure hardships without faltering or complaint, and the
aristocratic ability to rise to occasions.

For the first few years of John Marquand's life, particularly
those first seven prior to his grandfather's death, the little
family's existence was comfortable, pleasant, servant-protected,
and seemly. There was still all that money in the background.
To be sure, there were a number of moves about the American
landscape as, in addition to the bond business, Phil's father
tried pointing him in other career directions. After Harvard,
Phil had taken an engineering degree at M.I.T., and so there
was a period during which he worked as a civil engineer for
the American Bridge Company in Wilmington; that was how
John Marquand happened to be born there and not—as he
often said he *should* have been born—in Boston. Then there
were subsequent moves, first back to Newburyport, next to a
house on Pinckney Street in Boston, then to Concord, then to a
house at 51 East 30th Street in New York's fashionable Murray
Hill. Then there was a big house on the then-fashionable Bos-

ton Post Road in suburban Rye, a house that still stands and has become a nursing home. Rye was a far cry from the split-level, commuter-bedroom town it has become. It was a heavily wooded village of big estates that overlooked Long Island Sound, and among the Marquands' neighbors were the aristocratic Stuyvesants, Wainwrights, and Roger Shermans.

The growing-up years in Rye must have been particularly pleasant. Certainly they seemed so in retrospect to John Marquand since, as in any retrospective view, it was always possible to edit the vision, to concentrate on the hours that were comfortable and happy, and to erase from the canvas any ominous storm clouds that may have been gathering on a not-too-distant horizon. There was a big barn behind the house, and a horse called Prince, and a carriage and coachman to drive Phil Marquand, the Westchester squire, to the railroad station in the proper style.

There was a nurse for little John—no other children to share her attentions—and there was a cook in the kitchen to prepare the meals, a waitress to serve, and a lady's maid for Mrs. Marquand. There was a man in the garden to rake the graveled walks and driveways and to trim the tall hedges. Automobiles were a rarity in those days, but Phil Marquand had one, a two-passenger Orient Buckboard with its motor placed up behind the driver's seat. So there were Sunday drives, frightening all the horses along the way as they went, causing the neighbors to look up from their verandas and say, "There go the Marquands!" There were trips to the American Yacht Club to watch the week-end sailing races, or to the beach club for tennis or a swim or a stroll among parasoled ladies who nodded and smiled and acknowledged the attractive family. There was tea with honey in a gazebo, and a sense of gaiety and luxury and permanence that one might easily have supposed would last forever. Phil Marquand was losing money, but there was seemingly a bottomless supply.

It was an era so recent and yet so far past that it seems quaint in the description. It was a time in which certain things counted, and in which one counted on certain things. It was a period that was very English Colonial in feeling, and where the concept of Society, in the English sense, was not only accepted but stressed. One talked seriously of who the people of Quality were, who were gentry and who were not. Both blood and breeding mattered. Anything English was admired. Harvard was considered socially better than Yale because Harvard was designed along the lines of an English university and laid out in a town called Cambridge along a tree-lined river that looked very much like the Cam. To prepare for Harvard, there was Groton, which had been developed just a few years earlier in an unabashed attempt to copy such English public schools as Eton and Harrow, to educate the sons of American ladies and gentlemen, to sift the gentlefolk from the proletariat.

Copies of *Country Life* were placed on bedside candlestands, and English sporting scenes were hung on walls. There were even those people who displayed pictures of the Queen—Victoria, of course—and who gathered their children after meals to sing Kipling verses by the parlor spinet. Most important, there were Upper and there were Lower classes, and each class dressed and spoke and acted its part. The maid was called "Mary," and her mistress was "Madam." Gardeners doffed their caps and tugged at their forelocks when the Master and the Madam passed grandly by.

It was in this ambiance that John Marquand spent his early youth—rolling a hoop with a stick, under his Nanny's attentive eye among the hollyhocks, in a garden where it was perpetually summertime. Or so he later remembered and described it. As he used to say, "I was just a little boy living comfortably with my parents, and the rug was pulled out from under me."

The final blow, after losing his Stock Exchange seat, fell upon Phil Marquand half a dozen years later in the financial panic of 1907. As usual, Phil had been heavily "in the market." But this time his losses were the most grievous they had ever been, and overnight everything was lost. John Marquand was now a slender and handsome boy of fourteen. Already the ways of the rich had begun to hold a special fascination for him. He had been able to study them from two aspects, as an observer and as a participant. But now all at once he could be neither. There could be no more big house in Rye, no more servants, no more Sunday strolls to the beach and the tennis courts, no more of any of the pleasures and pastimes he had learned not only to love but to expect.

For several weeks after the panic, life was a disheveled affair for the little family as the Marquands tried to reassemble themselves and see where they stood. As usual, when misfortunes of this sort happened, John's father withdrew into silence, into a kind of towering sulk. "Damn it, I won't talk about it!" Phil Marquand would say, and that would be that. And so it was time for John's mother to take over and show her Yankee and Fuller grit.

It used to be said of Margaret Marquand that she "thought like a man," and in this case she certainly was required to, for there were a number of manlike decisions to be made. She pointed out to her husband that he still had his engineering degree from M.I.T. and that there were engineering jobs opening up throughout the still-expanding country, particularly in California. Phil would apply for one of these, and Margaret would accompany her husband to the West Coast. Until financial affairs were stable again, young John would go to live with two of his father's sisters, both maiden ladies, at the old family homestead outside Newburyport, called Curzon's Mill after John Marquand's great-grandfather, Samuel Curzon, who had bought the place in 1820. John's mother took him to Newburyport late in the summer of 1907 and arranged for him to enter Newburyport High School that fall. She then departed to join her husband in California.

Life at Curzon's Mill was very different from life in Rye. To begin with, there was the place itself, a forty-seven-acre tract of rolling and lovely though inferior farmland surrounded by groves of birch, oak, and white pine, lying between the tidal washes of the Merrimack and Artichoke rivers. The property consisted of three main buildings, all in a similar state of neglect and disrepair. There was the old gristmill itself, built in 1846 to grind corn with grindstones powered by the rise and fall of the tides on the Artichoke but no longer used except for storage of old family books and papers. There was what was known as the Red Brick House, a house without any great architectural distinction that various Marquand cousins shared during the summer months. Then there was the Yellow House, the pride of Curzon's Mill. The Yellow House was big and rambling, with eleven bedrooms with huge bay windows that jutted out from one side to overlook both rivers, with a square and stolid center chimney, and doorways hung with wisteria and rambler roses and banked with ancient forsythia bushes. The front part of the Yellow House, in the Federal style, was the oldest and had been built in 1782 as a hunting lodge for a rich man from Marblehead. Later generations had added rooms and ells and gables and porches to the rear. Inside, the Yellow House creaked and sagged and had the old and sleepy smell of more than a century of people who had lived and died there. Rooms opened on other rooms through a pleasant maze of low-ceilinged passageways and narrow staircases with uneven steps connecting areas of the house that had been built on different levels, at different times, for different purposes. There was a backgammon and domino room, for example. It was used for nothing else. Over the long and quiet decades, much of the Yellow House had been changed, but much also had remained the same. The Yellow House was not just the pride but the heart of Curzon's Mill. To Marquands and their scattered cousins, the Yellow House was home.

In spite of its considerable charm the Yellow House was, like so many old New England places, only moderately comfortable. There were always repairs to be done, and there was hardly ever enough money to do them all. The roof leaked, window frames chattered in the wind, and the caressing limbs of the big oaks and elms around the house loosened shingles from the eaves and bricks from the chimneys. Doors sagged from their hinges, and doorknobs came off in the hand. The house sighed and moaned in the night and, in winter, the winds off the icy rivers were so strong and penetrating that they came up through cracks in the old floor boards, causing scatter rugs to lift and billow in eerie little ripples from the floor. There were certain areas of the house that were impossible to heat, and on winter mornings you would rise, your breath smoking in the air, to find the water pitcher on your dresser frozen solid. Toilets and other plumbing required perpetual attention, and there was never a wall or ceiling that couldn't have stood a bit of patching or a coat of paint.

In *Wickford Point,* John Marquand would use the Yellow House as his model for the main farmhouse, changing the color only slightly to white. Jim Calder, Marquand's narrator-protagonist in the book, describes the life there this way:

> In those days . . . we were living on the comfortable tail-end of the Victorian era; but Wickford Point was so far removed from contemporary contacts that much of it was still early Victorian. Life still proceeded in the grooves worn by things which had happened before my parents were born. . . . My great-aunt Sarah never allowed the two huge brass kettles, used formerly for making soap, to be taken out of the kitchen closet. There was a tinder box on the table in the small parlor with which Aunt Sarah sometimes started the fire, because, she said, the sulphur matches smelled badly and the noise they made was startling. One was always sparing of the matches because they had once been novelties, and when the fires were going we always used paper spills to light the candles. One of the branches of the great elm by the front door was twisted because Aunt Sarah's mother used to have a pig hung from it in the winter. In the winter, as long as she was able, Aunt Sarah always put a few embers in the warming pan before she went to bed, and made tea from a kettle hung from a crane in the fireplace in the back parlor. She also had a collection of herbs in the long parlor cupboard.

The quirks and crotchets of the fictional aunts and cousins in *Wickford Point* are as nothing compared with the eccentricities of the real-life Marquand relatives who actually inhabited the Yellow House. John Marquand's Aunt Mollie was, for one thing, probably retarded. In the family it was explained that Aunt Mollie was "simple." But she was a sweet-faced little person who puttered happily about the house, she was inordinately fond of children and young people, and John became devoted to her. Her sister was something else again. Aunt Bessie was a frustrated spinster who was always casting about for new ways to occupy herself, which made her a perpetual troublemaker. Aunt Bessie had been a dedicated Unitarian and

at one point had actually gone to divinity school and obtained
her degree as a Unitarian preacher. After delivering her first
sermon, however, she announced that she had lost her faith.
She was an avid reader and a stern disciplinarian; during John
Marquand's long sojourn at Curzon's Mill, Aunt Bessie required him to listen as she read aloud every play of Shakespeare's, as well as the Bible from Genesis through Revelation,
and all of the classics, along with Scott's Waverley Novels.
Passages from these texts which Aunt Bessie considered particularly worthy or significant, she made him memorize by
heart.

Sharing the Yellow House with these two maiden ladies was
a third spinster, *their* aunt and John's great-aunt, Mary Curzon.
Great-Aunt Mary—the model for Great-Aunt Sarah in *Wickford Point*—was also an avid reader and considered herself an
intellectual. John Greenleaf Whittier had once had a considerable crush on Great-Aunt Mary and had often called on her at
Curzon's Mill. In that Golden Age of New England literature
all the greatest lights had been her friends, including Emerson,
Thoreau, William Ellery Channing, and Thomas Higginson,
the abolitionist. All these were household names at the Mill,
and Great-Aunt Mary would speak of Whittier's or Emerson's
visits as though they had happened yesterday. John Marquand
used to recall encountering Aunt Bessie and Great-Aunt Mary
one summer evening at Curzon's Mill walking barefoot in the
tall dew-covered grass and conversing animatedly in classic
Greek.

At eighty-five, Great-Aunt Mary had set certain rules. It was
she who had established the backgammon and domino room,
for example, and she liked to play a game of either after dinner.
That meant that someone, often John, was required to play with
her. The window shades in the domino and backgammon room
had to be set at a certain level, for that was the way they had
been set in Great-Aunt Mary's father's day. Great-Aunt Mary's
room in the Yellow House was the room in which she had been
born. "I was born here, and I intend to die here," she used to
assert. (And die there she did.) Great-Aunt Mary, too, liked to
read aloud. Her favorite was Pepys's *Diary;* every evening of

her long life she read aloud from Pepys's *Diary* for three hours before retiring, and everyone, including John, had to listen to these readings. As for conversation, her favorite topic was the Fire. The Fire took place in 1811 and destroyed her grandfather's house, his wharf, and one of his brigs, the *George Washington,* which had been docked at the wharf. In Great-Aunt Mary's opinion, the Fire was the most colorful and important event in American maritime history, eclipsing in significance the Civil War, the War of 1812, and the American Revolution.

All three aunts were strict, parsimonious, moralistic. They were not only sparing in their use of matches but kept a little box that was just to contain burned-out match ends. The stubs of candles were collected and saved so that they could be melted down and used for sealing wax when the time came to put up preserves. Paper wrappings from packages and parcels were smoothed out, folded, and put aside for future usefulness. Aunt Mollie had a dresser drawer that contained nothing else but buttons by the thousands in every variety of size and shape. John Marquand was once scolded for throwing out the broken half of a pair of scissors, since it could have been put to use as a letter opener. Compared with the easy affluence of the Rye days, this sort of thing must have been painful to endure.

In the meantime, John was quite aware that both his father's sisters, Aunt Bessie and Aunt Mollie, had, thanks to their father's trust, been able to hold onto their money. True, each aunt had an income that amounted only to about $2,000 a year —barely enough to keep Curzon's Mill going—but still, considering that John's father had lost his entire capital, it was impossible for John Marquand not to think of himself as very much the poor relation. And at Curzon's Mill there was always a great deal of talk about money and the lack of it; it took so much, after all, to keep the big old place going. Once during John's high school days a man pulled up to the Yellow House in a Cadillac and offered to rent the entire place for an enormous sum. That night at dinner there was an excited family conference, and John listened wide-eyed as each aunt outlined what she planned to do with her share of the windfall. Now they would all once again, it seemed, be living like millionaires.

Then, shortly after dinner, there was a telephone call saying that the ladies' prospective tenant had been safely returned to the Danvers State Mental Hospital.

To make matters seem worse—at least from the standpoint of John's feelings about his reduced circumstances—the third of his father's sisters, Margaret, who was called Greta to distinguish her from several other Margarets in the family, had married a man named Herbert Dudley Hale. He was the son of the celebrated Edward Everett Hale, editor and author of over sixty books, the most famous of which was then and still is *The Man Without a Country.* The Hales were a vast and prolific New England family, and now they were all "connected" with the Marquands. High in the illustrious Hale family tree hung such figures as Edward Everett, orator and statesman, and Nathan Hale, the patriot spy who regretted only that he had but one life to lose for his country. Some of the Hale cousins were certifiably crazy. Others were merely charmingly eccentric. Nearly all the Hales were amusing, if sometimes surprising, company, and Hales were always dropping by for visits at Curzon's Mill.

Aunt Greta's marriage to Herbert Dudley Hale was an imposing union, written up glowingly in society pages all over the country. The Hales moved to New York where, in young John's view, they lived in grand style. They had six children, and their two oldest boys, Dudley and Russell, were just about John Marquand's age. They were frequent visitors at Curzon's Mill, and as John saw them enjoy possessions and luxuries that he could never possibly afford, in his mind the economic disparity between the Hale family and his own grew and became exaggerated to enormous proportions. Actually, the Hales were not rich but merely comfortably off. Herbert Dudley Hale had a small income, and Aunt Greta had, in addition to her share of the Marquand trust, another small inheritance, all of which gave her an income of between $3,000 and $4,000 a year. To young John, this seemed a fortune, and he began to think of himself as a pauper, required to live Spartanly with three dotty old-maid aunts while his Hale cousins lived richly and happily and seemingly without a care in the world.

Herbert Dudley Hale died, and Aunt Greta then married a

man ten years younger than she named John Oakman. Aunt Greta and the new Uncle John began taking frequent trips to Europe, where they were taken up by the Paris art world. They returned to Curzon's Mill with heady tales of fabulous places and glamorous people—all of which seemed forever beyond the young boy's reach. John Marquand got along well with John Oakman; his uncle, after all, was only thirteen years older than he. Uncle John, who was a heavy drinker, taught young John to drink. They would go down to the old gristmill for their drinking sessions because Aunts Mollie and Bessie and Great-Aunt Mary would never have permitted alcohol to be consumed in the Yellow House. John Oakman hated his wife's first husband's family, the Hales. Edward Everett Hale's library had been stored in the gristmill, and when John Oakman got drunk he would begin throwing Hale's books into the Artichoke River.

In 1911, the year John Marquand entered college, the Oakmans gave birth to a daughter, Renée, giving John another cousin. To him, she was more like a baby sister, and Aunt Greta and Uncle John became, in the meantime, more like his own mother and father than the real parents whom he hardly ever saw.

Though there were always people coming and going at the Mill, and though there were occasional fond letters from his parents in far-off places, it was often a lonely life, for John, as a youth, had a shy and solitary nature. He took long walks down the old paths along the river, under the great stands of white and red pines, past the old boat landing and the rock that, in the family, had always been called "the picnic rock," reserved for summer picnics. There was even a spot where Sunday night suppers took place in good weather, and there was a family cemetery, at Sawyer Hill. On school days, dressed in what his aunts designated as his "good school suit," he took the riverbank path to the trolley stop, and the trolley into Newburyport to the high school, his books in a bag slung over his shoulder. Newburyport was then much as it is today, with its collection of fine old Federalist houses along High Street, with their cupolas and widows' walks, all painted a gleaming white with black shutters, arrayed behind white-painted fences and green lawns. It was an old seafaring town where everyone knew everyone else and, when John walked to school from where the streetcar dropped him, the people he passed on the street included retired captains of sailing ships, who still made daily pilgrimages to the wharves to look at the sea and the sky, and gray and faded little ladies, who wrapped their shoulders in paisley shawls to go out shopping or to tend their flower beds. There was a bookseller on the corner with his stock of musty volumes, brought out and placed on a little street-side shelf in good weather. All these people came to recognize the solemn young scholar, and nodded and waved to him on his way to school.

While John Marquand was toiling daily at Newburyport High School, his Hale cousins were off at the exclusive Morristown School for Boys in New Jersey. They came back to Curzon's Mill with stories of the romps and gaieties of boarding-school life, of larking trips to New York night clubs, of dances with beautiful girls imported from Miss Porter's, Foxcroft, and Madeira, all things John Marquand might once have expected but now could never enjoy. In the crisp and matter-of-fact way they had, John's New England aunts explained to him that there was no need for him ever to look forward to anything like that. There was no money for it, and that was that. It was what happened when one's father was a failure.

Failure and lost chances—they would become linked themes in John Marquand's best novels.

Chapter Four

*T*hey were called "The Mount Auburn Street Crowd," and Mount Auburn Street in Cambridge, Massachusetts, was known as the Gold Coast because all the richest and most social men at Harvard lived there. Today, the only relic of that gilded era is a dry-cleaning establishment that calls itself the Gold Coast Valetorium.

Mount Auburn Street was the district of Harvard's famous clubs. In the autumn of 1911, when John Marquand entered Harvard, the clubs were the backbone of the social structure of the college, and the Mount Auburn Street Crowd was the only crowd that mattered. If you did not belong to a club, you were as a nonentity, overlooked on every invitation list. Each club conveyed its own degree of social status. The two top clubs were Porcellian and A.D. These were followed by the Fly, the Spee, the Delphic, and the Owl clubs, but to grasp the vast social gulf that existed between Porcellian and Spee one need only know that at Harvard the local joke had it that Spee members, in order to recruit new men to their ranks, ran about the campus crying in mincing, pleading tones, "Oh, will-you-won't

you, will-you-won't-you come and join the Spee?" Socially,
Delphic and Owl were beneath consideration.

Porcellian, in the meantime, was The Club. Founded in
1791, it was the first college club in America. It was very Bostonian in its membership and, like the college itself, very English in its conception, for it was modeled on the men's city
clubs of London. One of the legendary features of the Porcellian Club was a tilted mirror affixed to the building permitting
members to look down on passers-by from an unseen vantage
point. The loftiest names in Boston's business and social history had belonged to Porcellian. Owen Wister had been a member, as had T. R. Roosevelt, father of Teddy, Oliver Wendell
Holmes, John Jay Chapman, and Louis Agassiz, along with
numberless Cabots, Lowells, Adamses, Saltonstalls, and Lodges.
Male members of the Sedgwick family were automatically Porcellian material. When asked about "P.C." or the Pig, as the
Club was nicknamed, Owen Wister is said to have remarked,
"Nothing has ever meant so much to me. It is a bond which
can be felt, but not analyzed." And, years later, in *The Late
George Apley,* John Marquand had Mr. Apley say in a letter to
his son,

> I am still quite well-known around the Club, you know, and
> your first object must be to "make" the Club. I believe that
> everything else, even including your studies, should be secondary
> to this. You may call this a piece of worldly counsel, but it is
> worth while. I don't know what I should have done in life
> without the Club. When I leave Boston it is my shield. When
> I am in Boston it is one of my great diversions. The best people
> are always in it, the sort that you will understand and like. I
> once tried to understand a number of other people, but I am
> not so sure now that it was not a waste of time. Your own sort
> are the best friends and you will do well not to forget it.

Life within the Club, meanwhile, centered largely around
the consumption of alcohol. Once a year it observed something
called "The Day of the Book," a holiday for which members
trained for weeks. On the Day itself, each member was required to consume the following: Before breakfast, a martini;
at breakfast, a quart of champagne; thereafter one martini per
hour until lunchtime, when two martinis were required; for

lunch, one more quart of champagne; throughout the afternoon, the same requirements as in the morning. After dinner, another quart of champagne was the rule, followed by one straight Scotch per hour until midnight, when the Day officially ended. Those left standing were declared the winners. For infractions of rules, members were fined in champagne, and after so-called business meetings the tables in the meeting room were strewn with as many as fifty empty bottles. Cass Canfield, a member of P.C., devised a red-wine fountain with a hose and spigot to make that liquid more available during the dinner hour, and once another classmate horsewhipped a fellow member for allegedly insulting his fiancée and then, after much champagne, thrust the offending hand that had held the whip into the fireplace until it was burned to a stump. Club members sat around watching this partial immolation. The class of 1915 in P.C.—John Marquand's year—was said to hold the all-time Porcellian record for liquor consumption.

Marquand was able to mock and satirize the Club in fiction, but at the time he entered Harvard there was no question but that he would have liked very much to have been asked to join Porcellian, A.D., or even the Spee. On the one hand he was already able to see through the pretentiousness and pompousness of the Club's attitudes, of values which set apart "the best people" from "a number of other people," one's own sort from the riffraff. And yet, on the other hand, there was something about these attitudes and values that he had come almost sheepishly to admire. Perhaps it was the air of security, complacency, and utter self-confidence that the average Porcellian Clubman managed to exude, a certain demeanor and set of responses that he seemed to have been born with. Clubmen seemed personifications of what it meant to be "to the manner born." At Harvard it was said that you could tell whether a man was of Porcellian caliber after a few moments' conversation with him. There were even some who insisted that you could identify the Porcellian sort simply by *looking* at him. Mixed up in John Marquand's ambivalent feelings about Harvard's social clubs and their values were his already complicated feelings about his Hale cousins and what seemed to him their better way of life. How pleasant, he must have thought, it would be to be asked into the Sphinx, which was the "waiting club" for both Porcellian and A.D., sort of a halfway club where an undergraduate waited for the nod of acceptance from above. *That* would certainly show the Hales!

And yet, throughout his Harvard years, John Marquand was never asked to join any social club at all.

Years later, John Marquand developed a rationale which he used to explain his "rejection" by Harvard's clubs. It was all because, he said, he had come to Harvard from Newburyport High School and not from one of the clutch of great New England private schools such as Groton, St. Mark's, Middlesex, and St. Paul's. But there were at least two other reasons.

For one thing, Harvard's clubs were expensive, with high initiation fees and dues, and Marquand, even if invited to join, could not have afforded it. He had come to Harvard on a scholarship, and even that scholarship had not been easy to get. He had applied, first, to the Harvard Club of Newburyport for a grant. In those days the procedure was a somewhat humiliating one. Young Marquand had been required to appear, hat in hand, at the Federalist mansion of Mr. L. P. Dodge, one of Newburyport's leading worthies, and to state his case, feeling suddenly acutely embarrassed at being the poor relation of a well-off family. He had tried to explain as best he could his wish to go to Harvard, his qualifications and ambitions—still largely undefined—and his need for financial aid. Mr. Dodge promised to consider his application but, a few days later, turned it down. Marquand, however, was able to obtain a scholarship that Harvard offered to students who were interested in chemistry. He had never cared much for chemistry, he wrote to his parents at the time, but perhaps chemistry would offer a career for him. His father, meanwhile, after various engineering jobs in Los Angeles and San Francisco, had found himself for a while in the Panama Canal Zone as a supervisor of sorts in the digging operations for the canal there. Soon he was back in Wilmington again, as a designing engineer for the Edge Moor Iron Works. John's mother had faithfully accompanied her husband on his wanderings about the world.

But an even more important reason why the Harvard clubs overlooked John Marquand was that John Marquand, in those days, was a very overlookable young man. Later on, fame and money helped him acquire poise, an easy heartiness of manner, and an ability to deal with situations. But in those Harvard days he was a shy and gangling youth who positively radiated lack of assurance. He had a good-looking face with high cheekbones, wide dark eyes, and a largish nose. But he wore his hair unfashionably long, parted at the exact center of his head, as though with a knife, and slicked down flat at the sides with a wet comb.

He had a way of standing, slouched a little to one side, his head cocked at a diffident angle, his feet seeming to shuffle as he talked. Helen Howe has described what she calls his "whipped look," which she suspects may have been "partly feigned, but expressive nonetheless of his true inner lack of self-confidence." He was a meticulous dresser, and his high-collared shirts were always clean and starched, his tie neatly knotted beneath his somewhat prominent Adam's apple, and his cuffs and jackets and knickerbocker trousers hitched up and buttoned and buckled in the proper places. To the supposedly sophisticated youth of Boston, John Marquand may have looked something of a bumpkin, a small-town boy out of his depth in a big university full of rich men's sons. There was little to suggest the man who would one day pose as a "Man of Distinction" in an advertisement for a liquor company.

Marquand was not then and never would be much of an athlete. He attacked sports with energy and determination but was hindered by a lack of coordination. At tennis he ran hard around the court, flailing awkwardly at the ball with his racket. His swimming style was vigorous but choppy, a stroke that yielded slow progress through the water.

Socially he seemed equally inept. Backgammon and reading aloud with three maiden aunts had given him little preparation for what were called the "swell" parties on Beacon Hill. These parties were ritualized and, according to some people, dreadful affairs, yet they were endured because they were and always had been a part of the only social pattern that existed. One went to a tea party during the winter "season," then on to a dinner party, and then perhaps to a concert, to hear a performance of the Boston Symphony, a string quartet, or a soprano soloist. Then one thanked one's hostess and went home. Liquor was seldom served at any of these parties. New Yorkers who came northward to Boston for the celebrated coming-out parties in the Somerset Hotel were appalled to find not even champagne in evidence.

At the same time, it was fashionable—again, this was very English—to be rude to anyone you did not know. The art of the social snub was practiced extensively. One grew accustomed, at Boston parties, to cutting remarks, icy stares, or blank unseeing looks directed at outsiders. John Marquand was invited once to one of the Somerset parties, and to a dinner preceding it at a big house on Commonwealth Avenue. He would recount, years later and in vivid detail, the agony of standing in that drawing room in his rented white tie and tails, rooted at a corner of the carpet while groups of young people drifted and swirled around and about him, laughing and talking to each other and completely ignoring him. After nearly an hour of this, having spoken to no one and having no one speak to him, he bolted from the party and made his lonely way back across the Harvard Bridge to Cambridge to the modest rooming house at 7 Linden Street where he and several other boys shared rooms with a parrot who could say, "Hello, boys!" The boys sarcastically called the rooming house, which was run by two maiden ladies reminiscent of the Curzon's Mill aunts, "Miss Mooney's Pleasure Palace."

Sometimes on winter evenings Marquand would wander over to Mount Auburn Street and stand quietly in the shadows watching the bold young blades in their tail coats and silk hats and walking sticks swagger as they emerged from Gold Coast parties with beautiful young debutantes on their arms. Marquand, with his developing inner eye, could now see himself not only as the poor relation but also the social outcast, the lonely boy with his nose pressed against the windowpane, watching the shimmering life that was led by the handsome, the witty, and the rich.

But his Harvard years cannot have been as lonely and unpleasant as he later made them out to be. By his sophomore year he had made the staff of the *Harvard Lampoon,* which in itself carried considerable weight on the campus. It was at the *Lampoon* that he first met aristocratic young Gardiner Fiske, who was the magazine's business manager, and who would remain John's friend for life. He was then invited to join Professor Copeland's "Tuesday Night Readings." The first stirrings of literary ambitions were clearly being felt. He did well in his courses, including chemistry, and made several good friends. Among the residents at 7 Linden Street was James Bryant Conant, who would one day become Harvard's president. From their fourth-floor rooms they would drop water bags on each other, and there were elaborate duels staged with brooms and pillows. Among the games the young men invented was something they called the Two-Drink Dash. To play it, each man left 7 Linden Street at a different time and, traveling by subway, went to a bar in Boston called the Holland Wine Company, had two quick drinks, and then made it home by the quickest route possible. The winner was the man who made the round trip in the fastest time. The game was made exciting by the fact that a variety of routes was available. Also, depending on the leniency of the bartender on duty, there was always the question of whether one might or might not be permitted to buy one's two drinks because of the age limit.

But once having cast himself in the role of Poor Social Outcast, John Marquand always played it to the hilt. It was in keeping with his growing habit of viewing his own life novelistically. Years later, Marquand ran into two of his classmates, Robert Nathan, the writer, and Archibald Roosevelt, one of Teddy Roosevelt's sons. The talk turned to Harvard days, and to all the bittersweet memories those days evoked.

Robert Nathan complained that although he had been snubbed and ignored as an undergraduate, now that he was a successful author he was forever being asked to make a speech for Harvard, to give money to Harvard, or to write something for some Harvard cause. "Now it doesn't seem to matter that I'm a Jew," Nathan said. Marquand pointed out that his own situation was identical, and he even lacked Nathan's excuse of being Jewish. "They would ask me where I had gone to school," Marquand said, "and I would tell them Newburyport High, and a look of horror would pass over their faces. Now I get nothing but letters from classmates addressed 'Dear Old Johnny,' and asking me for such and such."

Archie Roosevelt smiled and said, "You fellows had it easy. Look at my situation. I was the son of a former President of the United States, perhaps the most famous figure of his time. I had gone to Groton. Do you think anyone paid any attention to me? *I* never made the Porcellian."

John Marquand used to tell this story with amusement. And yet, at the same time, it seemed to puzzle him. He had convinced himself that the fact of Newburyport High School—that and nothing else—had kept him out of Porcellian, A.D., or even the Spee. Newburyport High School had become, as it were, the plot device by which the best clubs had bypassed him. But, in Archie Roosevelt's case, why? Novelistically, it made no sense at all.

Chapter Five

*C*hristina Sedgwick was a delicately beautiful blonde creature with slender legs and a tiny waist and an appealing,
almost childlike manner. John Marquand met her in Cambridge shortly after his graduation from Harvard with the class
of 1915. He had gone to work for the *Boston Transcript* as a
cub reporter and was managing a meager existence on a salary
of $15 a week. He fell hopelessly in love with her.

Years later, after nearly thirteen years of a sometimes-happy-
sometimes-not marriage and a bitter divorce, Marquand would
romanticize Christina, turning her into an exotic fairy-tale
heroine of perfect gentleness, goodness, and grace—into the
kind of wife he felt he *ought* to have had, rather than the
perplexing and complicated actuality that Christina Sedgwick
was. She certainly had charm, and a dainty and winsome gaiety
and humor that could be quite beguiling. But she also, having
been brought up as a proper New England lady, was completely impractical, incapable of coping with the realities of
life. She had led what is called a sheltered existence, and much
of its shelter was the creation of her own personality. Sometimes she seemed to be living on another star.

She never, for instance, seemed to know quite where she was. She would go out for a walk and soon find herself lost and, when she asked for directions and these were pointed out to her, she would smile sweetly and then turn and walk dreamily the opposite way. Her ethereal vagueness could be both endearing and exasperating, for in addition to being vague she was also forgetful. She would forget invitations and show up in the wrong places for appointments. She would make dates with Marquand and then fail to appear. He began proposing marriage to her soon after their first meeting, and sometimes she would accept his proposals and sometimes she would demur. When she accepted, she would have forgotten the acceptance a day later. Everything about Christina was haphazard and disorganized. One afternoon she was seen walking on Beacon Hill and holding one end of what was clearly a dog's leash, apparently quite unaware that no dog was attached to the other end. Once in a restaurant she was observed carefully gathering up *three* gloves. She was a child-woman who had to be guided and led, and in this capacity she had always been served by her mother, Mrs. Alexander C. Sedgwick of Stockbridge, Massachusetts.

Perhaps it was Christina's Princess Lointaine quality that supported John Marquand's feeling from the beginning that, socially, he was from the wrong side of the tracks. Certainly his Marquand-Fuller lineage was every bit as distinguished as Christina's. Still, she was a Sedgwick, and John Marquand was very much aware that, as they say in New England, "Sedgwicks are Sedgwicks." Sedgwick House in Stockbridge, the family seat, is an imposing yellow house that addresses a wide elm-shaded lawn facing Main Street, a local landmark pointed out with pride to visitors. In the Stockbridge Church the Sedgwick pews are placed in a chancel so that Sedgwicks can sit above everybody else. Beyond the church lies the Sedgwick burial plot, a circular piece of real estate known as the Sedgwick Pie. At the center of the Pie reposes an ancient ancestor, Judge Theodore Sedgwick, and around him lie all the other Sedgwicks, their heads away from the center in order that, at the sound of the last trump, all the Sedgwicks may rise and face Judge Theodore who, it is assumed, will have a verdict of his own to deliver to each of them. The Sedgwick servants, meanwhile, are buried separately, "below the salt." So seriously are the Sedgwicks taken in Stockbridge that it is said that in spring all the peeping frogs in the local ponds chirp "Sedgwick, Sedgwick, Sedgwick."

Though most Sedgwicks are comfortably off, there is no Sedgwick family fortune, as such, to speak of. But the Sedgwicks have long represented other things in Boston. More than money, they have stood for intellectual achievement, civic rectitude, cultural responsibility—qualities which traditional Boston has always admired. Sedgwicks have provided Boston with scholars, teachers, essayists, poets, clergymen. They have, meanwhile, not been shy about *marrying* money, and several Sedgwicks have married Cabots and Peabodys. Perhaps the most important fact about the Sedgwicks, as far as young John Marquand was concerned, was that Christina's uncle, Ellery Sedgwick, was then the editor of the *Atlantic Monthly*, the only magazine that proper Boston deigned to read and take seriously. In Boston, when one spoke of the Magazine, one meant the *Atlantic Monthly*, just as to speak of the President did not mean the occupant of the White House but the head of Harvard. To Marquand, a hack reporter for a daily newspaper, the presence of the great editor of the Magazine in Christina's family tree was awesome. Uncle Ellery, who set the literary taste of New England, became a gray eminence in the background as John and Christina's courtship started on its uncertain path.

It was the spring of 1916, and between his work at the *Transcript* and courting Christina John Marquand had also joined Battery A of the Massachusetts Field Artillery, a National Guard unit. "Preparedness" had become the popular if somewhat vaguely defined motto of those pre-World War I days, and young men all over America were starting to set their military courses. But John's joining Battery A was done, more than for any patriotic reason, to impress Christina and her family. Battery A was something of an elite corps. There were, to begin with, only 190 men in it, and nearly all of them were Harvard men of "good" families. There were two Peabodys, a Cabot, an Appleton, a Bradley, and an Otis, along with Gordon

Hammersley from the New York *Social Register* and a Philadelphia Strawbridge. Battery A provided a pleasant diversion, and its assignments were far from strenuous; the Tuesday night winter drills were held at Boston's exclusive New Riding Club, and, in spring, maneuvers moved out to the country club in suburban Brookline. Members of Battery A were permitted to exercise their horses in the bridle paths along the Fenway and Jamaica Pond, and they were frequently accompanied by young debutantes riding sidesaddle in dark blue habits with derby hats secured to their heads by black elastic bands under their chins. Locally, the young men in Battery A were called "The Blue Bloods," and it was said that the unit was composed of "millionaires' sons and willy-boys"—epithets which the carefree young blades hardly minded in the least. The swath they cut in their snappy uniforms on their thoroughbred horses was part of the fun of playing soldier. For John Marquand, membership in Battery A was an even headier experience because he had, in a real sense, been invited to join his very first club.

Then, on June 19, 1916—the day before Harvard Class Day, and just when everyone who was anyone had made his or her summer social plans—the blow fell. Pancho Villa, the Mexican bandit, had been causing trouble at the border, including several raids into United States territory, and, supported by the Mexican authorities, a detachment of American troops was ordered into Mexico under General Pershing. Federalized state guards were to back up the expedition. The Massachusetts Militia, including Battery A, was ordered to report for immediate duty.

Battery A at the Border! It became the rallying cry of a whole generation of young Bostonians, the source of an endless supply of comic anecdotes which only those who had shared the experience could appreciate or understand. From the outset, the adventure had a musical-comedy quality as weeping mothers and girl friends with parasols assembled in huge Pierce-Arrow touring cars to kiss the troops good-by from their departure point in Framingham. As their train made its way across the country into the Southwest, flag-waving crowds gathered at station stops to cheer on the youthful soldiers. Once, outside St. Louis, when the train made an unscheduled stop near an inviting stream, a number of young men took the opportunity to bathe and were forced to run naked down the tracks when the train started up without them. Song, ribaldry, and whiskey were the order of the day and night aboard the rattling cars.

When the group reached Fort Bliss, outside El Paso, a pattern of life was established. By day there was the dreary routine of army camp life in the dusty desert under a hot summer Texas sun. But the nights were cool, ideal for partying, or for going to dances at the El Paso del Norte Hotel, or for simply sitting around in tents telling stories. Baseball teams and track meets were organized, but, as the summer weeks wore on, tedium set in which was aggravated by the fact that not the slightest trace of an enemy appeared on the horizon. There was talk of abandoning the outfit and going home, and one evening, after much gin, a young Peabody and one of his Lowell cousins set out on foot to go back to Boston. They were found the next day, passed out, in the desert about fifteen miles from camp. No disciplinary action was taken against the two by the commander of this detachment of innocents.

Then, just as abruptly as it had been ordered into Texas, Battery A, in September, was ordered back to Massachusetts. In Boston, the men were given heroes' welcomes. Accompanied by local ice-wagon horses, they were marched through the city's streets past cheering crowds. The newspapers praised their courage and the fact that they had "sacrificed so much and had rushed away to serve if need be on foreign soil." Battery A had, of course, accomplished absolutely nothing; not a weapon had been fired. But the men of Battery A had acquired a shared experience that they would treasure for a lifetime, and John Marquand had made more friends in three months than in all his years at Harvard. They were, furthermore, friends of what he liked to consider his "class."

Six months later, America was in the war, and Marquand set off for Officers' Training Camp at Plattsburg, New York, embarked upon a much more serious military commitment. Plattsburg was quite different from the palmy life with Battery A, and Marquand found the routine there both wearying and terrifying—and yet, again for Christina's sake, he was

determined to succeed at it. One false step in the three-month
training program and he would have been sent home in disgrace. But he passed the course and, in July, 1917, received
his commission as a first lieutenant in the United States Army.

From Plattsburg, Marquand was transferred to Fort Devens
in Massachusetts, and from there to Fort Greene, North Carolina. Because he had learned to both write and speak French
at Harvard—though he spoke with a decided New England
accent—it was decided by army higher-ups that he could be
put to good use in France as an interpreter with a Military
Police unit. This struck Marquand as an interesting enough
assignment but, just before departing Fort Greene, he was
reassigned—in what always struck him as typical military
lunacy—to an artillery brigade with the Fourth Division, sta-
tioned outside Bordeaux.

From the time of his arrival in France, the war became a
nightmare experience for Marquand which, in later years, he
could never drive out of his mind and never really bear to
speak about. He fought—most of the time with the 77th Regi-
ment Field Artillery—in the bloody battle of the Vesle River,
and at St. Mihiel, and in the Argonne, and the war, for him,
consisted mostly of mud, the noise of shells exploding, and the
sickening sight of dead men's bodies lying everywhere. It was
his first sight of bloodshed, and it left an indelible impression,
one he could not erase. In November, 1918, he spent a few
hours in Paris and was there when the Armistice was declared.
His reaction to the news was one of exhausted relief.

Years later, he would turn his wartime experiences to
fictional use in a series of successful war stories. And the dis-
parate natures of his two wartime adventures—in Battery A
and in the bloody trenches of France—gave him a rather
special double-edged view of military life. He was to view the
military and its endeavors the same way he could view the
strivings of the American upper crust, both as an insider and as
one a bit removed, looking in. Fighting and killing he could
treat as comic, even ridiculous, on the one hand (as it had
seemed in Battery A, although touched with comradeship)
and brutal and deadly and dreadful on the other (as it had

been in France). Editors would regard his interpretation of war and killing as unique.

Immediately after his discharge from the Army, Marquand headed—after a brief, almost perfunctory, but of course required visit to his parents, who were back in Wilmington—to New York, where he decided his first task was to make some money. Only by making money—now that he had proved himself a man—could he win Christina and persuade the Sedgwicks to let him carry off their daughter.

For a while, he had a job as a Sunday feature writer for the *New York Herald*. While there, he became acquainted with another young writer named Robert Benchley, and one night, when the two men were having a drink and talking about ways to make money, Benchley told Marquand that there was more of it to be made in advertising copywriting than in newspaper work. Immediately John applied for a job at the J. Walter Thompson advertising agency and was taken on as a copywriter for the princely sum of $60 a week, nearly twice what he had made at the *Herald*.

Later on in life he would defend his move from the more prestigious world of journalism into the hustling, hard-sell, dog-eat-dog scramble of advertising by claiming that advertising copy was better for a writer than newspaper work since it dealt with "basic human fears and emotions." Perhaps he eventually came to believe this, but at the time he wrote ads sheerly for the money, and he hated the work. He wrote advertising copy and slogans for such Thompson accounts as Veedol, Tydol, Lux, and Yuban Coffee. For a while he was the chief copywriter on the Lifebuoy Soap account, a product for which he retained a lifetime aversion. He was at one point assigned to an account that advertised rubber heels and was sent out on a field trip with the following mission: He was to stand at a curb and count how many people stepped from the sidewalk onto the street toes first, and how many stepped off heels first. After several hours of curbside study Marquand returned to the office with his answer: "Two hundred on heels, three hundred and fifty on toes." "No," he was told, "that's not the right answer for our client. Go back and find another."

To save money, he had been living in New York with his
Hale cousins. One night after dinner he picked up a copy of
the *Saturday Evening Post* and carried it up to bed with him
to read. The issue contained perhaps half a dozen short stories
and part of a serialized novel. The next morning, Marquand
carried the *Post* down with him to breakfast and said to his
cousin, Dudley Hale, "You know, these stories are simple to do.
They're all about a man of low social standing who falls in
love with a girl who's socially above him." That night he came
home and laboriously typed out a short story. It was about a
prize fighter who falls in love with a debutante. He shipped
the story off to the editors of the *Saturday Evening Post,* who
promptly bought it. It was his first published short story. In
this casual, almost accidental way, John Marquand became a
writer of fiction. The flighty, otherworldly debutante in the
story reminded people who knew her of Christina.

Chapter Six

*I*n the spring of 1921, Stanley Resor, the president of J. Walter Thompson, called John Marquand into his office, said to him sadly, "John, I don't believe you have the business instinct," and suggested that he look for gainful employment elsewhere. Marquand was apprehensive about being out of a job and yet, at the same time, he was relieved. Business instinct or not, he had been able to sell several more short stories, most of which, to be sure, shared a common theme—poor-social-outcast boy falls in love with rich-socially-prominent girl; sometimes he would achieve variety by turning the sexes and social positions the other way around. George Horace Lorimer, the great editor who steered the *Saturday Evening Post* to its most successful years, was delighted with the new, young, and productive writer who could so easily turn out material that fit the *Post*'s formula.

Marquand had also acquired his lifelong literary agent, Carl Brandt of the firm of Brandt & Brandt, one of the finest in New York. With the help of Brandt, Marquand was soon being paid as much as $500 for each of his *Post* stories. Brandt also brought Marquand to the attention of another celebrated

magazine editor of the day, Ray Long of *Cosmopolitan,* and
began skillfully to parlay the enthusiasm of one editor against
the other, saying to Lorimer, "If you don't want this one, Long
does," and to Long, "If you don't take this one, Lorimer will."
In the process, of course, he was slowly but steadily nudging
Marquand's prices upward. And so, in a way, Marquand's dismissal from J. Walter Thompson could not have come at a
better time. He had paid off all his debts from college days
and had $400 clear in the bank, a respectable sum in 1921.
Also, Carl Brandt had been urging him to try a more ambitious
project, a full-length novel, the kind which the *Post* and other
magazines often bought and ran as serials. Serials paid much
more than short stories. What was more, John Marquand had
an idea for one—a costumed cloak-and-dagger affair that he
planned to call *The Unspeakable Gentleman.* That summer he
went back to Newburyport, moved in again with his maiden
aunts at Curzon's Mill, and started to write his book.

Years later, after the Pulitzer Prize and all the rest, he would
have liked to forget *The Unspeakable Gentleman,* for he looked
back on it as an unspeakable piece of work. "I regard it with
horror!" he would cry, cringing at the very mention of the title.
But, as his first novel, it was an unmistakable turning point in
his career as a writer. It was written in a florid, portentous
style that seemed to have been borrowed from the Victorians.
It started out, "I have seen the improbable turn true too often
not to have it disturb me. Suppose these memoirs still exist
when the French royalist plot of 1805 and my father's peculiar
role in it are forgotten." And the novel ended, many pages of
huffing and puffing later, "'Very much relieved,' he said, 'and
yet—and yet I still feel thirsty. The rum decanter, Brutus.'"

The memoirs almost did not exist. A few days after finishing
the manuscript, Marquand returned to New York where he
intended to deliver it to Carl Brandt. On the night of his
arrival, however, he met his Harvard classmate George Merck
for a drink at the University Club, and he carried the manuscript with him in a suitcase. Later, he and Merck took a taxi
downtown to meet two girls and take them out to dinner. Marquand placed the suitcase in the taxi's outside luggage rack.
When the men got to the address where they were to meet

the girls, Marquand discovered to his horror that the suitcase had fallen off the cab. There was no other copy of the manuscript. For days, Marquand was in a state of despair. He placed a pleading ad in the newspapers, and ten days later the suitcase and manuscript turned up. The episode taught him a professional lesson he never forgot, and thereafter he always kept a carbon copy of everything he wrote.

Though *The Unspeakable Gentleman* was undertaken more or less as a test, to see whether his skills as a short-story writer could be carried over into a longer piece of work, rather than as an attempt to write immortal literature, Carl Brandt immediately saw it as a marketable property. Because it contained ladies in wigs with fans and bombazine petticoats, Brandt offered it to the *Ladies' Home Journal,* which promptly paid $2,000 for serial rights. Marquand later liked to claim that the *Journal* bought the manuscript because the magazine had, lying around the office, some color illustrations that seemed roughly to suit the text, and because it had a new four-color printing process that it wanted to try out, but none of this was remotely true. *Ladies' Home Journal* liked *The Unspeakable Gentleman* because, for all its faults—such as its atrocious style—it was a fast-paced yarn. Scribner's also liked it and paid Marquand some more money to publish the novel. All at once John P. Marquand—and in those days he was very casual about how he billed himself, sometimes signing his stories with the middle initial, sometimes without, sometimes simply "J. P. Marquand"—was a popular novelist and, in his mind at least, a rich man, a success. This was in 1922.

With his windfall, he set sail for Europe, where Christina Sedgwick was traveling with her parents on one of the Sedgwicks' periodic Grand Tours. John met her in Rome, told her all that had happened, and she agreed at last to marry him. They became officially engaged that summer, after a seven-year courtship, and were married in September back in Stockbridge in a small ceremony at Sedgwick House.

In retrospect, even the location of the wedding seems ominous. For now that John Marquand was a part of the family, the Sedgwickian influence hung even more heavily over his life. There were, in particular, Christina's mother and her Uncle Ellery. While steamily romantic stories were pouring out of Marquand's typewriter, full of slave girls and pirate ships and society girls who were adored by bricklayers, Mrs. Sedgwick did not consider this "writing" at all. In fact, she hardly acknowledged that her new son-in-law worked. She considered his stories cheap pulp fiction and him a hack, and she told him so. Naturally, since none of it appeared in the Magazine, she never read a word he wrote and told him that also, adding to Christina that she hoped she wouldn't be bothered reading such trashy stuff either. From time to time she would condescendingly say to John, "Why don't you write something *nice* for Uncle Ellery?" John, at one point, asked Carl Brandt whether, indeed, anything of his would be suitable for the *Atlantic Monthly*. Brandt replied that he was sure John could produce an *Atlantic Monthly*–type story but reminded him that the *Atlantic Monthly* at the time paid $100 apiece for stories and that it added, if particularly pleased with a piece of work, a silver inkwell as a bonus. Marquand's stories were by now going for $1,500 apiece to the *Post* and *Cosmopolitan*.

It was a good thing that he was able to command these prices, because Christina—and her mother—had very definite ideas about the manner in which she should live. A cook was needed, and then a personal maid. When the Marquands' first child, John, Jr., was born a year after their marriage, a nurse was required for the child. A certain amount of entertaining was expected from the young Marquands, and Christina, along with her mother, demanded the usual evenings out with Boston society. The Marquand household very quickly became an expensive one to run. Christina's mother, in a gesture that was intended to be helpful, bought the couple a house in Boston at 43 West Cedar Street, on Beacon Hill, very much a proper address. John christened his mother-in-law's present "Gift Horse."

Mrs. Sedgwick ran Christina the way she ran everyone else in her life, and John soon discovered that Christina could not make her mind up about anything without first seeking her mother's advice. Guests were coming for the week end; what, Christina asked her mother, should she serve them for dinner? Mrs. Sedgwick planned the menu and then said, "Have John run down to the grocery store for these things. He's not doing anything."

John, meanwhile, though he had not written anything nice for Uncle Ellery, was writing at full speed for everybody else. He regarded himself as a man writing for a popular market, nothing more. And yet, at the same time, he refused to apologize for any of his work. He considered himself a professional and knew that whatever he chose to write about he could handle ably and well. He found the Sedgwicks' attitude oppressive. To escape from it, he took a small room in Charles Street and took his writing equipment there. There was no telephone, and when Christina began making interruptive trips to his hideaway he would lock the door and refuse to answer the bell.

In the early winter of 1926, Christina Marquand discovered that she was pregnant for a second time and became distraught. She rushed to her doctor and announced that she wanted to leave her husband; she wanted a divorce. A council of war was called between Marquand and the Sedgwicks, and Christina's doctor was called in for advice. An abortion was suggested, but Christina's doctor said that pregnant women frequently behaved in this unstable fashion and that John should stand by his wife and "do his best." With a frequently hysterical woman, this was not an easy order, and the next few months were turbulent ones. From time to time John found himself inventing excuses to escape from the confusion and disorder of his house. He would go to see his friends Gardi and Conney Fiske, who had a big and comfortable apartment at 206 Beacon Street. The Fiskes' apartment was ordered and well staffed and, since they were childless, it was admirably quiet. It became, little by little, a second home in Boston for John. By the time the new baby—a girl, whom they named Christina, after her mother—was born, dropping in on the Fiskes had become a habit with him and provided some of the most relaxed moments of his life.

Equally relaxed were his visits to New York to see Carl Brandt. Brandt had begun performing a service for Marquand that he would continue to perform throughout his life—cutting and editing his manuscripts and helping him space the breaks in his stories for serialization. Brandt also gave Marquand edi-

torial help in ways that not only increased the salability of his
stories but also their popularity with readers. Marquand
tended, for example, to display a certain reticence in his writing where matters of physical love were concerned. A typical
Marquand romantic scene would end with the lovers at breakfast the following morning. "I like to close the bedroom door,"
Marquand would protest. But Brandt, knowing that readers
were inevitably curious about what went on behind the closed
door, would insist on a bit more detail. A typical Brandt scrib-
ble on a Marquand manuscript would say, "Now, have him
kiss her here!" Once John Marquand set off for a meeting with
Brandt, saying solemnly, "I swear Carl won't make me put a
girl in this story, because if I put a girl he'll want a love scene."
But he emerged from the meeting having inserted both the
girl and the scene.

With the birth of little Christina, the expenses of the Marquand household went upward again, and John wrote harder
and faster than ever, grinding out stories to pay the bills. When
Christina was a year and a half old, she had a serious attack
of pneumonia, and she had barely recovered when she was
stricken by a second, even more severe, attack. For several
days it was doubted that the baby would live. A rib had to be
cut and the incision drained, and the child spent most of the
winter in Children's Hospital in Boston, while her father
worked long into the nights on a serial called *Warning Hill*.
The Sedgwicks continued to show no appreciation of how hard
John was working, or of what he was working for. Scribner's
had published John's first novel, and a second costumed affair
(which had also been a *Post* serial) called *The Black Cargo*.
But now Little, Brown in Boston offered a thousand-dollar
advance for *Warning Hill*, an exceedingly generous one, Carl
Brandt thought, and so did Marquand. He made a major career
decision: to leave Scribner's and make Little, Brown his publisher. Christina's reaction to this news was of the sort to be
expected. "Oh, I've heard of Little, Brown," she said. "I've
never heard of the other one."

With their daughter recovered, things returned somewhat
to normal, but not really. As a housekeeper, Christina was
hopeless. Weeks would go by without her sending out the

laundry. The wash would accumulate, stuffed in wads, under her bed. She would invite guests for dinner and forget her own invitation, and the guests would come to her door to find her in a bathrobe with her hair in curlers. During the increasingly fewer hours John spent at home, Christina would confront him with domestic problems. The water faucet in the kitchen sink would not turn off, there was no milk in the house for the baby, the maid had not shown up for work, and so what should she do? Once when little Johnny would not stop crying, Christina became very upset and was convinced the child had appendicitis. There could be no other explanation for it. Friends were called in for consultation. John said that he thought the boy merely needed a good spanking. Christina, weeping, begged him to take their son to the hospital. At last a friend went into the little boy's room and asked him what he was crying *about*. Rubbing his eyes, little Johnny said that he was crying because he wanted a pair of brown corduroy pants like those a friend of his had worn at nursery school.

When the Marquands entertained there was usually some sort of crisis which Marquand blamed on Christina's lack of talent as a hostess. Once, for a party at their house on Beacon Hill, Christina thought it would be an amusing touch to hire an organ grinder and a monkey. She forgot to tell John about it, and when the organ grinder appeared John was furious. He shouted, "Get that music and that man and that *animal* out of my house!" And once, at a Christmas Eve party, he became so enraged at the way Christina was handling things that he seized the Christmas tree—lights, decorations, and all—and hurled it out a window into the garden of 43 West Cedar Street. Christina went out into the garden to retrieve the tree, came back with a broken branch from which a few ornaments still dangled, and asked forlornly, "Why do we *do* this?" West Cedar Street quickly became a battlefield; when the Marquands weren't quarreling the servants that Christina hired were misbehaving. One of her maids went berserk and had to be carried away. John, coming home from his writing office, soon acquired the habit of asking her, "Well, what dreadful thing has occurred at the Marquand house today?"

To be sure, as those who knew him had become well aware,

John Marquand had a way of *contriving* problems for himself.
As a novelist, he loved scenes, and so he created them. Situations were his stock in trade, and so he set them up. This way
he could observe and study his characters as they came into
dramatic interaction with other characters.

It was the same thing where his feelings about the Sedgwicks were concerned. He had begun to complain bitterly to
Carl Brandt about his Sedgwick in-laws, and Brandt listened
sympathetically. What else could he do? And yet, at the same
time, there was something about the Sedgwicks that John admired, respected, even envied—a quality and substance of
familyhood, a sense of their being all of a piece, things that
he himself often felt he had been cheated out of as a boy. He
studied the Sedgwicks with a kind of fascination. He would
use them novelistically, later on, just as he would the Hales.

Chapter Seven

John Marquand first met the woman who would later become Carl Brandt's wife in the summer of 1926, in Paris. John's marriage to Christina was then not quite four years old. Carol Hill (as she was then) was a beautiful young woman of twenty-three, ten years younger than John and married to a man named Drew Hill, another writer. It was an era when, or so it seemed, every bright young American took up the pen and wrote—short stories, essays, articles, poems, novels—and everyone who wrote, or wanted to write, carried his ambitions and hopes and, in some cases, talents with him to Paris. The writers and would-be writers perched on the edges of the little chairs in the Left Bank cafés like so many birds after a long flight and sipped apéritifs, smoked Gitanes cigarettes, and talked about writing and other writers. Hemingway had come to Paris, and so had Scott Fitzgerald and Ford Madox Ford. Gertrude Stein was there conducting her salons, James Joyce could be found sniffing around Sylvia Beach's bookshop, Shakespeare & Company, and it was all very literary and young and Bohemian. Even when it wasn't, it tried to be.

John Marquand wasn't exactly in the category of these other

writers, nor did he make any real attempt to join the Paris
literary set. If anything, he did his best to avoid that sort of
company. For one thing, writers like these rather embarrassed
him; they were the ones who wrote nice things for Uncle
Ellery. Marquand had come to Paris to get away from Christina and the Sedgwicks, and he was enjoying himself immensely. Christina was also in Europe, traveling with her
mother, and there was some vague talk of John meeting Christina and Mrs. Sedgwick at some later point, but it was all
very indefinite, and in the meantime John was making the
most of his independence. Though his literary star had not
risen to the heights it one day would, he was already quite
well known, even famous, for his *Post* and *Cosmopolitan*
stories. He was now earning as much as $20,000 a year, and
so he could afford to relax and have a good time.

Things had already begun to go badly with the marriage.
It was Christina's exasperating sloppiness and carelessness
that got most on her husband's nerves. During his fairly long
bachelorhood, he had become a man who required a system
and order to things. He liked his shirts, ties, cuff links, studs,
shoes in neatly ordered arrangements on his shelves and in
his dresser drawers. But Christina, who was inevitably losing
something, would paw through drawers and closets in search
of the lost objects, disarranging everything, and whenever
John encountered another of Christina's havocs there would
be a terrible, bellowing scene.

John had begun to mimic and mock Christina in front of
their friends, just as he would later do with his second wife.
He would snarl and hiss out her name, "Chris*teen*a." It was
"Chris*teen*a doesn't seem to understand how I make my living" and "Chris*teen*a was so busy feeding Johnny an ice cream
cone that she drove the car into a tree instead of looking
where she was going" and "Chris*teen*a thought it would be
nice if I interrupted my work to come in and say hello to you
ladies. So here I am. Hello." He would say, "I have to remind
Chris*teen*a to take a bath, you know. If I didn't remind her
she'd never bathe at all." He liked to tell their friends that
a tradesman had said, "I like Mrs. Marquand. She's real common." And he liked to remind everyone that he had had to

rent the little room in Charles Street just to get away from Chris*teen*a.

These verbal attacks on Christina both amused and disturbed their friends, who privately wondered how seriously John's expressions of hostility were to be taken. Though Christina seemed outwardly unperturbed, there were signs that she was beginning to wither under the onslaught of accusations and complaints which her husband leveled at her head, and of hearing all the reasons why he felt she was making his life intolerable. He had begun to make an assertion that he would continue to make throughout his life: "Writers should *never* marry. At least *I* should never have." And Christina once wistfully confided to a friend, "You know, I broke my engagement to him fourteen times. Perhaps I shouldn't have ever—" and her voice trailed off into silence. And so, by the summer of 1926, there was the first of what would be several separations.

Christina had begun to say that she thought she was going to have a nervous breakdown—the threat had become one of her few defenses—and the omnipresent Sedgwicks, who were always waiting watchfully in the wings to come to the aid of their beleaguered child, suggested that she join them on the European trip.

Carol and Drew Hill, meanwhile, were young writers of yet a different sort. Drew Hill had, like John Marquand, worked for a while in advertising, despaired of it, and had come to Paris "to see if I can write," Paris being the traditional place where one came to find answers to such questions. He had written a few things and sold some of them, but he was having only a limited amount of success. Carol Hill, simply because everyone else was doing it and there seemed not much else to do, had also written a novel. But, because she wasn't sure quite how one went about such things, she had done nothing about showing it to a publisher. In fact, she had not even let Drew read it.

Carl Brandt was also Drew Hill's literary agent, and he had written to the Hills to say that John Marquand was in Paris, alone, and might want company or cheering up. Brandt suggested that the Hills get in touch with him. They did, and the three hit it off splendidly from the beginning.

Marquand had been staying at the Hotel Reservoir in Versailles, and he—who had at that point much more money to spend than the Hills—would motor to Paris and take his new friends out to lunch and dinner at expensive restaurants which they themselves could never have afforded. He took them for drives in the country, for trips on the *bateaux mouches,* and saw that they were invited to week-end house parties in the country.

One day, Carol rather shyly mentioned to John that she had written a novel. He insisted that she give the manuscript to him to read, and he took it back with him to the hotel that night. He returned to Paris the next day, told her that he thought the book was certainly publishable, and suggested several editors to whom she ought to send it. Carol Hill's novel—called *Wild*—was quickly accepted by John Day and was also sold for magazine serialization. *Wild* was a tale of flappers in the Flapper Era, written with a what-the-hell, devil-may-care attitude and erratic spelling and punctuation. But it was fast-paced and breezy, and Carol's views on sex were frank and airy and amusing, and the book eventually sold quite well.

It irritated Drew Hill a bit to watch his wife's little book, which she had more or less dashed off, turn her into the more successful writer of the two. But on the whole it was a happy summer for the three friends, and toward the end of it they all motored down to a big house party at a place called Maule. There was a garden behind the house and, in the center of the garden, a mulberry tree whose branches spread so wide that they seemed to embrace the garden, throwing it into a restful late-summer shade. Lunch was in the garden, under the mulberry tree, everyone drank a great deal of wine, and after lunch everyone went upstairs to rest. John Marquand and Carol Hill found themselves alone in the garden, and John confided that he felt depressed. He had been too upset to enjoy the wine. He was worried about Christina, about what was happening to his marriage. Carol said suddenly, "Look, you've done so much for me, can I do something for you? Why don't we sit down and work? It will get your mind off things." There was a typewriter in the house, and she carried it out into the garden, sat down in front of it, and said, "Now, dictate a story to me."

Marquand was doubtful. He was not at all sure that this approach to writing would work. He had never dictated a story before. He had either typed it out—and he was a very poor typist—or had written it in his tiny, slanted longhand which was so difficult to read it had to be transcribed. "Try it, anyway," Carol suggested. He did, and all at once he discovered that it worked quite well. In fact, it worked wonderfully. Carol quickly noticed that if John stood facing her as he dictated, he became distracted, trying to decipher her reactions to his words. If a line was supposed to be humorous, he would wait for her to smile, and so on. Carol solved this problem by turning around and typing with her back to him. The work went fast. Carol, who had been trained as a secretary, typed speedily and accurately, getting the words down on paper just as fast as John could say them. In a little over two hours, working that afternoon and the next, the story was done.

It was a long war story called "Good Morning, Major." Though the action of the story takes place in a stateside Army training camp, on a troop ship, and on a battlefield in France, it deals with a familiar Marquand theme: the differences that mark the upper classes and the lower. The narrator—the Major of the title—and his friend, Lieutenant Billy Langwell, are both newly commissioned officers, just down from Harvard. Billy Langwell, "one of those nice New York Langwells," is a "slender and almost delicate" young man, whose "family wanted [him] to be an aide." He wears custom-made boots and expensive whipcord breeches. His antagonist, General Swinnerton, is a hard-nosed, tough-talking Regular Army officer who has fought his way upward through the ranks in a hard career of mud and blood. Lieutenant Langwell observes that the General "isn't quite a gentleman." The General, for his part, senses the elegant young officer's feeling of social superiority and accuses him of thinking that the General is a "mucker," while the Lieutenant is a "dude"—expressions, of course, which nice families like the Langwells would never use. In the heat of battle, however, the General is required to turn to the younger officer for help in reading a map that is full of French words and place names, and later Billy Langwell's valor in carrying out a dangerous mission demonstrates to the old General that there is something to be said for upperclass values and education, after all. At the same time, the narrator, seeing with what bravery the General accepts the news of the death of his son, learns that there is also something to be said for the values gained from the school of hard knocks of a Regular Army man.

Marquand shipped the story off to George Lorimer at the *Post*, who was delighted with it. In fact, Lorimer considered it one of the very best stories Marquand had ever done. Apparently, so did a lot of other people. The *Post* published "Good Morning, Major" in the winter of that year, and the story was promptly scooped up and placed in a number of distinguished anthologies. It was reprinted in *The Best Short Stories of 1927*, in *C'Est la Guerre: Best Short Stories of the World War*, and still another book called *Best Short Stories of the War*. More than ten years later, the story was placed in a volume called *Fifty Best American Stories*. It was a story that might even have impressed Uncle Ellery.

And in the process of its creation Marquand had made a discovery about himself that was of overwhelming importance to his career as a writer, as an artist: He could talk his stories and novels straight into type. One whole awkward and painful step in the creative process had been instantly eliminated for him. The work not only went faster; it came out sounding, and reading, better. And so this became the new pattern of his work. He would dictate for a few hours, then read over the typescript. He would pencil in small cuts and changes, and have the manuscript final-typed. This lucky discovery— to Marquand it seemed next to miraculous—of a new and quicker and easier and better way of writing was very much like other odd bits of luck and happenstance that helped him forward as a writer and as a man. To implement the luck, of course, there was one thing he would always need: someone who could take dictation as rapidly and well as Carol Hill had that afternoon under the big mulberry tree at Maule.

That same afternoon he revealed to Carol his secret dream, which was to write at least one great novel—an American *Madame Bovary.*

Chapter Eight

.

*I*t was during Marquand's months with Battery A at the Mexican border that he first began developing his skill as a raconteur and discovered that he could hold an audience. Perhaps it was the intimacy and camaraderie of military camp, the sense of outing and adventure that goes with bivouac life, that brought out Marquand's storytelling knack. But certainly the ease with which he had learned to tell anecdotes helped him make the transition from physically writing his books and stories to talking them—and virtually acting them out—to a typist. His was something very close to a histrionic talent. At Harvard, he had not been known as a particularly funny fellow, or wit. And yet at the encampment of Battery A Marquand soon became the funniest man around, celebrated for his comic stories. On warm and lazy Southwestern evenings Marquand and his squadron mates would gather outside their tents. A bottle of whiskey would be produced, and soon someone would say, "John, tell us the story about —" and he would be off on one of his raucous tales, amid gales of laughter. It was in Battery A, too, that he met some of the men who would remain his best friends for life, such men as

William Otis and George Merck. These men had all been with him at Harvard but—they were part of the Mount Auburn Street Crowd—he had never really got to know them there.

Just what comprised Marquand's gifts as an anecdotist is worth considering. He had, for one thing, a deep and resonant voice, and during his four years at Harvard, and more years reading aloud with his cultivated aunts at Curzon's Mill, he had developed what is called the American educated accent. The American upper-class accent is designed to command attention and respect, and Marquand's voice did this. When he started to speak, others stopped to listen. But he would also imitate a number of regional accents, and these imitations were part of his humor. Then there were his exaggerated gestures, the violent flinging about of his arms as he talked, the contortions of his face into a variety of theatrical expressions, and the way he had of pacing up and down, shoulders hunched like a prize fighter, as he told his stories. Under strict analysis, one would have to admit that he over-told his stories just as he overwrote several of his books. Yet, though the reader might be aware that a Marquand book was overwritten, the reader was seldom bored. Neither were his listeners. In his tales he was a successful user, as he was in the novels, of the device of repetition. He would single out, for humorous effect, a certain word or phrase and repeat it, each time changing the inflection and emphasis slightly, and the cumulative effect of these repetitions, with variations, was hilarious. The more stories he told, the more he became in demand as a storyteller. And, in the process, the painful shyness that as a younger man had encased him like a shell simply fell away.

To be sure, when one had laughed one's way through one of John Marquand's anecdotes—as he did in the novels, he used the flashback technique, and so his listeners became involved in an intricate tapestry of time—one sometimes wondered what it was, exactly, that was so funny. Strictly speaking, when you examined his most popular tales they turned out to be of a rather primitive order. "John, tell us the story about Milo Junction, Maine!" his friends would cry again and again. The Milo Junction, Maine, story was one they never seemed to tire of. It is a ramshackle affair that meanders toward a punch line which asserts that when you look down into a toilet bowl you will *see* Milo Junction, Maine—and a resident of Milo Junction who looks up at you and says, "Well, how would you feel if you'd been pissed on all of your life?" For some reason, this bromide would bring down the house.

Then there was the story John told about the Yankee carpenter who refused to build a two-holer outhouse for a country farmer. After a lengthy build-up the story ends when the carpenter explains, "By the time you decided which hole to use you'd have shit in your pants!" It is a disservice to his storytelling to repeat these whiskery chestnuts, but it is a testimony to his theatrical artistry that he could not only hold an audience with them but also make them come out very, very funny. He was a personification of the cliché about jokesmiths: It wasn't so much the jokes he told as the funny way he told them.

Meanwhile, his talent as a funnyman was definitely helping to destroy his marriage to Christina because, with her natural ineptitude, she became the perfect target for his humor. There is no question that Christina hated being the butt of her husband's jokes. But still she sat there smiling her tentative smile as he told them, while their friends laughed at them and at her, the ideal sitting duck.

From their European wanderings, Carol and Drew Hill had returned to New York, and now their marriage was also in difficulty. Part of the trouble was the publication of *Wild*. But with Drew Hill there were deeper career problems. He not only seemed to lack the ability but also—and more important—the discipline that a writing career requires. It was not so much that he wrote badly but that he had trouble getting himself to work at all. He could not seem to make the vital first step that a writer must take, which Sinclair Lewis once described as "applying the seat of the pants to the seat of the chair." Instead, he made a series of wandering journeys, hitchhiking about the United States in order to get, he said, "the feel of grassroots America." Whether he got this or not, he was unable to get the words on paper, while his wife, as the money was running out, grew increasingly impatient with him.

With the publication of her novel, Carol Hill had also acquired Carl Brandt as her literary agent, and with Drew off on his cross-country travels she now saw as much of Carl as she did of any man. Frequently Marquand was there, and the three-way friendship began that was to last for so many years. Sometimes, when John was in New York, Carol would help him by taking dictation (he had found a secretary in Boston who could do the same thing), and often the three would have lunch, drinks, or dinner together. Drew Hill's absences from New York grew longer. At last Carol went to Carl Brandt privately to ask him the question that had been most on her mind: Was her husband *really* a writer? Sadly, Brandt shook his head and said that he thought not; he did not believe Hill possessed whatever mysterious ingredient it takes to write and suggested that he ought to consider going back into advertising or some other kind of work. "But John's a better judge of writing than I am," Carl Brandt said. "Why don't you ask John what *he* thinks?"

So, in the middle of the summer of 1927, Carol Hill journeyed up to Weston, Massachusetts, the Boston suburb where the Marquands had taken a house for the summer while Christina waited for the second baby, and met John there. John took her for a drive in his new Cadillac car, of which he was very proud since it was his first Cadillac and symbolized his success, even though it was full of bugs and crotchets.

They drove at random about the green New England summer countryside, through the old towns of Lexington and Concord, and at last paused for rest and refreshment at a rather garish little pavilion that had been erected at the edge of Walden Pond where, not that many years before, Henry Thoreau had found both surcease from pain and a tranquillity unclouded by domestic difficulties. They ordered ice cream. Carol, who already knew about John's troubles with Christina, now told him about hers with Drew and what Carl Brandt had said. John immediately agreed and added that if either one of them had the equipment to be a writer it was probably

Carol. They then sat there in silence, spooning their ice cream.
It was one of those moments where nothing more needs to
be said, where perfect agreement has been reached between
two people, and complete understanding. Each knew the exact
nature of the torments the other was undergoing, and the
shared feeling, over the prosaic plates of ice cream, made it
as tender and meaningful an afternoon, though meaningful
in a different way, as the afternoon just a summer before
when the two had produced a successful short story under the
mulberry tree at Maule.

Drew Hill was a handsome and a charming man but also,
in ways that his wife was slowly beginning to grasp, a weak
one. Carol, on the other hand, was a restless and ambitious
young woman with drives that were gradually defining themselves and becoming focused. Raised in suburban New Jersey,
the daughter of a man who owned a furniture business, she
had attended Barnard College for a while and then, eager to
get on with life, had left school and married Drew Hill—perhaps too hastily. Despite what John Marquand said that day
by Walden Pond, Carol knew that she also was not a writer.
She had written her novel "out of desperation and boredom,
because everybody else was writing." She was bright enough
to realize, as she has said, "that I would never be any better than
second-rate at writing." She was also a great believer in setting
goals for herself, of deciding what she wanted and going after it.
Her husband's inability to concentrate his energies in a specific
direction made her both impatient with him and apprehensive
about what their future together might be. Drew Hill, however,
did take John's and Carl's advice and went back into the advertising business. For a while he worked with an agency, and then he
took a job with the advertising department of Bankers Trust
Company.

On Memorial Day of 1929, Drew and Carol Hill and Carol's
father went on a picnic trip in a canoe on the Connecticut
River. The canoe, caught on a sudden fluke current, over-
turned. Carol and her father made it safely to shore, but Drew,
who had suffered a gassing in the First World War, disappeared, and his body was not recovered until ten days later.

It was a violent end to a life that had, for the most part, been unfulfilled and unproductive. It was also now necessary for his widow to find a job. Carl Brandt immediately came forward and helped Carol find a place with a fellow literary agent, Ann Watkins.

Carl Brandt was a gentle, kindly, and witty man, whose manner combined something of the courtly Old-World Southern gentleman with a certain bawdiness of humor that was very New York and very contemporary. No one liked an off-color joke better than he. And yet he could be professorial—even owlish—in his evaluations of authors and their works. He contained, much as John Marquand did, both a serious literary side and a comic side, and it was little wonder that the two men had fast become friends. Brandt's childhood had been not unlike John Marquand's. The son of a moderately prosperous doctor, the house physician at the Homestead Hotel in Hot Springs, Virginia, he had spent his early years in a cottage on the grounds of the resort. His father, however, deciding that Carl and his brother Erd were becoming "spoiled" by life among the wealthy Homestead guests, sent the two boys to live with a Baptist clergyman and his wife in a hamlet some fifty miles from Hot Springs where they were to learn Latin, English, and the Bible. Here, in a house without central heating or indoor plumbing, lit by oil lamps and with only corncob mattresses to sleep on, life was very much like John's at Curzon's Mill. The clergyman, Father Gwathmey, and his wife used corncobs for another and more intimate purpose in the outdoor privy that stood hard by the house, and once, as a cruel prank, Carl and his brother placed a corncob that had been soaked in turpentine in the privy for Father Gwathmey's personal use. It was about a week before Father Gwathmey could sit down again with comfort, and this became one of Marquand's favorite stories. "Carl, tell the story about Father Gwathmey and the corncob!" he would implore. Brandt had been orphaned at the age of sixteen and had had to work and fight hard for everything he achieved, just as John had, in a sense, been abandoned by his parents and sent out to make his own way.

Carl Brandt was a shrewd and exceptionally graceful trader,

who maneuvered his way through the often treacherous jungles of New York publishing with dignity and ease and charm, behind which lay a solid tough-mindedness. It was said that Carl Brandt cajoled—even wooed—good prices and favorable contracts out of editors and publishers for his clients, and that his soft-sell methods were so persuasive that one agreed to his terms without even sensing the hard-sell muscle that rippled underneath. Brandt's Yankee-like trader's instinct was still another thing that endeared him to Marquand.

Now that Carol Hill was herself a literary agent, she found Carl Brandt an invaluable tutor and adviser. Carol, widowed, and Carl, who had been divorced from his first wife for several years, saw even more of each other—socially, as well as in a business sense—and it wasn't long before Brandt asked Carol to marry him. For Carol, a lonely young woman of twenty-seven, nothing seemed more natural than to accept, and the two were married in May, 1931, not quite two years after Drew Hill's death. Carl Brandt was forty-one. This drew the threads of the three-way friendship even more tightly together.

John was not averse to making a certain amount of use out of his friends. After all, what were good friends for? Carl was his agent and editor. Carol could take dictation and type his scripts. He rewarded them with the pleasure of his company, and there is no doubt that, as his own marriage continued its unsteady course, he enjoyed being the third point in a triangle that included a happily married couple. In New York he had Carl and Carol Brandt; in Boston, Gardi and Conney Fiske. In these triangles he felt safe, comforted, loved—and assured of free lodgings, which he definitely appreciated. In New York it was Carl Brandt to whom he turned for carfare for the return trip to Boston, and to whom the dollar bills fluttered back through the mails.

In Boston, the Sedgwicks—Christina's mother in particular —seemed to be doing nothing that was in the least bit helpful in holding the Marquands' marriage together. Mrs. Sedgwick continued her domineering ways with her daughter and remained disparaging about her son-in-law's writing. There seemed to be no way to please her. On the one hand, she complained of John's "writing for money"; on the other, she claimed that John was not earning enough to support a wife and children in the proper Sedgwick style. Christina had grown more vaporous and imponderable than ever. In 1929, signs had been appearing everywhere that the glorious bubble of the twenties was about to burst, and suddenly in Boston there had been earth-shattering news. Kidder, Peabody & Company, one of the most respected investment banking and brokerage firms in the city, had announced that it was in serious financial difficulties. For days, Boston had been unable to talk of anything else. The collapse of Kidder, Peabody would be as stunning an event as if the sun failed to rise in the morning. To the Sedgwicks, it would have very nearly amounted to a family tragedy, since Cousin Minturn Sedgwick was married to a Peabody. A few days after the firm's crisis, John and Christina Marquand had been driving out to their summer house in Weston with Gardi and Conney Fiske, and all the way out the Fiskes and John had talked excitedly in the car. What did this all mean to the economy of Boston, to the country, to world banking? Suddenly Christina had spoken up in her high-pitched, fluty voice. "What's this I hear about Kidder, Peabody?"

It was inevitable that word of his marital problems should reach the ears of such men as George Horace Lorimer and Ray Long, who were buying Marquand's increasingly popular short stories and serials, and it was Lorimer's suggestion that John get away from Christina and the two children for a while by taking a trip to the Orient to gather new material for fiction. And so, financed by the booming *Saturday Evening Post,* Marquand sailed for the Far East. When he returned, it was summer again and the Brandts had taken a house for a few months in Bronxville. John joined them there for an extended visit and, dictating to Carol, began a novel to be called *No Hero,* the first of what would become a hugely successful series of books and stories about a whimsically obsequious, lisping Japanese detective named Mr. Moto.

Carol would return from her office on weekday afternoons, and John would dictate for two hours before dinner. Carol would type the manuscript in triple space. The next day, John would edit the previous evening's material and, by afternoon, would be ready to start dictating again. On Saturdays and Sundays, they would work for as many as seven to eight hours at a stretch. The work was concentrated and exhausting, but by the end of the summer the novel was finished. Lorimer was delighted with it.

In the year 1933, John Marquand earned $19,000, not at all bad for a writer in the depths of the Depression. Nonetheless that year the Marquands made a decision that on the surface seems foolish and was to prove ruinous. For reasons of economy as much as for anything else, they decided to move in with Christina's family at Sedgwick House.

It was, of course, a large house with many big rooms, and an argument could be made that it was big enough to hold all the Sedgwicks plus four Marquands, and there were also quaint and quirky details about the old place that rather appealed to Marquand's sardonic turn of mind as a storyteller, to his sense of the ridiculous. He had always been amused, for example, by the Sedgwick dog cemetery behind the house, a canine resting-place where, beneath tiny headstones in carefully tended graves, reposed Sedgwick pets going back for over a hundred years, their names—"Kozo," "Kai," "Benvenuto Cellini"—carved in the ancient stones above inscribed testaments to the departed dogs' virtues, written in Latin.

For all this, 1933 was hardly the happiest year of the Marquands' marriage. Christina's brother, A. C. Sedgwick, Jr., also lived at Sedgwick House and, in the Sedgwick tradition, he was "literary." That particular year he was at work on a poetic novel to be called *Wind Without Rain,* and the family was understandably excited about the book's emergence. Across the hall from A. C.'s workroom, John Marquand was writing one after another of his endless stream of serials and stories that were feeding and clothing his wife and two children— serials that were appearing in magazines with circulations totaling in the tens of millions but which, by Sedgwick standards, "nobody" read. One afternoon, while John was working, Mrs. Sedgwick tapped on John's door to ask him if he would mind taking A. C.'s dog, whose name was Chou-Fleur, out for its regular midafternoon walk. "I can't disturb him to ask *him* to do it," Mrs. Sedgwick whispered to John. "He's writing, you know."

With increasing frequency that year, John would find himself boarding the train at the Stockbridge station to escape to New York for a few days. Sometimes these trips were necessary in order to meet or lunch with editors, but as often as not he would invent reasons for his departures merely to get away from the Sedgwick world. In New York, he would move in with Carl and Carol Brandt. One time, returning to Stockbridge and the Sedgwicks, he brought with him a tankful of tropical fish. Tropical fish had always fascinated him. But this time he presented the tank and fish to Christina's mother as a hostess present. Mrs. Sedgwick, looking mystified, asked him, "But why would you give me tropical fish, John?" He replied, "It seemed to me a bit chilly up here." Mrs. Sedgwick rewarded him with her iciest stare.

When Carol Brandt suffered an attack of appendicitis in 1934, her doctor ordered her to take two weeks of vacation and rest. Since this occurred during one of Marquand's periodic flights from his family, Carl Brandt suggested that he and Carol go to Bermuda and then, rather hesitantly, asked, "Can we take John with us? He doesn't want to go back to Christina and the children yet." Carol wasn't certain whether a holiday *à trois* was a good idea, but she agreed. It turned out to be one of the happiest times the three had ever spent together. They stayed at the Castle Harbour, which had just opened, and for two weeks they swam, lay in the sun, played three-handed bridge, and drank something they christened "Liquid Sunshine," a murderous concoction which Carl devised out of several varieties of rum and brandy. Too soon it was time for John to go home and face troubles in Boston, for although these escapes from marriage were diverting they solved no problem.

In Boston he had begun to think about a novel quite different from anything he had written before. It would be a novel *about* Boston, about the social attitudes that prevailed there which were so different from those in New York, or any place else in the world, for that matter. These were the attitudes that had seemed to present him with nothing but obstacles in terms of Christina and the Sedgwicks.

When, in late 1934, John told Carl and Carol that he intended to divorce Christina, the Brandts were deeply disturbed. It seemed to his friends that for all its up and downs it was a marriage worth saving, and there were two small children in the picture. John, Jr. was then eleven, and little Christina was only seven. The Brandts begged John to meet privately with Christina to discuss matters, and to meet with her preferably on neutral territory, with no children or Sedgwick relatives on hand to distract the couple from facing their problems. Reluctantly, John agreed to try their suggestion, which was more Carol's than Carl's; Carl, having been through one divorce, was less sanguine about the chances of John's marriage surviving. Carol suggested that the meeting take place at the Brandts' apartment, which was at 270 Park Avenue, and on the morning of the meeting both Brandts departed for their offices to leave John alone to await Christina. That evening, when they returned, John was alone again, standing in the living room, a drink in his hand, swinging the glass in circles in that characteristic way of his. From his expression, it was clear that the meeting with his wife had been less than a complete success. It was also clear that John had had more than one drink.

"Well," Carol Brandt asked tentatively, "how did things go?"

John exploded. "Can you *imagine?*" he asked. "Can you *imagine* what she said? She said that before we discussed anything I would have to *apologize!* She said, 'John, before I say anything, I want you to apologize!' *Apologize!*"

And so that marriage was over. It had lasted, in its shaky and fragile way, more than twelve years. A divorce decree was granted to Christina Sedgwick Marquand on May 19, 1935, in Pittsfield, Massachusetts, and another chapter in the life John Marquand was writing for himself came to an end.

PART TWO
A Middle

Chapter Nine

*O*f all Marquand's friends, the person whose literary taste and judgment he admired the most was Conney Fiske. Carl Brandt might help him as an editor, telling him where to cut and splice and fill, and Carol—or any other good stenographer— could make the creative process easier by taking down the novels and stories as he dictated them, but only Conney Fiske, in Marquand's opinion, had true critical ability. Throughout his life he expressed nothing but disdain for book reviewers, particularly those who sought to elevate their calling by claiming to be "critics." "Nothing but a bunch of ex-obituary writers," he used to say, and he insisted that he hardly ever bothered to read what they wrote about his books and never paid any attention to anything they had to say. But he paid attention to Conney Fiske, and early in their friendship he began his lifelong practice of letting her read his manuscripts as they progressed, a few chapters at a time, and listening to her opinions on the work in progress.

Conney Fiske today is a small, gingery lady who, by her good tweed suits, her little hats, and her quiet demeanor, would be recognized almost everywhere as a Bostonian. Like others of her own and of other generations, she possesses the curious ability to carry the distinctive stamp of Boston with her wherever she goes. Boston is in every inflection of her speech, every gesture, every turn of mind and shade of thought. Her sense of quality is *Bostonian,* which means that more emphasis is placed on duty, probity, good manners, and quiet accomplishment than on money or show. Conney Fiske was born rich, the daughter of a hugely successful manufacturer, but she would probably shudder at the thought of indicating that she was anything more than comfortably—and respectably—well off. It is typical of her sense of propriety that in her sprawling old farmhouse ("It's not really old, only nineteenth century") in suburban Framingham, the furniture should be old and fine, but upholstery is threadbare and rugs are thin and worn. An air of shabby gentility hangs over the whole place and, in summer, when one jumps into the icy waters of her somewhat old-fashioned (and certainly unheated) fill-and-draw swimming pool, one is joined by tiny and quite unobtrusive green frogs. Now in her seventies, Conney Fiske has all her life been an ardent horsewoman and is proudest of her stable, her thoroughbreds, and her private jumping course. When she foxhunts, which she does regularly "in season" from her winter home in Southern Pines, North Carolina, she rides using "the Queen's seat," that is, sidesaddle, a position that seems appropriate to one who is clearly a Boston gentlewoman.

But Conney Fiske is also, by Boston standards, something of a sport, a maverick. Though she has been widowed for a number of years, her existence is hardly typical of the "proper" Boston widow who spends her days paying calls and pouring tea. Conney Fiske travels extensively and almost compulsively in her own country and abroad, always seeking out new places and experiences and people, satisfying her restless curiosity about the world and its beings. "In Boston, they think I am a little crazy, of course," she often says. Though she toils for proper Boston causes—the hospitals and Radcliffe College, of which she is a trustee—she is far from the typical committeewoman. She also possesses a definite *chic,* which is not at all what one thinks of as Boston standard-dowdy. She is justifiably proud of her slender figure and slim legs, and of tiny feet which are always handsomely and expensively shod.

At the same time, she possessed—and possesses—a quality that particularly appealed to Marquand: a sense of humor about her own situation and social caste and about the values of upper-class Boston that have shaped Constance Morss Fiske into the definite lady she is. She has John's ability to see both sides of her position and station in life. Like John, she could always laugh at the rituals and mystiques surrounding such venerable Boston institutions as the Athenaeum, the Chilton Club, the Somerset Club, and the enormous and mysterious importance of living on the Hill. At the same time, Conney Fiske would seem to take her membership in all these institutions very seriously; lunching in town she usually prefers the Spartan dignity of the downstairs ladies' dining room in the Somerset Club, and during the years when the Fiskes kept their big house at 206 Beacon Street Conney Fiske did so with an awareness that this was a most impeccable Boston address, and that an impeccable address matters seriously in Boston.

Conney Fiske's detachment was not typical but exceptional for Boston. She could get amusement from observing the old and proper families such as the Lowells and the Lawrences and the Peabodys, people who saw each other over and over again, year after year, who traveled to London and stayed at Brown's Hotel because only here could they be sure of finding other Bostonians, and who, confronted with people from out of town, would simply refuse to engage them in conversation, preferring "our own sort." And yet she was herself very much a part of this formalized world, part of this pattern, and knew its contours and its rules.

Perhaps her curious combination of serious adherence to form, along with a gentle and detached self-mockery, is best seen watching Conney Fiske on horseback, in the Moore County Hunt. Though she rides the Queen's seat with dignity and authority in her well-worn but expensively tailored riding skirt, and with her sensibly coiffed hair tucked under a black derby hat, it is somehow also clear that she knows perfectly

well that she is an oddity, an anachronism, and is getting huge
enjoyment from this knowledge.

This specialness of her humor was what endeared Conney
Fiske to John Marquand. She was everything that the Sedgwicks were, but with self-awareness added. She, in turn, understood what John had had to endure from the Sedgwicks and
admired his curiosity and industry and grit in the face of it.

Gardiner Fiske, meanwhile, was if anything even more Bostonian. Though Conney's family was richer, the Gardiner and
Fiske families bore the more prestigious lineage—the Gardiners, in particular, who include in their family tree all the
ancient Lords of the Manor of Gardiners Island, New York, a
private fiefdom granted to the Gardiners by the Crown long
before the Revolution, and still in the family. In Boston,
Gardiners and Fiskes have taken themselves enormously seriously for generations, and men like Gardi Fiske's father,
Andrew Fiske, and his aunt, the maiden lady Miss Gertrude
Fiske, were so thoroughly Beacon-Hill oriented that one could
hardly imagine them more than a block away from Beacon
or State Streets; they could not have breathed the air. Gardi
Fiske had a bit of this in him too, but he was also a movie-
star-handsome, athletic—one might even say dashing—man,
who simply did not look the part of a Boston Brahmin. He had
a romantic past. During World War I he had been a flying ace
who, at one point, had fallen out of the plane he was flying,
seized hold of one of the rear struts, and clambered back
aboard. He was not at all frightened at the time, he told Marquand, who never tired of hearing about this astonishing feat,
because "I know the Bishop, who is Up There, and if there are
any good clubs, he'll get me in." He was referring, of course,
to Bishop Lawrence of Boston. Gardi and John had been good
friends since *Lampoon* days. Gardi, after the war, had gone to
work as a cotton broker and was a member of the Boston Air-
port Authority, earning a respectable, if not giant, salary, and
Marquand had admired Gardi for doing this. It would have
been so easy, Marquand often pointed out, for a man in Gardi
Fiske's position to live off his wealthy wife. Most of all,
Marquand admired Gardi's integrity, his insistence on sticking

to his principles. With Gardi there was black and there was white, and no shadings in between.

John Marquand had developed an admiration for the novels of Edith Wharton and Jane Austen. A dog-eared copy of *Pride and Prejudice* could usually be found in his jacket pocket, and he read and reread it many times. Before his divorce from Christina, he had turned out two novels that reflected the Jane Austen influence and were suggestive of the major novels that would one day follow. The first of these two, published in 1930, was called *Warning Hill,* and the second, published in 1933, was titled *Haven's End.* Both had been first written for magazine serialization, and both had New England settings. Of the two novels, *Haven's End* is the more interesting and the more successful and, later on, *Haven's End* was the only one of his early novels which Marquand chose to list on the traditional "ad page" at the front of each of his books, an indication that he considered *Haven's End* the only title worth owning up to, and that he would just as soon let the others be forgotten.

The fictional town of Haven's End, where the finest houses "still are very fine. They stand on a ridge above the Main Street, where they may overlook the river and the sea," is very reminiscent of the Newburyport John Marquand knew as a boy, and the Swales, who have ancient roots there, sound very much like his own ancestral Marquands. He was gradually, and somewhat hesitantly, abandoning the costumed melodrama of his first books and coming to grips with his own experience. In the process, his writing style was becoming less turgid and labored, moving toward the honeyed smoothness of the writing in his best books, a style so polished and restrained that there hardly seems to be any style at all. Also in *Haven's End* he made use—somewhat crude and primitive use, to be sure— of the flashback technique that would become the great Marquand trademark in the later books, the perfectly structured and sweepingly cinematic movements backward in time that carried readers deep into the past of the Marquand characters. *Haven's End* opens with the village auctioneer about to put the splendid old Swale mansion on the block. The novel then shifts—too abruptly to be as dramatic as a good flashback should be—into the past history of the Swales. Three-hundred-odd pages later, the story jumps back into the present again as the auctioneer's hammer falls on the final sale.

Conney Fiske encouraged John with both these New England novels—he was writing, after all, about a world which she also knew, perhaps even better than he—and together they would discuss nuances of the Yankee's character: his sense of probity and thrift, and also his strong feelings of continuity of family as expressed through property, through roots.

Meanwhile, John's Mr. Moto stories were achieving huge popularity, and each new tale of the lisping, bowing, and foot-shuffling little detective was immediately being snapped up for movies that starred Peter Lorre. Despite his complaints about the amounts of money he had had to settle on Christina and to support his children, Marquand was becoming a rich writer. This gave him time and leisure to work on the big novel he had been thinking about, the Boston novel. When he had once mentioned it to Christina, her reaction had been, "We'll have to leave Boston, of course." Now this had become the novel he and Conney Fiske talked most about during the long and pleasant afternoons at 206 Beacon Street, and which he was giving her to read, chapter by chapter, as it progressed. Its central character was to be a Boston Brahmin, a man not unlike Gardi Fiske's father. It was a character who would be approached with Conney's, and John's, kind of double sight. That is, the hero of the book would be a man whom one would laugh at for his foolishness and pomposity, but whom one would also love for his integrity and fidelity to his code. As a novel, it would be an important departure for John, the most ambitious project he had ever undertaken—a bid, though he did not come out and say so—for greatness. It would be, perhaps, his *Pride and Prejudice.* As the novel moved along, Conney Fiske could tell that her husband, in all probability, would not like it. It dissected their own world too surgically, mocked it too cleverly. But Conney Fiske sensed that a major book was under way, and her encouragement was therefore steady and insistent. She also sensed Marquand's extraordinary excitement with what he was doing. It was an excitement he had not experienced before in anything he had written. With this book, which he planned to call *The Late George Apley,* he was not writing as a journeyman professional, turning out commercial fiction. He was writing with a true creative joy.

He could not come out and say this either, but he was writing a novel that could thumb its nose at Uncle Ellery. And at Christina.

Chapter Ten

*C*onney Fiske, in a gentle and friendly way, had for a long time been trying to get Marquand to tone down his writing style, to restrain it, to make it somehow quieter and less fervid —more civilized. Along with a tendency to overwrite, he had a tendency to exaggerate. Exaggeration can present problems to a writer, particularly when he is attempting to write humor. If humor is not reined in and kept under control, it can easily fall over the line and become slapstick. Satire, pushed too far, slips the track completely and becomes farce and, in the process, loses every vestige of credibility. Conney objected, for instance, to a detail in one of Marquand's short stories in which a woman character is described as appearing in a cocktail dress "from one of New York's most creative couturières" which was "of hand-painted silk with a brilliant motif of violet and red mixed drinks in long-stemmed glasses." Conney didn't believe that such a dress could ever exist, except in a novelist's somewhat bitchy fancy, and, if it did, that it would have been worn by this character, an expensive lady in an exclusive club at a fashionable resort. But John liked the detail, considered it humorous, and kept it, and there it stands in the story today, looking very much as though Conney Fiske had been right. In writing *The Late George Apley*—to be a long satiric novel— the problem of maintaining balance, of avoiding overstatement, faced Marquand with each new paragraph. Looking back on his struggles with the novel years later, Marquand confessed that he was not sure that he had been completely successful, or that he had fully resisted "a constant temptation to indulge in slapstick farce." At times his characters, he admitted, "often more than verge on the preposterous." It is an honest admission.

Marquand began writing *The Late George Apley* in 1934, left it half finished until the end of 1935, after the divorce, and completed it toward the end of 1936. It is an extraordinarily subtle and complex piece of work. To begin with, it is constructed as a series of letters between Apley and his children, friends, associates, parents, grandparents, and other relatives. This epistolary form of construction was, of course, nothing new, but over this device Marquand laid a parody of the memoir form which was most original. He had run across, in and around Boston, memorial testaments written about deceased worthies of the city—long-winded pieces of biographical puffery designed to place the subject in the most flattering possible light and to overlook, even bury, any of his shortcomings or weaknesses. Marquand had been amused by these testimonials—which usually were privately printed, on heavy vellum, for distribution to members of the family following a funeral, and were usually atrociously written—and decided to parody one of these biographies to tell the story of the late George Apley's life. Marquand picked, for his fictional biographer, the character of Horatio Willing, pompous Bostonian, prig, prude, bigot, social snob, a man who totally lacks perception or humor and who is otherwise without redeeming social value.

An indication of how successful Marquand was with this device, and how believable a character he was able to make out of the self-important Willing, was that a number of readers— and a few unwary critics—were caught off their guard and deceived into thinking that Marquand was unintentionally responsible for Willing's jaw-breaking prose style, with its frequent lapses from proper English syntax, and accused Marquand of writing "bad grammar." They failed to grasp the point that the bad grammar Marquand wrote for Willing was part of the parody, part of the fun.

One of the hazards of a Horatio Willing, as a device, is that every detail of Apley's life, every relationship and every event, is commented on by Willing, comes to us through Willing's consciousness, and is subject to his whimsical interpretation. But the reader learns, early on, that Willing is a man not to be trusted. He misinterprets everything, shows an utter lack of sensitivity about his subject, does his best to conceal an interesting or revealing fact once he has discovered it, and commits other acts of biographical treachery and deceit.

And yet, it works. Through the smoke screen thrown up around Apley's life by Willing, we somehow manage to see Apley even more brilliantly and—since Apley is himself a prude, a snob, a bigot—more understandingly.

There is, for example, the carefully dusted-off account which Willing gives of the young George Apley's early love affair with a girl named Mary Monahan. Mary Monahan was not only from the wrong side of the tracks, she was also—her name tells the whole story—Boston Irish, and a Catholic. She was, Willing allows, a beautiful girl and "had many of the externals of a young person of a higher position." In fact, out walking once with George on Commonwealth Avenue she was actually mistaken by some passers-by as a Baltimore society belle. In other words, she could almost pass as true Quality, but not quite. Willing dismisses Mary Monahan—or "the young Monahan woman," as he prefers to call her—as a "youthful lapse" of Apley's, something hardly worth taking note of in the book, and points out piously that "anyone at a certain stage in life may be beset by vagaries which must not be considered seriously." At the same time, from the few scraps of Willing-edited correspondence between George and Mary which he selfishly permits his readers to see, it is quite apparent that theirs was a deep and passionate romance and that Mary, not at all a lapse, was the only great and enduring love of George Apley's life and his only chance to break away from the rigid mold into which Boston and the heavy fact of Apley-dom were determined to cast him. Willing promises his readers—though how could he know?—that physical sex was never a part of the relationship between Mary and George, and that "if latitude was offered him by the young Monahan woman . . . he took no advantage of it. This is the one pleasing aspect of an affair which obviously could not be of long duration." Do we believe Willing? Not for a minute.

We watch with a kind of horror as Boston and the Apleys move in on George and Mary and take charge of things. George's letters to Mary grow desperate as he tries to convince her that as soon as his parents get to know her they will love her as much as he does. "Once they do," he promises, "you'll find that all the Apleys stick together, and that you will be one of us." But of course this can never be. Mary Monahan suddenly drops from sight, and the next we hear of George Apley he has been shipped off to Europe for a long rest. His mother writes comfortingly that she had not realized how "overtired" her dear boy was and assures him that when he comes home he shall have "a mother's love, a father's love, or sister's love." On a grimmer note, his father writes, sending money, to explain that an early return to Boston is out of the question, as is any further discussion of "various matters," and, employing a familiar type of emotional blackmail, he explains that this is because of the precarious state of George's mother's health. "I will not have her upset further," his father tells him. "You will view matters in quite a different light after a change of scene and will understand your obligations as a member of our family." George Apley's sister, Amelia, writes to him to say, "There is one thing which I think you will be glad to know. No one is talking about you. I have told everyone that you were overtired by your examinations and everyone is most understanding." She adds, "If you see any sort of brooch in Paris or any pin with pearls, I wish you would buy it for me."

From this point in the novel onward, the clamp of Boston conformity closes relentlessly upon George, and every ounce of rebellion is squeezed out of him drop by drop until he becomes what he was predestined to be: another Boston Apley. In the meantime, the Mary Monahan episode—which consumes scarcely half a dozen pages in the text—throws the entire

balance of the novel into sharp perspective, making the reader
see the aridity of George's eventual marriage, the painful
difficulty he has in understanding his children, the slow coming
to grips with an awareness that his life, taken out of its Boston
context, may have very little meaning, his agonized grasping
at straws at the end for something—family, friends, duty,
tradition—that will make it all have some sense. It is, all in all
—despite the richly humorous details of Boston life observed
in the process—a journey of heartbreak that we are watching
unfold. And the omnipresent biographer, Horatio Willing, is
there to congratulate Apley on every disappointment and rub
his hands on the occasion of each defeat. The more we loathe
Willing, the more we admire and sympathize with George
Apley for being able to carry on, with as much dignity as he
does, in such a world.

If the novel has one flaw it is perhaps that the reader is
never quite convinced that Willing is writing Apley's biography
with the endorsement—at the specific urging, in fact—of
Apley's son, John. Through the pages of the book, John Apley
emerges as a very up-to-date, intelligent young man. At the
outset of the book, in a letter appointing Willing as his father's
biographer, John Apley says he hopes Willing will tell his
father's story straight and true. "My main preoccupation is that
this thing should be real," John Apley tells Horatio Willing. It
soon turns out that Willing is a man of demonstrated dullness,
obtuseness, and biographical inability. Couldn't John Apley
have found someone better for the job? Of course if he had
there could have been no book, for Horatio Willing is as essential to the success of the novel as George Apley.

In an introduction to a new edition of *The Late George
Apley* that was published in 1956, John Marquand reflected
that "the writing of this novel represented for me a species of
personal revolution. I was obviously weary of the many in-
hibitions which were placed on all writers of salable fiction
twenty years ago. I was also weary of many of the restrictions
of my environment—a phase of living with which most of us
have coped at some time or other. Besides, I like to think that
in an exacting literary apprenticeship I had gained a degree of

technical skill and maturity that made me wish to move to a new writing area."

When, in the autumn of 1936, Marquand had come close to finishing the novel, and when Conney Fiske had read it and pronounced it excellent, Marquand sent off the manuscript to the New York offices of Brandt & Brandt. What happened next almost cost him his friendship with Carl and Carol Brandt. The first person in the office to read the manuscript was a young woman named Bernice Baumgarten. Miss Baumgarten—in private life she was the wife of the novelist James Gould Cozzens—had started out in the Brandt office as a secretary, had been elevated by Brandt, and was rapidly gaining a reputation in her own right as one of the brightest and toughest literary agents in New York. Brandt had developed great respect for her judgment. Bernice Baumgarten read John Marquand's venture into "a new writing area" and was dismayed. Her immediate reaction was that the book was unpublishable. In all fairness to Miss Baumgarten—who has since moved to pleasant retirement in Florida—she probably could simply not understand the book, and what she *could* understand she could not believe. Her own background was middle-class-Jewish New York. Upper-class life on Beacon Hill in Boston was as remote from her experience as life on Mars. At the same time, she had been helping John Marquand get top prices for his fast-paced serials and stories of war, romance, and Japanese detectives. *The Late George Apley*, she felt, was too leisurely a tale for Marquand's already large audience to accept. His readers would not only be bored with it but infuriated by it. The book was simply too much of a departure from Marquand's standard for Bernice Baumgarten to swallow. She took the manuscript to Carl Brandt and outlined her objections to it, which were vociferous and heated.

Brandt read it next, and then Carol. Both Brandts—Carl more so than Carol—liked the book better than Bernice did. But they too were somewhat baffled by it, and neither saw in it any sales potential. Again, for them, it was a long way from anything they had experienced—Carl who had grown up in the South, Carol in suburban New Jersey. And it seemed such

a violently revolutionary change for John. If he wanted to
alter his literary style, did he have to do so as drastically and
suddenly as this? Wouldn't he be wiser to work up to something like this gradually?

Next, John wrote to Alfred McIntyre at Little, Brown:

> The last two months I have been working on a thing which
> I have often played with in the back of my mind, a satire on
> the life and letters of a Bostonian. I have now done some
> thirty or forty thousand words on it, and the other day showed
> it to a friend whose literary judgment I greatly respect, who
> feels it is a great pity for me to waste my time in going ahead
> with it. I suppose the most damning thing that can be said
> about the whole business is that I, personally, have enjoyed
> writing it, and think it is amusing, and think that it is a fairly
> accurate satire on Boston life. I certainly don't want to go ahead
> with the thing, however, if you don't think it holds any promise,
> and is not any good. Besides this, I do not, for purely artistic
> reasons, feel that the thing can be helped by any great changes
> such as injecting more plot, or by making the satire more
> marked. In other words, if it is not any good as it stands, I think
> I had better ditch it and turn my attention to something else.
> As this is the first time in a good many years that I have been
> in a position to write something which I really wanted to write,
> I naturally feel bad about it. I know you will tell me frankly
> just how it strikes you, and its fate rests largely in your hands.
> Tell me quickly.

McIntyre told him both quickly and frankly, "John, I personally think it is swell. I can't tell you whether it will sell
more than 2,000 copies—it may be too highly specialized. But
by all means, go ahead with it!"*

* John Marquand agonized over the production of this novel as he had done
before over no other piece of work, endlessly querying his friends and literary
advisers—in the publishing fraternity and out of it—as to the "wisdom" of
doing such a book. Needless to say, the opinions he received were varied, but
Alfred McIntyre's reaction, since it carried the weight of Little, Brown with it,
was certainly the one he valued most. As a result, for many years after the
publication of *The Late George Apley* Marquand used his letter to McIntyre,
and McIntyre's response, as a prime weapon in the novel's defense. He allowed
Edward Weeks to quote from this exchange of letters in his book *The Open
Heart*, and when Kenneth Roberts, in 1956, was writing his introduction to
Marquand's *North of Grand Central: Three Novels of New England*, Marquand
gave Roberts the letters to publish again.

Privately, others at Little, Brown had doubts about the undertaking. If readers outside Boston would find the book mystifying, readers *in* Boston would be mad as hell. The novel seemed to poke fun at Boston. The gentry who lived on Beacon Hill would certainly be offended. So without doubt would the Boston Irish, and their church, over the depiction of "lower-class" Mary Monahan.

Gently and tentatively a feeler went out to Marquand: If, he was asked, he really wanted the novel published, wouldn't it be wise to do so under a pseudonym? John was outraged and deeply hurt. (Over the years, the hurt would continue to rankle. Marquand was never sure just who first made that suggestion. He rather suspected Carl. Many years later he claimed in print that it had been "an officer of Little, Brown." If so, it could only have been Alfred McIntyre. At the Brandt office, a belief persists that the person who suggested the pseudonym was Bernice, but Bernice is certain she never made such a suggestion, though she does remember being "extremely worried" about the book. As time passed, it became something that John and Carl, by tacit mutual agreement, never talked about.)

The Late George Apley was published early in the spring of 1937—not without a certain amount of nervousness—above the signature of John P. Marquand, as he had insisted. The *Saturday Evening Post,* which bought the novel for serialization (George Lorimer was one of the book's earliest supporters), printed a cautious disclaimer with the first installment, warning its readers that they would not find this the usual Marquand fare. There was, as it happened, no great reaction—no wave of critical acclaim or of admonition. If anything, the critics tended to overlook the size of John Marquand's literary step and to underrate the book's importance. In Boston, there were a few bristling reactions from Irish lay Catholics and a few scolding comments from the Catholic press and pulpit. And, on Beacon Hill, there were some disgruntled mutterings that John Marquand had been "a traitor to his class." Gardi Fiske tended to take this view of his old friend's book and privately confessed that he hadn't cared for it (there was a good deal of Gardi in Apley), while Conney Fiske took pains to keep the book from such as her Uncle Wells and Gardi's father, Andrew Fiske, who might easily find too much of themselves in the characters. In its hard-cover edition, the book sold scarcely more than 50,000 copies—enough to make it reach the best-seller list, but several of Marquand's other titles had sold better.

And yet the book made a powerful impact in a lingering and cumulative way. Though the number of copies sold was not outstandingly large, it seemed that these copies were being bought by a different sort of reader than John had been able to reach before, a more sensitive reader, perhaps, better educated and more articulate—not the kind who had found much that was appealing in John's other tales of romance and derring-do. These readers found John's insider's view of Boston utterly fascinating, and they talked about the book and passed it around among themselves. Publishers used, more than they do today, to distinguish between a mass market and a class market for their books. *The Late George Apley*, ignored by the former, became the darling of the latter. These were people who, just as Marquand was weary of his environment, were weary in 1937 of a national Depression, of a controversial man, Franklin Roosevelt, in the White House, of bread lines and apple peddlers in the streets, of the Spanish Civil War and of John L. Lewis, of the rash of government acronyms coming out of Washington, or reading about Stalin and Hitler in Europe and a Dust Bowl in the Middle West. To these readers, *The Late George Apley* brought, among other things, assurance that somewhere—in Boston, specifically—life went on in an unchanging pattern, generation after generation, with those values and amenities and manners that were specifically upper class still observed religiously, where a world could be found where there was, if nothing else, seemliness and order.

An anonymous critic in the "Notes and Comment" section of *The New Yorker,* in an obituary tribute to John Marquand, wrote of *The Late George Apley* that it was "the best-wrought fictional monument to the nation's Protestant élite that we know of" and added that the book is "the finest extended parody composed in modern America . . . a detailed Valentine to a city—Boston—such as no other American city can expect to receive."

In the spring of 1938, when the judges of the Pulitzer Prize Committee announced their awards, the prize for the best book of fiction published in the previous year went to John P. Marquand for *The Late George Apley.*

The title was carried on, through a successful Broadway play and motion picture adaptation with Ronald Colman in the title role. For some reason, Hollywood decided to drop the crucial role of Mary Monahan. Bosley Crowther, then the film critic for the *New York Times,* claimed that *The Late George Apley* had been "botched, but good" by Twentieth Century-Fox. He complained that Joseph L. Mankiewicz's screenplay and Ronald Colman's performance had turned George Apley into a kind of Boston "swell" and had given the story an artificially happy ending. Nonetheless, the words George Apley—as a name and as a symbol—had entered the American language.

At the time of the announcement of the Pulitzer Prize, Conney Fiske wrote to John in New York to tell him how happy and proud she was for him. She remembers how, in his reply, he told her that he thought that she and Gardi, for their help and moral support throughout the book, should have received the prize instead of him.

The success of *The Late George Apley* taught John a somewhat more bitter lesson. There is, in the novel, an episode some twenty pages long concerning George Apley's efforts to bring a crooked Boston-Irish politician with the not uncommon name of O'Reilly to justice; Apley says, "Before I have finished, this man O'Reilly will face the jury of the criminal court." In many ways, the episode is hilarious. In others, it is chilling in its exposure of the Boston Establishment's bigotry and anti-Irish, anti-Catholic bias. Quite often, in these pages, it is quite clear that Apley's sentiments about O'Reilly have less to do with O'Reilly deeds than with his faith and country of origin. For example, Apley says, "This O'Reilly cannot be very popular as many persons in every walk of life are anxious to have him punished. I have looked up his record. He went to the Boston Latin School which proves that I was right in always thinking that this school has been losing its grip since my father's time." Horatio Willing calls O'Reilly "a lawyer and a faithless civil servant," an "unscrupulous Irish politician," and —in the course of the twenty pages in question—a great deal else that is either snobbish, unpleasant, or downright insulting.

John Marquand failed to reckon, quite clearly, with the existence of a Boston-Irish lawyer-politician who, rightly or wrongly, saw himself as the object of Apley's fictional attack. Mr. Peter M. O'Reilly of Boston promptly filed a libel suit against Little, Brown & Company claiming "pecuniary damages and loss of business," saying that he had been "greatly injured in his reputation in his profession" and that the book had caused him great losses in his "earning capacity, his credit and his good name." The lawsuit was filed in the Superior Court of Suffolk County, Commonwealth of Massachusetts, on February 4, 1938.

Years later, John Marquand would caution beginning novelists to be sure—if they did nothing else in their fiction— that there were no people with similar names, in similar occupations, and living in similar towns as their fictional counterparts. "Before you name a character, look him up in the local telephone book," Marquand warned.

Chapter Eleven

*T*here was a theory in the nineteen thirties that if a well-to-do American mother couldn't marry off a daughter, one thing she could do was send the girl to Peking. In Peking in those days there were all sorts of eligible marine and naval officers, embassy officials, and attachés, many of whom hadn't seen an unattached white girl in months or even years, to whom the sight of any woman—particularly a rich American one—was welcome. A girl traveling to Peking wouldn't expect to meet an American novelist, but that was what had happened to Miss Adelaide Hooker in 1935 when she met John Marquand —wearing shorts and a pith helmet—on a beach on the Gulf of Chihli on the Yellow Sea. Adelaide was traveling with her sister Helen, who was en route from Tokyo to Ireland to marry Ernie O'Malley, the Irish revolutionist. A third sister, Blanchette, had already married John D. Rockefeller III, while a fourth Hooker girl, Barbara, like Adelaide, was unmarried. At first, the Hooker girls mistook John Marquand for an Englishman. Adelaide, who was Vassar Class of 1925, had been out of college for ten years, and John Marquand, who was forty-two, was touring the Orient for material for his Mr. Moto

stories. At home in Boston, his marriage to Christina was in its
final throes.

The Hookers were an altogether extraordinary family.
Adelaide's father, Elon Huntington Hooker, was a direct descendant of Thomas Hooker, who founded Hartford in the
early seventeenth century and drafted the constitution of the
State of Connecticut. By Elon Hooker's generation, the family
was rich; he not only headed his own electrochemical manu-
facturing company but was also chairman of the board of the
Research Corporation, chairman of the Executive Committee
of the National Industrial Conference Board, and a director
of the American Association of Manufacturers. An unrecon-
structed Republican who considered F.D.R. anathema, he
had been Deputy Superintendent of Public Works under
Governor Theodore Roosevelt. He was also a strident and
devout Prohibitionist, though apparently he enjoyed pleasures
other than drink. John Marquand liked to tell the story that
when Hooker died a drawer in his desk was opened and found
to contain nothing but dozens of unused condoms. He also liked
to devise curious entertainments for his friends. Once he gave
a stag dinner party at an office in downtown Manhattan. The
men all showed up in dinner clothes and, since there would be
no drinks served—Hooker being a teetotaler—their host advised that there would be a special diversion. At a signal, a
stage curtain went up, and behind it stood a row of girls in
skin-tight panties and bras. A big barrel of cotton snowballs
was then produced, and Hooker announced, "Now you may
throw the snowballs at the girls."

He was an overpowering father, more than a bit of a bully,
and he stressed sports for his four daughters. Tennis, golf,
riding, calisthenics, and other forms of athletics were part of
their upbringing. So avid was Hooker about the importance of
tennis that for a number of years he kept a full-time tennis
professional on his household payroll. As children, his daughters
were trotted all over the countryside to tennis tournaments;
Adelaide, by the time she met John, said that she had become
so sated with tennis that she could not bear the game. Mrs.
Hooker, meanwhile, was a gentle lady who founded the
Women's University Club and, with her sister, Mrs. Avery

Coonley, gave Vassar College the Alumnae House on its campus. Mr. and Mrs. Hooker divided their time between their estate, called "Chelmsford," in Greenwich, and their large apartment at 620 Park Avenue in New York.

Adelaide Ferry Hooker, when John Marquand first met her, was not as heavy as she eventually became, but she was on the plump side. It was almost as if—though now in her thirties—she still retained some of her baby fat. She had a round and pleasant face, and thick and curly blondish hair. She was an ebullient woman with a quick and hearty laugh, generous to a fault. She loved to buy presents for her friends. At school, nicknamed "Tommy," she had been known as a good sport, athletic, a good organizer. She had had a proper New York girl's schooling, had graduated from Miss Spence's School and Vassar, had been presented to society in the customary manner, and had joined the Cosmopolitan Club and the New York Junior League. She had done a routine amount of travel. On the surface, for a woman of her position, it was all very ordinary.

But the unusual thing about Adelaide was that all her life she had a restless passion to do something creative, to be someone on her own, to be something other than a commonplace rich man's daughter. Early in her girlhood she determined to be "different," to stand out from the crowd, and she chose a variety of means in her attempt to do so. She professed a disdain for fashion and, instead, got herself up in costumes— Indian dresses, peasant dirndls, Scottish kilts, dangling beads and bracelets, boots and sandals. She wore ballooning lounging pajamas and slacks long before they were fashionable. She once showed up at a party with a stuffed bird perched in her hair. She espoused off-beat causes and, at Vassar in the early days of Fascism, she went about campus making speeches in praise of Mussolini. She also considered herself artistic and struggled to find outlets for her artistic urges and, if they existed, her talents. But for the most part her efforts were met with frustration and failure.

She had a pretty singing voice, and she had thought that there might be a career for her on the concert or operatic stage. After college she had gone to the Eastman School of Music in Rochester and had earned a Master of Arts degree.

She had also had a disastrous love affair with a music teacher. After that, she had gone to Germany, where she spent several years studying voice under Lilli Lehmann. At one point she decided that if she could not find success as a singer she would try composing, and she wrote the entire first movement of a symphony before abandoning that idea. Still without a career, she came back to New York and, as a bachelor girl, kept at her endeavors determinedly. She took up writing. She wrote the program notes for the Women's Symphony Orchestra and short pieces of music criticism for various of the "little magazines" that flourished in the twenties and thirties. She wrote a few travel articles. One of the things that undoubtedly attracted her to John Marquand was that here was an actual living, producing writer, a working artist, and so much more a creative personage than her music teacher.

In New York, Adelaide worked industriously to gain a reputation as a hostess who gave "interesting" parties that were filled with creative people—not just ordinary society people, but people who were doers and movers in the world of the arts and sciences. Some of her parties were indeed unusual. Inviting friends to one of her evenings, she once excitedly announced, "Two marvelous explorers are coming, and they're going to bring a giant panda!" The explorers arrived with the panda, which was carried in on a sedan chair. The huge owl-eyed beast was solemnly borne around the dining room in the chair and presented to each guest at the dinner table. One of the explorers gave a short dissertation on pandas, their habitat and mating patterns. Then the animal was carried upstairs and placed in a bathtub for the rest of the evening.

After John and Adelaide made their separate ways back to New York in 1935, and after John's marriage to Christina had been terminated that same year, his name appeared with increasing frequency on Adelaide's guest lists for her parties. Soon it was noticed that he was escorting her to other affairs. Marquand was now dividing his time between a bachelor apartment in the East 70s, where he was tended by a Filipino manservant named Pete, and the summer place he was building for himself at Kent's Island in Newburyport. But there were week ends at Adelaide's parents' big place in Greenwich

—week ends which John disliked since they were aggressively nonalcoholic. There were little dinners in Tarrytown with Adelaide's sister and brother-in-law, the Rockefellers. These John tended to enjoy more because—well, here was the poor little boy from Newburyport High School having dinner with the Rockefellers! It was a fictional situation.

Late in 1936, John Marquand had begun to admit privately that he intended to marry Adelaide Hooker. Friends like the Brandts and the Fiskes were somewhat surprised. "What do you see in her?" Conney Fiske asked him outright. John hesitated and then said, "She's very good-natured."

Good-natured or not, she was certainly nothing at all like Christina. The breeds of Christina Sedgwick and Adelaide Hooker had been developed at opposite poles. Where Christina was all gauzy softness and indecision, Adelaide was iron-hard determination and gumption. Christina was gentle, Adelaide was strident. Christina was feckless and vague, Adelaide was energetic and ambitious—with an energy and an ambition that would be a good match against John's, his friends noted uneasily. Having failed with a Tinker Bell, he was now going to take his chances with a Brünnhilde. Certain of John's Hale cousins, who knew both ladies, commented that Adelaide reminded them of John's mother. Their engagement was formally announced on February 26, 1937. *The Late George Apley* had just been published and had made its way onto the best-seller list. Prominent notice of the announcement was taken by the Boston and New York newspapers. It was big social news.

It was, of course, still another way of getting back at the Sedgwicks. The Hookers' New England lineage was as good as, if not better than, the Sedgwicks'. Furthermore, the Hookers were ever so much richer. It would not exactly be fair to say that one of the reasons John wanted to marry Adelaide was for her money. He was making, for a Depression year, quite a lot— $55,000 in 1937, and the following year, due to the success of *The Late George Apley*, his earnings would jump to $73,000. Adelaide at the time, mostly from shares she had been given of Hooker stock, had a small independent income of about $7,500 a year. But she also had, in the phrase of the day, great expectations. And John Marquand had, as was becoming apparent as he became successful, an acquisitive side to his nature. He not only disliked spending money, he was like a magpie; he enjoyed collecting it and storing it away in banks. Adelaide's money was certainly something he had not overlooked when asking her to marry him. But there was more to it than that. "Poor Adelaide," one of the Hales remarked later, "never realized that she was being used as an instrument of revenge." John would make further use of her, of course, as a plot device.

Their engagement wasn't very old before John's stubbornness began to collide with Adelaide's intransigency. John, for example, had not wanted a formal announcement made of the engagement. Considering their age, and that it was a second marriage for him, he thought that even to be "engaged" was a little silly—or so he said. When Adelaide won out, and the announcement was made, he cannot have been too displeased with the *New York Times* headline that read "Adelaide Ferry Hooker Will Become Bride Of John Phillips Marquand, Noted Author." Next, Adelaide wanted a diamond engagement ring. If she was going to become engaged and married, she wanted what other girls had—even though she was no longer a girl herself. John also protested this detail, which he considered ludicrous. But Adelaide would have her way, and so John, who knew nothing whatever about stones or settings, telephoned Carol Brandt, who enjoyed jewels and had already started a small collection. Together they went out to shop for Adelaide's ring. When John presented the ring to Adelaide, and when she was exclaiming over the size and beauty and luster of the stone, he remarked casually that he was glad she liked it and that Carol had picked it out. He did not understand why Adelaide seemed less than pleased at this news.

Adelaide had wanted a large church wedding, which John did not, and she was finally willing to compromise here. The wedding was large, but it was not held in a church. They were married in Adelaide's parents' apartment at 620 Park on April 16, 1937, rather in the fashion in which John and Christina had been married at Sedgwick House. Adelaide wore a coronet of flowers in her hair. The Marquands' was considered one of the most important society weddings of the season, and John and Adelaide Marquand moved to an equally important social address: 1 Beekman Place, a large and airy duplex apartment, overlooking the East River, which had formerly belonged to Gertrude Lawrence. The artists were in residence.

Chapter Twelve

*A*n extraordinary thing had happened to Marquand in Peking, during that same 1935 trip when he met Adelaide. He had been staying at a hostelry called Mrs. Calhoun's Boarding House, which had a sunny courtyard and a number-one boy to do the guests' bidding, and one night, dining with a Chinese acquaintance, his companion suddenly clapped his hands for the number-one boy and commanded, "Send in the fortune-teller!" Instantly, out of the twilight shadows of the house an ancient Chinese with a long Mandarin mustache appeared, in a kimono, and stood with folded hands, gazing intently at Marquand. For several long minutes he riveted John with his penetrating stare, and then he began to speak in a soft, high, musical voice. John's Chinese friend translated. "In China, there is no social classification for this man," the fortuneteller said with his eyes still fixed on Marquand. "He is not a student, but he is almost a student. He is quick-tempered and success-ful. Should he gain knowledge of the complexity of social re-lationships, he will live to be seventy." Suddenly the soothsayer stepped backward several paces, and a terrified look came across his face. "Please," he said to Marquand's friend, "I

implore this man to wear a mustache, even if it is a small one."
When questioned about the importance of a mustache, the
fortuneteller was vague but still almost desperately insistent.
It had something to do with restoring the proportions of
Marquand's face, of bringing out its true character and quality,
of giving the face balance. It had something to do with the
Chinese concept of fêng-shui, which is the particular domain
of soothsayers. Fêng-shui, literally translated, means "wind and
water," but philosophically it is usually interpreted as "the
balance of things." In China, the soothsayers have the final
say on matters of fêng-shui, and their advice must always be
taken because, though its effects may be small and subtle and
in ways almost unnoticeable, this advice is inevitably helpful.
Sometimes, Marquand's companion explained, the soothsayer
must study a man's face for hours before coming to a pre-
diction and recognizing an individual's fêng-shui. It was
highly unusual that this man, the friend said, had been able to
make such a quick and positive appraisal. For Marquand, the
episode was a thoroughly unsettling experience, and he immediately began to grow a mustache—the short-clipped,
British-style mustache that did indeed give him the appearance
of an Englishman. He also never forgot the soothsayer's remark about learning "the complexity of social relationships." It
encouraged him to write novels along the lines of *The Late
George Apley*.

Everything about the Orient fascinated Marquand. He loved
this land of soothsayers and evil spirits, of household gods and
goddesses who had to be consulted and whose whims and
wishes had to be respected. There was, he had decided on that
first China trip, something of the Oriental in his own cast of
mind, something that admired and understood the Chinese
love of solitude and mystery and order—of balance. Balance,
in fact, became his guiding artistic principle. But there was
more to his love of China than this. He had journeyed out onto
the Gobi Desert and watched the tribes of nomadic Mongols
with their camels, seen them pitching their tents and cooking
their meals over dung fires, and had been stirred by the solitude and wandering of these people of the vast plains. In his
somewhat romantic self-appraisal, he had begun to see himself

as a lonely wanderer, a man passing through life who could see
and touch but never really reach other people. Aloneness was
becoming one of his favorite themes. In response to the considerable amount of fan mail he was receiving about *The Late
George Apley*, he had set up what was practically a form letter
of reply. "Writing is a lonely occupation . . ." it began.

He also continued to say, "A writer should never marry."
And yet he himself had wanted marriage—twice. He had not
enjoyed his bachelorhood and had spent much of it visiting
friends such as the Brandts and the Fiskes. For a while he had
courted the monologist and writer, Helen Howe, but then one
day at Adelaide's insistence he had brought Adelaide around to
see her—uninvited, for which Helen Howe never quite forgave
him. (Later, she satirized him unpleasantly in a novel, *We
Happy Few.*) He demanded solitude but was restless with it
the moment he achieved it. He talked of needing peace and
quiet and yet, in any situation that was remotely peaceful, he
was quickly bored. And so, married to Adelaide and an established success, with no real money problems to worry about, he
entered upon a way of life that was like that of the nomadic
Mongols—moving from place to place, never satisfied for long
in a new encampment, always restless to get on to the next. In
New York he would want to get back to Boston, and once in
Boston he would begin making plans to go back to New York.
So it went. And, just as it had gone with Christina, he was
quickly finding himself dissatisfied with Adelaide as a wife.

She didn't understand, he claimed, his need for solitude. She
was forever barging in on him with noisy suggestions or
changes of plans. She wouldn't leave him *alone*. Furthermore,
Adelaide, unlike Christina, was no shrinking violet and for all
her supposed good nature was showing herself to be a singu-
larly stubborn person. Like so many children of the rich,
Adelaide Hooker Marquand was used to giving orders and
having them obeyed; she had done this all her life. She not
only disliked—she could simply not comprehend—not getting
her own way.

From the beginning there were disagreements over seemingly trivial matters. Traveling in the Southwest on their

honeymoon, John and Adelaide stopped for the night at a small-town motor inn. Adelaide explained that if they left their shoes outside their door before retiring, they would be picked up by a minion during the night and shined. John was quite sure that this would not happen, but Adelaide assured him that it would, just as in any respectable hotel in Europe. Seeing the shoes outside the Marquands' door the next morning, the chambermaid hurried back to the front desk and said, "Who *are* those people, and what do they want?" "It's all right," the manager assured the mystified girl; "it's the American novelist Mr. Mark Twain and his wife."

Adelaide had a definite talent for interior decorating, and it wasn't long before 1 Beekman Place was, under her hand, transformed into one of the handsomest apartments in the city; it was the sort of apartment which one entered on the second floor, then descended to other rooms below, and it made excellent use of the sweeping East River view. She had also gone to work on the country house he was building at Kent's Island, adding a room here, an ell there. But there were inevitable divergences between John's and Adelaide's tastes. Adelaide had always wanted to own a Grant Wood painting. John not only had no interest in Grant Wood, he actively disliked Wood's mannered and sentimental realism. Wood's prices were also high, and John argued that they could not afford one of his pictures. Breezily—and characteristically—Adelaide said, "Then *I'll* pay for it." The painting Adelaide had set her heart on was called "Parson Weems' Fable," Mr. Wood's depiction of the legend of young George Washington, the cherry tree, and his inability to tell a lie. Adelaide loved the picture. John hated it. It seemed to him actually disrespectful to George Washington's memory—perhaps even unpatriotic—since Wood had painted Washington as a small boy in knee breeches, holding a hatchet beside the felled tree, but as a humorous touch had given the youth the old man's face (hard-jawed from the ill-fitting teeth) of the celebrated Gilbert Stuart portrait. Adding to the effect of parody, or travesty, was the fact that Wood had painted in the figure of Parson Weems, who stood at one side of the painting, slyly holding aside a curtain to reveal

the scene. It struck John as though Weems were offering the
viewer a kind of peep show. But Adelaide bought it and hung
it on the wall. Once it was there, John refused to look at it.

Then there were certain difficulties with John's new in-laws,
the John D. Rockefellers. He found them a somewhat perplexing couple. With the publication of *The Late George Apley*,
John Marquand had become a kind of expert on New England,
particularly the Boston area. The Rockefellers, who had been
fascinated by *Apley*, decided that it would be a pleasant change
from Seal Harbor, Maine, where Rockefellers generally sum-
mered, to take a summer house on Boston's North Shore. Quite
naturally, they turned to John for advice, giving him their
personal specification of the sort of summer place they were
looking for. The trouble was, as John explained it to Conney
Fiske, that the Rockefellers had never ventured anywhere without knowing exactly what to expect. They regarded New
England as some exotic uncharted place, and their requirements
for a holiday retreat struck John as baffling. They wanted, they
explained, simplicity, and yet at the same time they wanted a
place where there would be attractive people, a good country
club with good tennis, and beaches and boating. They wanted
to entertain and be entertained, and yet they did not want to
go where there were cocktail parties. It seemed to John as
though the Rockefellers were looking for a place that didn't
exist. John turned over the problem to Conney, who suggested
that the Rockefellers journey northward for a visit. For years
afterward John would relish the story of how, when Conney
Fiske mentioned to her Irish maid that the Rockefellers were
coming, the maid dropped the tea tray on the floor.

The Rockefellers arrived, and one of the first aspects of New
England they commented on was the multitude of fine old
houses. John remarked that it was traditional in Boston to
leave things as they are, that old houses were carefully kept up
but not moved around or subject to elaborate restoration.
There was a somewhat awkward moment when John D. Rockefeller chose to take this remark personally. Quietly, almost
apologetically, Mr. Rockefeller said, "Of course we had no idea
that Williamsburg would be so successful."

John took the Rockefellers on a tour of North Shore towns,

but it was a fruitless journey. The Rockefellers, he reported to Conney, seemed to find Ipswich too much like their home-town Tarrytown, and the whole North Shore they decided was too social to be to their liking. They looked at a lot of places on the Cape, so many that they could not distinguish one from another, and the place that they liked best, whose name they couldn't remember, had been washed away in a hurricane. John had a wonderful time mimicking—and exaggerating—the plight of his vacation-starved in-laws.

Then there was Adelaide's mother, Mrs. Hooker. John liked Mrs. Hooker but felt that at times she took herself and her good works a trifle too seriously, and he added Blanche Hooker to the list of people of whom he did his merciless parodies. He ridiculed the way she made a fetish of her health, telling the story of how, when Mrs. Hooker had joined John and Adelaide in Jamaica in 1938, where they had stopped on a West Indies cruise, the good lady had been bitten by a mosquito, thereby contracting something John labeled "Double Tertiary Malignant Malaria." In John's version of Mrs. Hooker's illness, teams of specialists and round-the-clock nurses were required, along with elaborate medications, injections, serums, and transfusions.

Then there was the problem of John's aging father. John's mother had died suddenly in 1932, and the one emotional strut supporting the old man's life disappeared completely. When John married Adelaide, his father was seventy-one, completely retired from engineering and his son's full responsibility. He had become increasingly a burden. John had arranged for his father to go and live in the Red Brick House at Curzon's Mill. For a while he spent winters in the South with the younger Marquands, but he was happier at the Mill—where all Marquands and their Hale cousins came at the end. Only the Mill was home to him. But one of the attractions of the Mill to Phil Marquand was quite clearly its proximity to Rockingham Park race track, and John was forever having to step in and bail out his father or cover his losses.

Senility was overtaking him. He drove an automobile so erratically that his driver's license was finally taken away. To give him something to do, John bought him a motorboat, but his father kept running the boat up on rocks and ledges. In 1929, John's mother had inherited a small amount of money from a Fuller relative. John had immediately convinced her to put the money in a trust, so that his father would not squander it. John's father had considered that an act of terrible filial treachery and never forgave him for it. Phil Marquand had been certain that that money, wisely invested as he knew best how to do, could have been nourished into a vast fortune. At times he would come upon John and stare at him balefully a moment, then say, "If only you hadn't put that money of your mother's in trust!" and turn away.

For a while, John had tried to set his father up in the chicken business at Newburyport, raising Rhode Island Reds. It almost seemed as though the old man might finally be successful, for Marquand's eggs were considered the finest in Eastern Massachusetts, and the business was showing a tidy profit. Then one day a check arrived for $1,500 for a shipment of baby chicks. Quietly Phil Marquand got dressed in his best suit, put on his best coat and hat, picked up his walking stick, and— looking every bit like the country gentleman from the good old days in Rye—announced that he was going to Boston on urgent business. A strange smile was on his face. For two days nothing was heard of him. Then he returned, the smile gone and the money gone too. John asked him what had happened. "I blew it in, and it's none of your damned business," Phil Marquand said.

From his house on Kent's Island, John would drive over to see his father at the Mill. One winter day Phil Marquand suddenly seized his son's arm and said, "John, it's time for spring planting. Let's get out of here." John took his father to the window and pointed out to him the falling snow that was gathering in drifts outside the house. "It's winter, Papa," he said. The old man stared at the snow for a long time and at last said, "By God, John, you're right." When the couple whom John had hired to take care of his father left for a two-week vacation, Phil Marquand came to stay with John at Kent's Island. For John it was a painful ordeal because, with his father underfoot, he was made more aware than ever of his father's mental deterioration. John's father would follow him around the house, asking John to take him home, and when John would patiently explain that he could not go home for a while the old man would say that, in that case, he would walk. Minutes later, forgetting the conversation that had just taken place, he would begin it again. John knew that his father should be placed somewhere where he could get better care, but John could not bring himself to place his father in a nursing home. And every now and again Phil Marquand would turn to his son and say in a bewildered way, "Where is the money, John? Where is the money?"

But perhaps the greatest difficulty that pervaded John's marriage to Adelaide from the beginning was Adelaide's feeling that she could be some sort of assistant to her husband in his work. She saw how Carol Brandt—or any other crack secretary—could help John by taking down the novels, how Carl Brandt could help him cut and edit them, and how Conney Fiske could serve him as a consultant in subtler matters of taste and themes. It wasn't that Adelaide was jealous of these other people's positions in her husband's creative life, exactly, but she could not see why she herself couldn't also be given some sort of supporting role. She was, after all, artistic, and had done some writing. And so she saw no reason why she should not be permitted to go into his manuscripts, read them, and then come forth with proposed changes and revisions, substitutions and deletions. These efforts of Adelaide's to improve her husband's output were particularly galling to the man whose bailiwick this had long been, Mr. Alfred McIntyre, John's editor at Little, Brown. McIntyre, a shy and timid-seeming little man until he had consumed his customary six martinis for lunch—at which point he became brilliant and quite extroverted, to say the least—had worked successfully with John for a number of years. John had the highest respect for McIntyre, and for his wife, Helen, who worked with him as sort of a team. (McIntyre's literary assessments were highly personal and typically idiosyncratic. "If a story can make me cry after four Scotches," he used to declare, "it's good.") McIntyre complained bitterly to John about Adelaide's interfering efforts, but when John tried to dissuade her from them she protested, "But I want to feel a part of your work, John!"

At last a solution was proposed to Adelaide: She could be useful as a sort of copy editor—in other words, she would be in
charge of correcting spelling errors, punctuation, syntax, and
the like. Adelaide agreed to this. But it was next to impossible
for Adelaide Hooker Marquand—a woman not accustomed to
confinement—to restrict herself to these areas alone.

In the meantime, two of John's best and oldest friends, Gardi
Fiske and Charley Codman, from the days in Battery A, had
been planning something for him that would mean more to
him, perhaps, than anything that had thus far happened to him
in his life—more than his financial and critical and popular
success, more than the Pulitzer Prize, more than being married
to John D. Rockefeller III's sister-in-law. Quietly but firmly
the two men had been promoting John's membership in the
Somerset Club, Gardi as proposer, Charley as seconder. In the
spring of 1938 they were successful, and John received a notice
that he had been accepted into the most exclusive club in the
most exclusive city in the country. He had made it. Upper-class
Boston had accepted him at last. He had made it, furthermore,
in spite of having written *The Late George Apley,* which many
of the Boston Old Guard would always resent. He could now
go to the elegant old club on Beacon Hill, sit in its deeply
buttoned black leather chairs, sip its famous sweet martinis,
nibble on its special muffins called corn dodgers—not as a
guest, but as a member.

He was overwhelmed with the news. Surely, he said, the
club's and Boston's standards must be slipping badly. "However," he wrote to Gardi Fiske, "this in no way dims my gratitude for the trouble you have taken in accomplishing a feat
which was almost gargantuan." John Marquand, at the time,
was forty-four years old.

On one of his early visits to his new club, John Marquand
commented to an elderly member that he had heard that old
Mr. Sears—whose town residence the gray brick mansion that
houses the club had originally been—had required his daughters, when he received them in the drawing room, to walk
backward from Mr. Sears' presence when it was time for them
to depart. The older member's comment was, "Times have
changed since then."

Chapter Thirteen

*J*ohn Oakman (the pleasantly ne'er-do-well "artist" from Springfield who never painted much of anything, who had married John's Aunt Greta, and who became John's secret drinking companion during his teens at Curzon's Mill) gave his wife a daughter, born in 1911, whom they named Renée. Both Oakmans were Francophiles. "My father decided to name me either for a French queen or a prostitute," Renée Oakman used to explain. It is also likely that she was conceived in Paris; the Oakmans used somewhat coyly to refer to her, as a child, as "our little French baby." Renée, though not technically a Hale, joined the small band of Hale cousins who were always dropping in and out of the various houses at Curzon's Mill, which they considered home.

When John was a young man in the 1920s, just beginning to get himself launched as a writer of popular fiction, Renée Oakman was a budding adolescent—and a budding beauty, at that. More than her name seemed alien in a family where women had always straightforwardly been called Margaret, Laura, Elizabeth, and Mary. The Hales had never been much on looks, being of stolid and plain-faced Yankee stock—

the Hale men almost Lincolnesque—and so Renée, as a presence, struck an odd and somewhat disturbing note in the family. She was almost dismayingly beautiful, with fine, soft blonde hair and lavender eyes. A newspaper reporter once described her as "orchidaceous," and she acquired, by the time she entered her earliest teens, a habit of making men fall in love with her. Like most beauties, she early became aware of what she possessed and learned from the beginning to make the fullest use of it. Renée was, at the same time, like her Hale half brothers and sisters, to say nothing of her cousins and aunts, something of an eccentric, with a fey wit, a mercurial temperament, and some unlikely notions. She believed, for example, that she could communicate with wild animals. All this, of course, merely added to her strange allure.

There was no question that John Marquand was captivated by—even, perhaps, in a way in love with—this eighteen-years-younger first cousin, this exotically gorgeous sport that had appeared in an otherwise homely family. There was even a period when John considered giving Renée an elaborate coming-out party for her eighteenth birthday—a lovely dream of giving the loveliest party for the loveliest girl, the kind of party John had never been invited to during the years at Harvard. He would turn Renée into one of his debutante heroines. In fact, Renée even got him to promise to give her such a party, though it was a promise he never managed to keep. John eventually soured on Renée somewhat or, rather, realized how flirtatious and fickle she was. Once, at a Newburyport party, when Renée was nineteen going on twenty, she disappeared with the young son of Dana Atchley, John's doctor. They were gone for hours. The boy was only thirteen. Also, by that time, Renée Oakman had settled upon a more practical career than that of a debutante. She had gone to New York and had quickly been signed up by John Robert Powers, who ran what was then one of the largest modeling agencies in the country.

Although *Wickford Point*, the novel that John began working on soon after his marriage to Adelaide, carried the customary disclaimer, "All the incidents in this novel are entirely fictitious, and no reference is intended to any actual person, living or dead," it was quite clear, once the novel was published, that the character of Bella Brill bore more than a glancing resemblance to Renée Oakman and that other members of the fictional Brill family could find awfully close counterparts among the real-life Hales. Wickford Point in the novel, in fact, sounded in its description exactly like Curzon's Mill, and a number of people wondered why John had bothered to change the name of the river from the Artichoke to the Wickford.

The Hales, furthermore, saw themselves portrayed as a family of barmy nitwits, all unemployed and probably unemployable. In *Wickford Point*, Greta Hale Oakman recognized herself in the character of Cousin Clothilde, a lovable if daft creature who spends her mornings in bed summoning members of her family to her side for long and aimless conversations, smoking their cigarettes, and borrowing their money whenever she can. Then there was the character of Sid Brill, perennial sufferer from stomach pains and tinkerer with useless inventions, who, when his car runs out of gasoline, siphons some out of a cousin's automobile, always thoughtfully careful to leave "a little bit" in the tank, at least enough to get it to the service station. There was, the Hales decided, more than a little of Robert Hale in this character. Robert Hale's brother, Dudley, reminded several people of Harry Brill in the novel, the Harvard snob who was always sure that his family connections plus the influential people he knew would get him an address on Easy Street without any effort on his part, and who regularly attended parties to which he had not been invited on the theory that not to invite Harry Brill must have been merely a careless oversight on the part of his hostess. Cousin Mary Brill in the novel—who relentlessly chases every man she meets, only to lose him in the end to her beautiful sister Bella, "Bella the Bitch"—seemed perilously close to the real-life Laura Hale, half sister of the beautiful Renée Oakman. Great-Aunt Sarah in the book, dotty and living in the past, who insists on reading aloud from Pepys's *Diary* night after night, cannot have been based on other than John's Great-Aunt Mary Curzon. Cousin Clothilde's second husband, meanwhile, a shiftless and unsuccessful muralist named Archie Wright who never quite gets the commissions he wants, sounds not unlike Aunt Greta Hale's second husband, John Oakman. And the specter who looms over the entire Brill family in the novel, John Brill, the father of Cousin Clothilde's first husband, is a minor ninteenth-century pastoral poet whom the family takes very seriously and refers to as "the Wickford Sage." Surely John Marquand cannot have meant this character as anything but a cruel parody of Edward Everett Hale, from whom all the Hales descended and whom all the Hales did indeed take very seriously.

John Marquand immediately and categorically denied that there was any kinship whatever between the Brills of his novel and the Hales, his cousins, and his denials may have been particularly vociferous because, in the first few months after *Wickford Point* was published in 1938, there were mutterings from certain Hale quarters about lawsuits for libel and invasion of privacy. Though these died down as the Hales —probably wisely—decided that the publicity attending a legal action would only focus more attention on them and on John's book, John continued to claim that the book was "at least eighty per cent a figment of imagination," and to profess amazement that Wickford Point could be construed to bear "any close resemblance to real estate in Newburyport, Massachusetts." He admitted, with writing *The Late George Apley,* that "For almost the first time in my life I had written about something that I thoroughly understood. I had translated something of myself and my own experience into *The Late George Apley,* and I had achieved through my experience an unforeseen depth and reality." And he confessed that *Wickford Point* was an attempt to further plumb his own experience, past, and territory he knew well. But as for the characters in the book, he wrote—in a preface to a later edition—"When someone utters the trite remark that truth is stranger than fiction, he might as well be saying that truth always is very awkward in the fictitious world. A fictional character, for example, is always a combination of observed traits drawn from an indeterminate number of people. I doubt whether any individual of one's acquaintance, no matter how vivid his behavior, could effectively stand alone in print."

All this, of course, cut very little ice with the Hales. But the fact was—and this was at the heart of the trouble—that John was right. It would indeed have been awkward to have portrayed the Hales as "truth." So he had taken the Hales' skeletal characteristics and distorted them, twisted them, heightened them, and exaggerated them. He had fictionalized the Hales, which is to say falsified them, in order to turn them into creatures of comedy. He had intended the comedy to be gentle enough, but the Hales found it a decidedly unpleasant experience to see themselves projected into this new dimension in which they saw certain facts about themselves, and yet not really.

John had worked harder on *Wickford Point* than on *The Late George Apley*. He was determined to prove, to readers as well as critics, that he was now a writer of "serious" fiction—fiction that made significant social comment—and not just *Post* and *Journal* potboilers. He was aware that his second "serious" work would be judged much more harshly, by much more meticulous standards, than his first, and that book reviewers —not always an overly generous lot—would be waiting eagerly for the follow-up to the Pulitzer Prize Novel to be an artistic disaster, for Marquand to prove himself a "one-book author." John wanted *Wickford Point* to be accurate in every detail, and he fussed endlessly over the manuscript—not only polishing scenes and dialogue but making certain that not the tiniest fact or social nuance could be labeled as false or incorrect.

He was worried, for instance, that some of his readers might feel it was wrong to have the Brills eat salmon in August; perhaps it should have been shad. When one entered an ocean liner, he asked Alfred McIntyre at Little, Brown, did not one customarily come off the gangplank onto the promenade deck? From there, did one go up, or down, to B Deck? Marquand spent a great deal of time worrying about the word "pants" in connection with Bella Brill. In a scene in which Bella skips into an automobile, her mother notices that she is not wearing pants. Alfred McIntyre wondered whether the word shouldn't be "panties." John, however, having surveyed his women friends, was convinced that women of 1937 thought of these garments as *pants,* not panties.

He worried for fear his Brill characters called each other "darling" too much, and he asked McIntyre to have his staff recheck the manuscript for repetitions of the word. He wondered whether the character of Pat Leighton—the love interest of the narrator, Jim Calder, in the novel—was perhaps awkwardly or artificially introduced. Pat Leighton, a New York career girl who is an early likeness of the celebrated Marvin Myles of *H. M. Pulham, Esquire,* does not come on stage until fairly late in the narrative, and so, to introduce her and establish her as a character in the story, Marquand had Jim Calder receive a letter from Pat Leighton—a letter that draws comment from Cousin Clothilde. Marquand feared that the letter was an obvious plot device. (It was, but not one that most readers would notice.)

He spent a great deal of time worrying about the ending of the book, always, along with the opening scene, a crucial moment in any novel. As originally written, the novel ended with Professor Allen Southby and Bella Brill announcing that they intend to marry each other. It is in fact the way the novel *must* end; no two characters in fiction ever deserved each other more. And yet, at the book's end, Bella and Southby have only just met each other, and Marquand began to fear that an announcement of marriage on such brief acquaintance was too abrupt to be believable. Perhaps, he considered, Southby should marry Bella's sister Mary—whom he had known longer but which would have been quite an anticlimax. Finally John decided to close the book in a more subtle manner. The reader is never told, precisely, that Bella and Southby will marry, but one knows that Bella is after Southby and that Southby is smitten. There is no question that the two will marry at some point in that vague area of fictional time after the final sentence.

Marquand was also quick to change the name of a character originally called "Russell Berg." A real-life Russell Berg had been discovered in the vicinity of Newburyport, and Mr. O'Reilly's libel suit was still pending. A line that referred to "that Doctor Cooney, that good-for-nothing one," was also changed to "that dentist."

And so surely Marquand cannot have been too surprised to

find that the Hales resented the treatment he had given them. Whether or not the statistic of "eighty per cent" imaginary which he claimed about his *Wickford Point* people could ever be proved, there was enough there that was recognizable—and recognizable as the object of ridicule—to hurt his cousins deeply.

Did John Marquand set about to do this deliberately? Perhaps—half deliberately, anyway. He had written *The Late George Apley* not only as a reflection of his own experience and knowledge of Boston; he had also, in making parody of, and poking fun at, the whole tapestry of Boston snobbism and Boston's overweening self-pride and pride of family, rather successfully polished off the entire Sedgwick clan, from Uncle Ellery on down. Now, in *Wickford Point,* he was going back to his growing-up jealousies and bitternesses about the Hales—who had more money, and who made him (or who helped him make himself) feel threadbare. In *Wickford Point,* the narrator, Jim Calder, is a successful purveyor of serials to magazines such as the *Saturday Evening Post, Ladies' Home Journal,* and *Cosmopolitan.* He sounds very like John Marquand. And, because of some subtle social difference between Jim Calder and his Brill cousins—his feeling that he is somehow not good enough for the Brills—he loves them and yet he resents them. He is very conscious, for example, that when he walks about the town where he grew up and went to school, he is addressed familiarly, by his first name, Jim. His Brill cousins, on the other hand, are not treated that way; they are politely addressed as Mr. and Mrs. and Miss Brill. John Marquand, while learning the value of writing from his own experience, was also learning how to use fiction as a means of getting back at all the people who he felt—rightly or wrongly—had misused him in the past.

There is, for instance, in *Wickford Point* the comic character of Allen Southby, whom Cousin Clothilde perpetually mis-addresses as "Mr. Northby," a pompous, tweedy, pipe-smoking Harvard professor who has written a book of criticism and is a take-off on every self-important literary pundit who ever existed. Southby, whose letterhead reads "Martin House Study" and below it, in smaller type, "Dr. Southby," who quotes Chaucer and delivers profound literary pronouncements, is a man who has become more Boston than Boston in his study pine-paneled with hand-wrought nails, filled with pine-topped trestle tables and old leather-bound books tossed carelessly about. He serves his guests beer in old pewter mugs. His room lacks nothing but a spinning wheel to appear authentically New England, Jim Calder observes sarcastically. And Allen Southby—who is not from Boston but from Minnesota—is not sure whether Jim means that or is being funny. Allen Southby—who high-hatted Jim Calder at Harvard and who, naturally, places Calder's craft at little more than "putting words on paper"— is John Marquand's obvious (perhaps a bit too obvious) attempt to get back at all the literary and academic critics who refused to take him seriously as a writer. Southby, of course, is punished with Bella.

Allen Southby is probably a composite of a number of stuffy and self-important literary critics whom Marquand had encountered over the years, but there is an indication that he intended the character to parody certain aspects of Edward A. Weeks, who succeeded Uncle Ellery Sedgwick as editor of the *Atlantic Monthly*. Edward Weeks had high-hatted John in Boston during the early days. Like Allen Southby, Edward Weeks, arriving in Boston, had promptly become thoroughly Bostonian, even though—as John wickedly liked to point out— Weeks was originally from Elizabeth, New Jersey. Edward Weeks had not gone to any of the proper New England schools. He had gone to Elizabeth High School and something called Pingry Prep. Weeks had not even gone to Harvard but to Cornell, a college considered only "perhaps" in the Ivy League.

Marquand's feelings about Edward Weeks bordered on the paranoiac. Weeks had a series of lectures which he went about the country delivering, and which was called "Authors at Home"—chatty insights into the private lives and thoughts of literary figures. John Marquand had a fantasy scheme which he always wanted to exercise. In it, he would, under an assumed name, engage Edward Weeks as a lecturer and hire an auditorium. A date would be set, and the topic: "John P. Marquand at Home." On the day of the lecture, with Edward Weeks on the platform and Marquand as an audience of one in the auditorium, John would sit back in his seat, put his feet up, clasp his hands behind his head, and say, "Okay, Ted—do your stuff!" Alas, he never got up the courage to do it.

There is another writer character in *Wickford Point,* Joe Stowe. Joe Stowe is a writer of good, serious fiction. In a very real sense, Jim Calder is Marquand before *Apley,* and Joe Stowe is Marquand after. In the novel, the two men are best friends. Both are Marquand alter egos.

Some critics have claimed that *Wickford Point* is John Marquand's best novel, and at the time of its publication one reviewer marveled on the book's structure, "like a braided Indian basket, spiraling from bottom to rim, firmly interwoven, but dizzying to follow." It is indeed a bit dizzying because the novel leaps backward and forward in time. The flashback technique, which was to become Marquand's trademark to the extent that he was sometimes given credit for inventing it, works better here than in earlier books but is still somewhat creaky. Whatever else it is, *Wickford Point* is certainly John Marquand's most comic novel, with all the disheveled Brills bickering and nattering and accomplishing nothing, yet clinging to their old place like weary barnacles to a rock. And, with the character of Bella the Bitch, who puts men through her life like shirts through a wringer, Marquand proved—to critics who had been observing that his female characters were less successful than his men—that he was capable of creating, and sustaining, a memorable woman in fiction.

Meanwhile, for all his emphatic denials that his *Wickford Point* characters were based on anything more than their author's imagination, Marquand was still somewhat nervous about his Hale cousins' displeasure. He was also, in view of the O'Reilly claim against *Apley,* more than a little lawsuit-shy. So was his publisher, Little, Brown. The O'Reilly suit was still in litigation and showed signs of dragging drearily on for months. John Reed, a Little, Brown editor, suggested to Marquand that he write an article about all the various people, the country over, who had seen themselves in the *Wickford* tribe. Marquand thought that this idea might not only be amusing but also useful. He had in fact picked up at various soirees and cocktail parties in New York a list of people with whom the novel's characters had been identified. John Brill, for example, the Wickford Sage, had been variously spotted as John Greenleaf Whittier, Edward Everett Hale, Thomas Wentworth Higginson, and Longfellow. Joe Stowe had been similarly recognized as a portrayal of Sinclair Lewis, Sidney Howard, Ernest Hemingway, and Kenneth Roberts.

Allen Southby had been identified as Van Wyck Brooks, along with three Yale professors, and as Kenneth Roberts, and Charles Townsend Copeland. The Brill family in its entirety had been said to be " 'just like' a family in New Hampshire, one in northern Massachusetts, central Massachusetts and southern Massachusetts, also one in Virginia, and is said to be drawn from the Sanger family in 'The Constant Nymph.' " The Brill boys had been recognized as brothers by a lady in Massachusetts and two ladies in New York, while Cousin Clothilde had been identified as Edna May Oliver. Meanwhile, a reader had written Marquand to say, "It is not a story of a specialized group of people . . . but a record of family life that has something in it that all families must recognize as their own."

To the list of persons in real life whom readers had identified in the novel, Marquand suggested to Reed that he ask some people in the office if they could pick up some more, saying that he thought it would be nice if Reed could work into the publicity this theme of universal application and back it up with the varied identifications. But Marquand wanted to look at the release before it went out, and was concerned that the word "identify" might not be quite the right one. "Resemble" might be better. The lawyers had taught him to choose his words carefully. He incorporated these various resemblances in a nervously humorous piece called "Do You Know the Brills?" which the *Saturday Review* published in April, 1939, and in which Marquand stated flatly, "I can only say, in conclusion, that I do not know the Brills in *Wickford Point*. I know a great many people who possess a few of their peculiarities, but that is all."

While all this was going on, John and Adelaide Marquand were moving back and forth between 1 Beekman Place in New York and Massachusetts, where finishing touches were being put on the house at Kent's Island, just a few miles down the road from Curzon's Mill—the enemy camp, as it were. It was inevitable that there should be a certain amount of friction between the two places.

There would have been friction anyway, even without *Wickford Point*. Like the Brills, the Hales were always quarreling, in a perpetual if halfhearted way; often you couldn't remember who was quarreling with whom or what the battle was about. Adelaide didn't care for the Hales and said so. She found them entirely too fey and quixotic for her down-to-earth tastes, and shabby gentility was not her Greenwich- and Park-Avenue-bred cup of tea. But she admitted that there were some nice old pieces of furniture at the Mill, and between the three houses—the big Yellow House with its eleven bedrooms, the Red Brick House, and the Mill House that Aunt Greta had fixed up so that it was habitable during the summer—there were a lot of nice old things to pick and choose from.

Adelaide liked nice old pieces. So did John. His success and very likely his marriage to Adelaide—with her wealth and her Rockefeller connections—had brought out a strong streak of acquisitiveness in his nature, a distinct lust for property and possessions. Now they had a big apartment in New York, and they had Kent's Island. Soon they would have the house at Hobe Sound, then a house in Aspen, then an island rented in the Bahamas, then a second house in Aspen. Adelaide bought houses the way some women buy shoes; she once casually announced to friends that the Marquands owned eight houses. She bought a house in Massachusetts, which she never lived in, simply because it had "nice apple trees." In their thirst for real estate, she and John had at least one thing in common.

For all these places, furnishings had to be collected. In Newburyport, this seemed easy. Up the road, at the Mill, were certain pieces of furniture that John, over the years—rightly or wrongly—had grown to think of as his own. The Mill, after all, was as much a part of his birthright as it was the Hales'. And so he and Adelaide would make little trips over to the Mill to pick up a tilt-top table here, a candlestand there, a portrait that struck their fancy, or a Chippendale chair. Quite often, however, the Hales, returning to their old summer place from wherever they happened to be, took violent exception to these offhand Marquand appropriations. There were stormy scenes, telephone calls, and trips down to Kent's Island to snatch a portrait off the wall or a night stand away from the bedside. Accusations were hurled back and forth, which Aunt Greta—still the matriarch—did her best to arbitrate. But Aunt Greta was growing old. In *Wickford Point,* Jim Calder suddenly asks about Cousin Clothilde, the Aunt Greta of fiction who holds the discordant Brills together, "Suppose . . . she dies." Jim is hastily told not to think about such things; Cousin Clothilde must never die.

In *Wickford Point,* John Marquand wrote, "There was one good thing about the family: at the last moment we could all pull ourselves together and behave quite well." In real life, however, this would turn out not quite to be the case.

Chapter Fourteen

*E*arly in 1938, George Stevens, the editor of the *Saturday Review of Literature*, approached Conney Fiske to ask her if she would like to write an informal profile of her friend, John Marquand. Conney was delighted with the idea. She was not, of course, a professional writer. Had she been one, she would doubtless not have taken the assignment, for most professional writers are reluctant to write about their friends; candor about a friend is an almost certain means of losing him. But Conney agreed and wrote a piece that was warmhearted, feminine— and somewhat indiscreet. Carl Brandt was given the story in manuscript, read it, and was furious.

To this day, Conney Fiske feels that the reason Carl disliked her story was that she was not a famous or a "name" writer. But Carl's reasons were actually somewhat different. Conney felt—with a certain amount of justification—that she had been among those people who had been influential in guiding John away from writing his strictly commercial romance and spy fiction and had encouraged his turning to novels of satire and social comment. As a result, in her article, Conney Fiske tended to dismiss John's earlier popular fiction as not "serious" and as having been written mostly with tongue in cheek. She made the point—which she liked to believe was true—that John had written for the mass magazine and motion picture market only as a means to earn freedom to do his important literary work. No one was quicker than Carl Brandt to realize how professionally damaging to John such implications might be. John, after all, was still writing fiction for the *Saturday Evening Post, Ladies' Home Journal, Cosmopolitan,* and *Good Housekeeping.* In between *The Late George Apley* and *Wickford Point* he had brought out two more Mr. Moto novels—*Think Fast, Mr. Moto* and *Mr. Moto Is So Sorry*—both of which had been serialized in the *Post* and sold to the movies. How would Marquand's magazine editors and motion picture producers enjoy learning that one of their most popular and productive writers was turning out work for them about which he was not even halfway serious?

Conney also implied that John wrote only under a compulsion to make money. Again, there was a certain amount of truth in this—John had an obsession about money and about the rich—but Carl felt that to state this in a public way could do nothing but harm to John's career, in which Carl had a professional stake. In a long and heated letter to George Stevens, Carl wrote:

> No artist that I know is more conscientious or capable than Mr. Marquand is with any work of his that goes in front of the public. To say that he has written pot boiler stuff through the years only to write the Apley or his new books, I for one, and I have been pretty close to him, know not to be the truth. He has taken pride, and rightly so, in the work that he has done for magazines. Out of that work there are things which can stand the test of time to the same extent as GEORGE APLEY or the forthcoming book. To say that he writes only for money is . . . decidedly untrue. Despite the fact that he, like many another writer, says he would never write another line except for the money in it, he is actively uncomfortable if he does not get an opportunity to do his work. This is particularly true after a long trip or a real vacation.

Perhaps—to Carl—the most distressing aspect of Conney's piece was that it came right out and stated that the characters in *Wickford Point* were based on John's own colorful collection of aunts and cousins at Curzon's Mill. This fact was something that John had attempted to glide over as gracefully as possible; now it was to be starkly in print. Conney's article not only left the impression that John wrote autobiographical fiction but also implied that John wrote only about New England. After *Apley* and *Wickford Point*—and with a third New England novel already in the planning stages—John's publishers were already beginning to drop strong hints that he might profit by broadening his canvas somewhat and transporting his central characters beyond a fifty-mile radius of Boston. In his letter to George Stevens, Carl Brandt reminded him that John had written a clutch of Civil War stories and that he had extensively used China as a background, as well as Hawaii, the South Seas, and France during World War I. He had also written a series of short stories with horses and horse racing as subject matter.

In his letter to Stevens, Carl begged the editor to cancel or postpone publication of the article and suggested that another writer—"let us say, Quincy Howe"—be substituted. Carl added, "I am quite aware that I am arrogating to myself the privilege of interfering with your editorial judgment. I ask your forgiveness of this simply on the grounds that John is my oldest friend and it hurts like the devil to see a public presentation of him which I know will not do him justice." Stevens, however, declined Carl's request, and the article was published with all the material in it to which Carl objected, including the sentence that described him as "a versatile and prolific writer of fiction for the popular magazines . . . which has also given him the time to devote to more serious work."

What Conney caught very well was John's habit of self-dramatization. He enjoyed crises, and, to hear him tell it, his life consisted of nothing but narrow escapes and near disasters. Something terrible was always happening, or had just taken place, and urgent help from friends was always required. "According to himself," Conney wrote, "he has always found it extremely hard to cope with the ordinary mechanics of living. He has no ability to catch trains, he usually has no money in his pocket, his sheep on his farm in Newburyport

have developed some strange and sinister disease, he has recently been mistaken for a forger of travelers' checks at Aber-
crombie & Fitch, and has escaped being thrown in jail by the
narrowest of margins. He engages in various sports earnestly
but awkwardly, and although he has taken lessons from pro-
fessionals in golf and tennis, he is always prepared for failure."
She described him at Kent's Island as leading the life of "a
rather distracted country gentleman, followed by dogs who
do not obey him very well," but pointed out that "his apparent
ineffectiveness disguises a keen appreciation of fundamentals.
He can sum up any situation or personal equation with in-
cisiveness, with tenderness, and always with a strong flavor
of that disturbingly amusing cynicism that is Yankee humor."

John rather liked Conney's article and tended to dismiss
Carl's objections to it. But it continued to rankle with Carl.
It created a rift between Carl Brandt and Conney Fiske that
never completely disappeared. It was fortunate they lived in
different cities, and that John could continue his friendship
with both people. In clashes of this sort, John usually came out
the winner, or at least the nonloser. It was one of a series of
collisions that would result, directly or indirectly, from the
two kinds of fiction that he had taken it upon himself to write.

He had also, since the publication of *The Late George Apley*
and the Pulitzer Prize—both of which roughly coincided with
his marriage to Adelaide—become excessively preoccupied
with the sales figures and royalty statements for his books.
The Late George Apley had sold something over 50,000 copies
in the hard-cover edition. *Wickford Point* appeared not to be
doing quite as well, largely due to the highly unstable condition of the book market in those darkening prewar days of
1939. On April 30 of that year, *Wickford Point* reached the
number-one position on the *New York Herald-Tribune*'s list
of fiction best sellers, but John's editor, Alfred McIntyre,
wrote to him to warn him against excessive optimism, saying,
"I wish I could tell you that this meant lots of reorders,
but the fact is that the jobbers and most of the larger booksellers have not yet sold out their initial orders." The novel
had been serialized before publication in the *Saturday Evening
Post,* and—though the *Post* had presented only a condensed

version—McIntyre speculated that prior circulation might have hurt the book's hard-cover sale; readers who had read it in the *Post* were not buying the book.

This has long been an unanswered and probably unanswerable question in publishing. Book publishers tend to believe that previous serialization in a magazine reduces some of the impact of a book's appearance. Magazine publishers argue that, on the contrary, publication in condensed form in a magazine merely whets the reader's appetite for the full book and helps get the book talked about before it appears. There is evidence to support both arguments. Authors and their agents, of course, prefer to hope for the best of both worlds —prepublication sale of a book to a magazine, followed by a successful hard-cover sale. In his letter to John, McIntyre added, "We are still advertising it and still hoping for a long continuing sale, but it looks now as if our earlier views as to the likely sales . . . would not be realized."

McIntyre's less than hopeful tone put John in a dark and discouraged mood. Thanking McIntyre for publishing a book that appeared to be, as John saw it, "a financial flop," John told McIntyre that *Wickford Point*'s career convinced him that he would never be able completely to break away from his slavery to the big-paying magazines and that, with his current financial obligations, it looked as though it would be a long time before he could afford to tackle another serious novel. Perhaps he could never afford to do so. Instead, he was immediately going to begin another of his *Post* serials. So much for the Great American Novel.

Sensing that his letter had seriously damaged John Marquand's self-confidence, McIntyre dictated a second, gentler letter reassuring him. "Naturally you are discouraged by my letter, but a book that sells over 40,000 copies is not a 'financial flop,' and we haven't given up hope that 'Wickford Point' will sell a good many thousand copies more. Whatever may happen to 'Wickford Point,' we haven't really yet tested the fate of a serious novel by you on the basis of your 'breaking away from the Post.' We don't know how many readers of the Post read 'Wickford Point' in its columns instead of in book form."

Nor was there any way of possibly knowing. But McIntyre and a Little, Brown vice-president, Roger Scaife, came up with a promotion idea that was daring and—considering that Little, Brown had always been known as a traditional and conservative Boston firm—surprising. They placed a large newspaper advertisement for *Wickford Point* with a headline that read: TO ANYONE WHO TELLS YOU "I'M READING IT AS A SERIAL." The copy went on, in effect, to attack the *Saturday Evening Post's* serialization of the novel and to assure readers that there was much more to enjoy and discover in the finished book than in the hacked-up *Post* condensation. In publishing, Little, Brown's ad created an immediate furor. Nothing like it had ever been done before.

The ad also drew an immediate and angry response from Stuart Rose of the *Saturday Evening Post,* who advised Alfred McIntyre that his advertising broadside was a serious attempt "to interfere with our business" and that the *Post's* lawyers considered the ad "actionable." Furthermore, Rose warned, if Little, Brown persisted with such tactics, the *Post* "will notify all authors and agents concerned that we are no longer interested in their manuscripts . . . there is no point in our paying large sums for literary material only to submit to deliberate public attack." He added:

> I am afraid that your whole strategy is based upon the fallacious idea that Post serialization will injure your book sales. Were your premise sound there might be some point in what you are doing, but I think you'd find yourself in difficulties if you attempted to demonstrate that premise. Take, for example, Walter Edmonds' DRUMS ALONG THE MOHAWK. This novel appeared in part in The Saturday Evening Post, yet as a book it sold four or five copies for every one of any previous novel by Walter Edmonds—and none of Edmonds' previous novels were serialized in The Saturday Evening Post either in whole or in part. I could cite numerous more or less parallel cases.

Mr. Rose, in passing, took a swipe at John Marquand, saying that although the *Post* had not published *all* of *Wickford Point,* nonetheless "We, as editors, might easily assume the position that we published all of the manuscript that was, in our opinion, publishable."

Little, Brown apologized for its ad, and Mr. Rose and others at the *Post* eventually simmered down. But it would remain a dilemma for Marquand—and for Carl Brandt as his agent—whether to accept a serialization offer, which might run to as much as $75,000 in those still-depressed days, or to refuse on the chance that the hard-cover book would earn that much and more as a result. For this reason as much as any other, John Marquand was continually badgering his publishers for sales figures. Each thousand copies more or less that each book sold became a matter of terrible importance. Biweekly and even weekly sales reports to the author were required, and in between there were harried telephone calls between John, wherever he happened to be, and Boston. He was also convinced that his having won the Pulitzer Prize for *Apley* should have had some impact on the sales of this book as well as his others. Actually, the awarding of literary prizes—unless they are surrounded by violent controversy—has never had much effect at the bookseller's cash register. But Marquand felt otherwise. For a new edition of *Apley* that Little, Brown brought out in 1938, John wanted the words "Pulitzer Prize" placed on the book jacket in large boldface letters, but when he saw the result he was dissatisfied. He complained to Bernice Baumgarten that the book would certainly sell more copies if the words "Pulitzer Prize" were set in heavier type. What about a band diagonally across the jacket? Somewhat wearily, Miss Baumgarten passed along Marquand's thoughts to Alfred McIntyre. But two weeks later Marquand was still unhappy with the jacket, and Miss Baumgarten wrote to McIntyre again, saying, "the Pulitzer Prize line on the bottom of the jacket does not stand out at all. Can we persuade you to put a two-inch band around the book, with *Pulitzer Prize Winner* in large letters on it? John seems very much concerned about this."

Not long after the publication of *Wickford Point*, John and Adelaide's first child, a daughter, was born to the somewhat middle-aged parents. Adelaide was thirty-seven, John forty-seven. They named the little girl Blanche Ferry Marquand, after her maternal grandmother, but since neither John or Adelaide cared much for the name Blanche, she was called by the pretty name "Ferry."

At about this time, Adelaide became interested in the activities of that curious pre-World War II phenomenon known as the America First Committee. From its inception in the summer of 1940, America First had attracted a number of prominent American names, headed by General Robert E. Wood of Chicago, board chairman of Sears, Roebuck and Company, and including in its membership such people as R. Douglas Stuart, Jr., General Hugh S. Johnson, Kathleen Norris, Chester Bowles, Norman Thomas, Henry Ford, Sr., Eddie Rickenbacker, Lillian Gish, and Edward L. Ryerson, Jr. America First was composed not only of pacifists, like Kathleen Norris, but also of outspoken isolationists such as General Wood, and the Committee had been created specifically to counteract the activities of William Allen White's Committee to Defend America by Aiding the Allies, which advocated coming to the aid of Britain in her struggle against Nazi Germany. The America First Committee was only too happy to welcome on its board Mrs. John P. Marquand, wife of the celebrated novelist. It was already a panel of imposing names. In April, 1941, America First had acquired none other than Colonel Charles Augustus Lindbergh.

Adelaide pitched into America First work with her customary vigor and enthusiasm. She pinned to her shoulder the little American flag that was the badge of America First and was quick to pick up the America First slogans and repeat them. "We can't solve the age-old feuds of Europe" was a particular favorite, and she was once overheard to observe, "Some Americans are more American than others." She took to signing all her letters, whether business or social, with the words, "Yours for better Government." John was first amused with America First and Adelaide's involvement, and then appalled.

One of the disturbing aspects of the America First Committee was the undercurrent of anti-Semitism in some of its members. An effort had been made to avoid any public confrontation with this issue when the Committee had placed—at General Wood's insistence—Lessing J. Rosenwald, a prominent Chicago Jew and another director of Sears, Roebuck, on the executive committee. But when Henry Ford—who had led an anti-Semitic attack in his *Dearborn Independent* in the 1920s with the publication of the spurious document "The Protocols of the Learned Elders of Zion"—was announced on the committee in the same news release, the outcry among American Jewry was so great that Mr. Rosenwald was forced to resign in embarrassment. A huge rally for America First was arranged to be held at New York's Madison Square Garden in 1941, and at it the notorious Joe McWilliams, a Jew-baiting Christian Mobilizer, made a dramatic appearance. On the speakers' dais were Colonel Lindbergh and, in a flowing white gown, Adelaide Marquand.

The bleakest moment for America First came on September 11, 1941, when Lindbergh appeared before an audience in Des Moines, Iowa, and declared, "The three most important groups who have been pressing this country toward war are the British, the Jewish, and the Roosevelt administration." These "war agitators," he continued, "comprise only a small minority of our people; but they control a tremendous influence." He went on to deliver the only faintly veiled threat, "Instead of agitating for war the Jewish groups in this country should be opposing it in every possible way, for they will be among the first to feel its consequences. . . . Their greatest danger to this country lies in their large ownership and influence in our motion pictures, our press, our radio, and our government." In the shocked reaction that followed, the Lindberghs found themselves cut off by a number of their oldest friends and admirers. But Adelaide Marquand announced that she heartily approved of everything Colonel Lindbergh had had to say. One night at a party Adelaide got into a violent and not altogether sober argument with some other guests over Lindbergh and America First. Later, John's friends labeled it "The Night of Horror."

Privately, Carl Brandt approached John. Adelaide, he pointed out, was in the process of doing him irreparable harm in terms of his reputation and his reading public. Couldn't she, instead of making her announcements as "Mrs. John P. Marquand," call herself Adelaide H. Marquand, or even employ her maiden name, Adelaide Hooker? Wearily, John said, "I wish she would, but she is my wife, and that is her name."

Before she married Carl, Carol Brandt had been warned both by his brother, Erd Brandt, and their friend Samuel Hopkins Adams, that Carl had a serious drinking problem. When one is in love with a man it is easy to ignore such warnings. The trouble had started during Carl's first marriage, and it expressed itself in a unique way, if indeed every case of alcoholism is not unique. Carl would go for weeks, even months, able to drink in a normal, comfortable, social way, and it would be possible to believe that nothing was out of order at all. Then, for no discernible reason—not because of any visible career or emotional upset—he would disappear from sight, be drunk for days, and then return, or be found, shaken and ill and ready to be committed to a hospital or sanitarium. Carol had tried various means to cope with and even control this behavior. She had scolded, had withdrawn, had tried to reason with him during his sober periods.

"Through all these bad times," Carol Brandt recalls, "John was a wonderful comfort to me. He'd come over to the apartment to see me and to visit with the children, who adored him. I used to be terribly angry, furious with Carl for his behavior, but John would always urge me to be calm, to be more sympathetic and understanding. He always believed that Carl was a schizophrenic and should be treated like a person with a mental illness—not ranted at as I tended to do. During these times, John was like a rock for me to lean on."

But after ten years of marriage and two children—a son and a daughter—she had toughened herself to endure these terrifying episodes and to recognize a few if not all of the advance warning signs. She had also had to accept the fact that Carl's drinking had brought him to the point of sexual impotence.

It had, at least, in terms of his relationship with his wife. He could, he confessed to her, achieve sexual satisfaction with other women, but with her no longer. It was a painful thing for Carl to acknowledge, a difficult period for them both. Theirs had from the beginning been an uncommon sort of marriage. The second marriage for them both, they had entered into it with a full awareness that a perfect relationship between two people is almost never possible to achieve. They had married fully prepared to adjust, to make exceptions, to adapt to situations, to compromise. At the same time, though they were not at all alike, their temperaments balanced. Both were ambitious and in a true sense self-made people, with successful careers they had carved for themselves. Both were tough-minded and humorous about life and its possibilities, but while Carol was strong and taut, Carl was gentle and malleable. "He was the kindest man I've ever known," Carol has recalled. "It was his extraordinary kindness that first drew me to him. I have always believed that it's a man's world, but I don't believe in a woman getting kicked in the teeth for it. Carl's nature was such that he hated to hurt anybody. I'm a little short on kindness myself, and so I treasured that quality in him." The Brandts' marriage had reached another point when one of a series of assessments had to be made. Sometimes these assessments could be made together, and at other times, because of Carl's disappearances, Carol had to make them on her own. This time, discussing their marriage over a quiet dinner at home, they decided once more to try to make it last.

When, on December 7, 1941, the Japanese bombs came raining down on Pearl Harbor, Carl and Carol happened to be staying with friends in Washington who heard the news even before it went on the air. Immediately Carol telephoned John in New York, who said something like, "I want to see you and Carl the minute you get back to New York. I don't think I can live like this any longer, with what's going on." To Adelaide, he said, "I want to be with the two people who understand how I feel about this," and, as soon as the Brandts returned to the city, John went to stay at their apartment.

It wasn't many days later that Carl—perhaps it was the pressure of the war news, who knew?—disappeared again, and when he was found he was taken to the Silver Hill Sanitarium near New Canaan, Connecticut, for prolonged rest and treatment. Carol and John, both lonely, unhappy, dissatisfied with the courses their lives were taking, found themselves alone together.

They had been alone and unhappy in New York at the same time once before, it turned out—but they had been apart. Neither had known the other was there. It had been in 1930, right after Drew Hill's death. Carol had been a young widow working in the city and John, during one of his periodic separations from Christina, had taken a small bachelor apartment. The friendship that had begun four years earlier in Paris might have continued during that year, and if it had their respective lives might have taken quite different turns. It was interesting to speculate, they both thought, about what might have happened in 1930, before each had committed himself in a different direction. But for some reason, though they had several friends in common, neither had learned—in 1930—that the other was living just a few city blocks away.

Now, in 1941, they rather ruefully admitted, as two mature people, it was somewhat late to ponder over lost possibilities. But it was something to think about just the same. And so, in those unsettled days at the beginning of the Second World War, it was in this way—hesitantly, at first, and then with great seriousness—that they became lovers.

"It was more than the physical attraction, which was great," Carol Brandt recalls, "or the fact that I have always liked older men, and John was ten years older than I. It began to seem as though this was an inevitable extension of our days together in Paris in the twenties, when, as I look back on it now, I first fell in love with him, almost without knowing it. But the main thing was that I have always loved writers, and found them the most fascinating people in the world. John was simply the most important literary figure I had ever known. I was *impressed* by him. All writers need help and support, and Lord knows he was not getting that from Adelaide. He had great admiration for Conney Fiske's literary taste, but she was not as aware as I was of the difficulties of the writing process. Carl could help John in important ways as an agent. But John always felt that Carl was too concerned with making money. I knew I could help John in small and practical ways, as well as with love and sympathy and understanding, and perhaps even help him grow as a writer in some small way. I wanted him to depend on me."

Chapter Fifteen

*A*t least one thing had become settled in John Marquand's life before Pearl Harbor brought the United States into war, and that was Peter O'Reilly's lawsuit. It had dragged on for over two years, and though, at its outset, Little, Brown's lawyers—and John's—had variously labeled Mr. O'Reilly's action as "ridiculous" and "absurd" (of all the Irish names in the Boston telephone book, John had been unlucky enough to pick the name of a litigious politician), the lawyers had had agonized second thoughts, as lawyers often do. The case was approaching the expensive pretrial stage. It was quite possible, the lawyers reasoned, that in a city such as Boston a majority of the jurors selected to decide the case might be Irish Catholics. So, very easily, might be the judge. George Apley's views of the Boston Irish Catholics had not been exactly charitable, and it might not be easy to explain the subtle nuances of fictional satire to members of a traditionally hot-tempered tribe. Some sort of settlement seemed indicated. Finally, in payment for his "great pecuniary damages and loss of business," his "injured" feelings and reputation, the "disgrace" and "loss of reputation" he had suffered, along with the damage to his earning capacity, credit, and good name, Mr. O'Reilly was persuaded to accept the sum of $600. Little, Brown paid this settlement, which went with a release stating that the money was "not to be construed as an admission of liability on the part of Little, Brown & Company (Inc.) or of anyone else." Little, Brown and John split the legal fee, which amounted to somewhat more than the settlement.

It is interesting and perhaps no coincidence that at just about the time Marquand began his affair with Carol Brandt he was putting the finishing touches on a major novel which had adultery as one of its underlying themes, a novel that dealt with a confrontation between love, marriage, and male friendship, and also the novel in which one of the major female characters —Marvin Myles—reminded many people who knew her of Carol Brandt. *H. M. Pulham, Esquire* is the third of what might be considered a trilogy of New England novels, and, like *Wickford Point,* it is strongly autobiographical. There is something of John Marquand in the title character of Harry Pulham, but there is even more in Pulham's best friend, the restless, womanizing Bill King, who commits adultery with Pulham's wife and who is always "here today and gone tomorrow."

Though Bill King betrays his best friend by taking his wife to bed, the reader somehow does not despise him for it. Partly this is because Kay Pulham appears to get so little joy from the affair. But even more it is because of the vastness of Harry Pulham's trustingness and naïveté. Again and again in the novel Harry Pulham is confronted with evidence that something very off-center is going on between Bill and Kay, and again and again he dismisses it as something that could not be happening. Bill, after all, is a "gentleman," and gentlemen just don't sleep with their best friends' wives. By the end of the book, the reader is almost furious at Harry Pulham for not discovering what is going on under his own roof, practically in front of his very nose, and shortly after the novel's publication the late Wolcott Gibbs wrote a parody of *H. M. Pulham, Esquire* for *The New Yorker* in which the hero comes upon his wife and his friend in bed together and, after an initial moment of slight surprise, accepts the explanation they offer him—they got into bed together to keep each other warm.

And yet, at the same time, the reader respects and pities
Harry Pulham, who says, "I guess I've always been a straight,"
and one of whose friends keeps referring to him as a "norm."
Like George Apley, Harry Pulham once tries to break away
from the restraint of Boston and goes to New York and works
for an advertising agency where, though his job involves ex-
tolling the dubious qualities of a laundry soap, he nonetheless
feels alive, part of a team, and where he falls in love with the
beautiful businesswoman, Marvin Myles. Marvin at first can't
decide whether he is "dumb or clever" but soon is perceptive
enough to see that he is neither. She tells him, "You're just
yourself. I've never seen anyone like you." And looking at the
photographs of the Pulham family that are arranged on Harry's
dresser top, she says to him, "All of you is there, isn't it? All
that you're going back to? It must be queer, being in two
places at once." And so, of course, did John Marquand think
of himself as being in two places at once; he was at one and
the same time the wanderer who loved independence and
women and travel, and also the man who talked wistfully of
putting down roots in peaceful and quiet and changeless old
places like Newburyport, Curzon's Mill, and Beacon Hill.
When Harry Pulham brings Marvin Myles back to Boston for
a visit, he cannot help noticing that she is by far the best-
dressed woman there. This means that she does not and cannot ever belong.

Just as it did George Apley, Boston reclaims Harry Pulham,
and he returns to a life where, as his father explains it, "I can't
recall ever wanting things to happen. I've spent all my life
trying to fix it so that things wouldn't happen." He gets a job
selling bonds and with a terrible innocence says, "I don't want
to sell bonds." "My boy," says a member of the bond firm, "no
one wants to, but that's the way we live."

Of the pathetically small number of people who pass through
Harry Pulham's life, he understands Marvin Myles the best,
perhaps because she is the beautiful alien, and he says, "I know
the whole secret of Marvin Myles—that she wanted things
to belong to her, because what belonged to her gave her a
sense of well-being. . . . Once something belonged to her, she
would give it everything she had. I know, because I belonged

to her once." He admires this spirit in Marvin Myles, and he also admires and envies the rootless and unfettered existence —going from girl to girl—of his friend Bill King. These two become Harry Pulham's windows into the world that lies beyond State Street and Beacon Hill. At the same time, both Marvin and Bill see in Harry a figure of stability, strength, and truth to his code, quite different from most of the men encountered in their own topsy-turvy worlds.

Seeing the inevitability of the path Pulham's life will take, Marvin says to him, "It makes me frightened when I see you do things that I can't do. They take you away from me, all those little things." One of those little things is Kay Motford who, when Harry Pulham first meets her, strikes him as a "lemon." He cannot understand why his friend Bill does not think Kay is a lemon. Again, she is a type too familiar to Harry Pulham, but to Bill she is an exotic. Of Kay, Harry's mother says that she is one of their kind, "a dear, sensible girl. She's one of those girls who doesn't think about herself, or think about her looks. She thinks of other people." She does not, like Marvin, want things to belong to her. After Harry's return to Boston and the bond business—Marvin writes, "Darling, aren't you coming back?"—Harry Pulham and Kay Motford show up at the same dances and teas and debut parties, appear as usher and bridesmaid at the same weddings, and it is soon apparent to everyone that Harry will marry his lemon; there is absolutely no one else for either of them. On their honeymoon, Kay has a small favor to ask him. Could he please stop saying "Of course?" Harry Pulham replies, "Why, yes, Kay. Of course."

And so *H. M. Pulham, Esquire* becomes a story of love and marriage based on compromise, where there is little point in looking back on what might have been. Of course, one does look back, but one is always brought up to the realities of the present and such matters, trivial but persistent, as whether the dog has been let out or whether the pilot light is working properly on the kitchen range. One is sustained in such a life only by adhering to a certain code, a certain set of values. At one point, toward the novel's end, Harry Pulham enters his house and hears through the closed parlor door his wife's and his friend Bill's voices, and Kay saying bitterly, "Let's not go all over it again. We can't go back." For the briefest moment, Harry Pulham wonders: Is there something between Bill and Kay? But he pushes this unchivalrous thought out of his head immediately, thinking that such an idea is unworthy of him. After all, Harry reminds himself, "Bill King was my best friend, and besides he was a gentleman. . . . As I say, I was ashamed of myself. It made me feel like apologizing to both of them when I opened the parlor door, and I told myself I must never consider such a thing again—not ever."

Harry opens the parlor door, and what follows is one of the tenderest and yet funniest scenes in all of John Marquand's novels. Harry asks Bill solicitously if he has everything he wants, and Bill replies harshly, "That's a damned silly question, and you know it, boy. Nobody ever has everything he wants." Because Kay looks so distraught, Harry concludes that she has been "doing altogether too much lately," and, because her hands are cold to the touch, he suggests a hot water bag. "Anything," Kay says, "anything but a hot water bag!" Harry helps Kay to her feet and she kisses him, which he thinks is "very generous" of her. The ironic point is swiftly and brilliantly made that in Harry Pulham's ignorance is his only awareness and only happiness. Only ignorance, in Harry Pulham's world, can make that world even remotely tolerable. He is a man who must say "of course" to life.

Kay, at the same time, suffers from a similar lack of perception. When she discovers, years later and by sheerest accident, that her husband had a love affair with Marvin Myles, she cannot imagine what a woman such as the glamorous Marvin could possibly have seen in a man as dull and ordinary as her husband.

It was probably inevitable that critics should have drawn a comparison between *H. M. Pulham, Esquire* and *Babbitt,* the 1922 novel by Sinclair Lewis, since both novels are about men in ruts unable to get out, who go through life wearing blinders. It was said that Marquand's satiric novel was like Lewis's but "without the bite." Actually, it might have been pointed out that Marquand's satire was much more subtle, much more delicate, written with much more feeling, without Lewis's

stridency and harshness and generally tin ear for human speech.
Compare the husband-and-wife confrontation scenes which
close both books. When George Follansbee Babbitt and his
wife, whom he calls by such names as "old honey," and "you
old humbug," intended as terms of endearment, are reconciled
at her bedside (Mrs. Babbitt is to be rushed off for an emergency operation, a convenient device with which to end the
book), she says, "I was wondering what was the use of my
living. I've been getting so stupid and ugly—" Babbitt replies,
"Why, you old humbug! Fishing for compliments when I ought
to be packing your bag! Me, sure, I'm young and handsome and
a regular village cut-up and—" Lewis writes, "He could not go
on. He sobbed again; and in muttered incoherencies they
found each other."

Against the "muttered incoherencies" we have the quiet
dignity, almost elegance, of Kay and Harry Pulham's reconciliation. "So we have to be kind to one another always, don't
we?" Kay says to her husband. "We're all alone. There's only
you and me."

Meanwhile, John Marquand and Carol Brandt had no intention of turning Carl Brandt into a Harry Pulham, or of de-
ceiving him about the change that had occurred in their
relationship. All three, after all, were sophisticated people, and
the only civilized and decent thing to do was to tell Carl
what had happened. Adelaide was something else again. She
had already begun to suspect John of having affairs with other
women, and his tendency to philander had become—as it also
had with Christina—one of the problems facing their marriage.
The Bill King side of his nature was, to John, something he
accepted about himself and thoroughly enjoyed. He had, in
fact, since Harvard days. Christina had been unable to accept
it. Neither, now, could Adelaide. She was suspicious of every
trip he took away from her. She was sure that something was
going on between John and each new secretary, and quite often
there was. John found it very difficult to sympathize with
Adelaide's jealousies. He had been born, after all, in that
"tail-end of the Victorian era," and he believed in a double
standard. But from the beginning it was agreed that Carl

should be told. "John and I talked it over," Carol Brandt recalls, "and decided that I should tell Carl as soon as possible after he got back from Silver Hill. I also thought that John should tell Adelaide. It seemed fairer. But John said he couldn't bring himself to do that. I didn't want to be bothered with all the lies and deceptions of trying to lead a double life. But John knew the kind of scenes Adelaide was capable of making, and he simply was terrified of telling her."

It is always pleasant to suppose that at crisis points in life, or when circumstances abruptly change, all of us can rise to occasions, accept inevitabilities with dignity and courage and even a bit of grace, and carry on. In actual fact, though, few of us find ourselves equipped to do so, and most of us can be counted upon to behave quite badly. And so Carl Brandt's reaction, when he had taken it in—that his friend who was also his most productive client was now his wife's lover, and that Carol and John both wanted to continue the affair, that it was much more than a casual interlude that could soon be forgotten—was crucial to both John and Carol, to the future of their respective marriages. "When Carl came home from Silver Hill, we had dinner at the St. Regis," Carol says, "and I told him what had happened. His first reaction was anger—not at me, but at John. He took the attitude of 'How can my best friend do this to me?' which has always struck me as a very strange way for a man to behave. After all, if a woman is to have an affair with a man, isn't it likely that it will be a friend of her husband's? As for me, Carl knew me very well. He knew that I was a woman who, if I wasn't sleeping with my husband, had to sleep with someone. He knew that since the trouble in our marriage had come up there had been other men in my life. But he also knew that, in any choice between another man and Carl, Carl would always come first and that I would never leave him.

"And so, after he had accepted what had happened, I telephoned John, who had gone back to the apartment on Beekman Place, and told him of Carl's and my conversation. Then Carl talked to John. They talked very quietly and sanely, and both men agreed that they didn't want the triangle of our friendship broken. Carl also urged John to tell Adelaide, so that all four of us could spread the situation out on the table and look at it as grown-ups. But John said no, that was out of the question, he couldn't do it, and that was that."

That was almost that, but the new and perhaps strange plateau upon which the Brandts' marriage, and the relationship it bore with John Marquand, had moved needed, in Carl Brandt's mind, some sort of definition from him. He wanted to put it in writing, and so, alone one night soon after their dinner at the St. Regis, he penciled it on a few sheets of yellow foolscap and addressed it to his wife. It is an extraordinary letter from an extraordinary man, who was certainly no Harry Pulham:

Darlink:

Don't please feel you ought to defend anyone, John or me or you, but believe me with all your power that I am being exactly honest with you. If you ask me how I feel, what I am thinking, I'll tell you, all on the primary basis that I am alone at fault. But no matter the grievous sin, the bastardly actions, the man can still be hurt even by his own blows. I would like to be different, I'd like in a certain way to be completely abject, but if I were I would be, I suspect, lost not only to myself but to you.

I'm going to say this once and for all time. Wild horses will never again, god helping me, drag it out: If you insist I'll simply say I've buried my dead in this grove of statement . . . R.I.P.

So:—

John knows in his deepest heart that he did me a bastardly trick—it is in his nature to have the strength of the weak for a very long time, and then to crack and do the easiest and most pleasant (to him) thing. It is in his acquisitiveness, his parsimony, his snobbishness, born all of these out of his early frustrations and rejections. He has made me ashamed of my weakness coming from my real love and admiration for him, in believing that he was my friend and *our* friend first. And, having all faith in that, I gave him utter trust. I can accept and have accepted the blame that he could justify his taking advantage of that affection and trust. I cannot force myself to *feel* unhurt that he did a Pearl Harbor instead of declaring war.

But it is gone and over the mill. I will not ever let him

know either that I have felt this way, or that, despite my heinous behavior, I have any pride or dignity left.

I will, out of my great gratitude to you for wanting to keep the pattern, and out of my love for the guy which is unchanged, go the whole hog in the rearrangement of his life . . . and I'll not let you down.

Any future that we may have as a trio will be a healthier one and a happier one because I will not be the prisoner of my simplehearted trustingness. I have become more civilized, more sophisticated, and consequently harder in my own fashion. But whatever should not eventuate I can take because I will be able to fight for my own side, or not fight as it seems wisest.

I repeat in all solemnity that I have had my say. I have been honest with you, and that I feel as I do (that I *can* feel as I do) is what remains to me of my manhood out of a self-devastated ruin. I'll put all this into the deep unconscious forever and aye—and I can do it *because* I see it and can bring it into the light. Back it goes, kerplunk.

I love and love and love you—and I love John.

Always,
Carl

Chapter Sixteen

*T*he America First Committee, formed as an attempt to keep the United States out of the Second World War, had, as soon as America entered the war, immediately collapsed of its own weight, and Adelaide Marquand found herself once more at loose ends, without a crusade or a cause. Though she had, when she first married John, a modest income of about $7,500 a year, her mother had died and she had inherited several millions of Ferry Seed Company money and stock. When the Marquands were thrust into a loftier tax bracket, the Boston firm of Welch & Forbes, which for a number of years had served as John's business managers, came up with a plan designed to conserve some of the Marquands' tax dollars. Welch & Forbes suggested that Mrs. Marquand be considered a "collaborator" or "assistant" to her husband in his literary efforts so that certain deductions for travel, entertaining, and office expenses could be taken that might otherwise be lost if she remained Mrs. John P. Marquand, Housewife.

This idea delighted Adelaide, who had always liked to think that she was, in a real sense, a true aide to her husband in the production of his books. Though both John and Alfred Mc-

Intyre had tried to confine Adelaide to the restricted role of copy editor, she was simply too energetic and enthusiastic a woman to be held down. She *had* to make editorial suggestions, and she was compulsively critical; she could not keep her fingers out of the novelistic pies, and of course this led to arguments—and to much worse than arguments. To formalize the tax setup, Welch & Forbes proposed that the books be jointly copyrighted by John and Adelaide, that royalties be divided between them, and that letters be passed between John and Little, Brown acknowledging the degree of Adelaide's assistance. Little, Brown was at first hesitant about this arrangement but eventually agreed, and John agreed also— though somewhat grudgingly, since the agreement had the appearance of giving Adelaide more credit than she deserved. *H. M. Pulham, Esquire* was the first Marquand novel to bear the joint copyright. Adelaide was overjoyed.

Actually she had done a certain amount of work on the book. John was not a particularly good title man—as, indeed, many novelists are not. The titles for most of his books had been selected by Little, Brown. John had originally wanted to call the Pulham book "Reunion," since it is a twenty-fifth reunion of his class at Harvard that sends Harry Pulham's thoughts off into the long central flashback. John had then toyed with the title "The Wild Echoes Flying," and an even worse one, "Golden Lads and Lassies Must." In the *McCall's* serial, the book had been called "Gone Tomorrow." Little, Brown had just about settled on the title "H. Pulham, Esq.," without a middle initial, when Adelaide had a suggestion to make. It seemed to her that people didn't usually write "Esquire" after a name with just one initial. John's letters, she pointed out, usually came addressed to John Marquand, Esq.," or "J. P. Marquand, Esq.," but never "J. Marquand, Esq." Somehow "H. Pulham, Esq." just didn't sound like a Boston name. Little, Brown thought enough of her comment to give Henry Pulham the middle name of Moulton.

The sales of *Pulham* were somewhat better than those of *Wickford Point*, which encouraged John, who liked to worry about such matters. Published in February, 1941, the book was high on the best-seller list by mid-March and by the middle of

May had sold 47,290 copies in the United States. By June, it had sold 49,011, and by August the sales had leveled out to just over 51,000 copies. It had been a Book-of-the-Month Club selection and in that less expensive edition had sold 156,800 copies. John had every reason for good cheer. But in the spring of that year an incident took place that was as exasperating as it was comic. At an April meeting of the Boston City Council, that august body voted unanimously to ban *H. M. Pulham, Esquire* in Boston. The book, the Council stated, constituted a "slur on Boston womanhood" with its depiction of the adulterous Kay Pulham.

Ordinarily, in publishing, it is considered something of a blessing to have a book banned in Boston, since the publicity that such an action generates more than compensates for any loss in sales. But in the case of *Pulham* there was—to John— the galling fact that sitting on the City Council at the time was none other than Mr. Henry Shattuck, described in the newspapers as "Acting President of Harvard University," who had voted for the ban. Mr. Shattuck's vote not only gave the ban a certain academic cachet but gave it from an institution that was world famous for its liberality and was Marquand's own alma mater. To make matters even more grotesque, John had had, just a few weeks before the Council's action, a letter from Mr. K. D. Metcalf, Librarian of Harvard University, asking in the most gracious sort of way whether Mr. Marquand would consider donating the manuscripts of both *The Late George Apley* and *H. M. Pulham, Esquire* to the library where, Mr. Metcalf assured him, they would be placed in the "New Treasure Room."

Marquand was indignant. It seemed to him that if Mr. Shattuck's attitude reflected that of the university, Marquand's own manuscripts would be more happily housed in some institution that did not tolerate censorship, and he told Metcalf so. It was pointed out to John that Shattuck was not really acting president of Harvard but that he had merely presided over faculty meetings in President Conant's absence. This struck John as a very minor technical difference, especially since Shattuck had refused either to apologize or to discuss the matter with the press. All of John's old bitterness and mixed feelings about Harvard, and what he felt had been his rejection there, came back, and he could not help feeling that Harvard had managed somehow to snub him all over again. Quietly and with great determination, he packed up all his manuscripts and shipped them to Yale, in whose library they presently repose.

Elsewhere than in Boston, *H. M. Pulham, Esquire* had been received with good notices, and by the end of 1941 he had begun somewhat wistfully to think the novel might earn him a second Pulitzer Prize. He had mentioned this to Alfred McIntyre, suggesting that there might be ways in which Little, Brown could get it prominently placed before the Pulitzer Prize Committee. In his personal evaluation of his books, John considered *Wickford Point* better than *The Late George Apley,* and *H. M. Pulham, Esquire* better than *Wickford Point,* and there were prominent critics who agreed with him. *Pulham* was a good candidate for the Pulitzer, which is awarded by a committee that never reveals what books are under consideration. But the fiction prize for 1942 went to Ellen Glasgow for her novel, *In This Our Life.*

John was disappointed, but he took his disappointment gracefully. He liked Ellen Glasgow as a writer. He remarked that she had long deserved the prize, and that at least it hadn't gone to a "punk" such as T. S. Stribling, who had won it for *The Store* in 1933. Privately he admitted that the prize should probably not be awarded twice to any one novelist, since there were so many good ones around. In the theater, on the other hand, where the supply of talent seemed poorer, it seemed to him permissible that both Eugene O'Neill and Robert E. Sherwood had at that point each collected three Pulitzers, and George S. Kaufman had won two.

Adelaide, meanwhile, had become convinced that her husband was being unfaithful to her with another woman or, perhaps, with several other women. When she had come into her inheritance, it had seemed to John logical enough that she could now be treated as a more or less independent person and therefore—in a sense—ignored. She had her own money, could go where she wished and buy what she wished; there would be no more financial arguments. But to Adelaide this was not enough. She wanted nothing less than to be a complete wife and could not accept the somewhat arm's-length relationship which John preferred with all his women. One of the great attractions of Carol Brandt was certainly her lack of dependence on him and her lack of possessiveness. She was a successful businesswoman with a career of her own. After marrying Carl she had left the literary-agency business—it represented a conflict of interests—and had gone to work for Louis B. Mayer of M-G-M as his East Coast story scout, with a contract that provided her with $50,000 a year and a chauffeur-driven car. Also, John had always wanted a woman who could organize his life for him and keep track of the small details that were always distracting him, such as appointments and hotel reservations and servants' pay checks. In terms of sloppiness, Adelaide was even worse than Christina; she simply could not organize anything. There was also the annoying problem of her perpetual lateness. She was never ready on time, and friends learned not to be surprised when the Marquands showed up hours late for a dinner party—or failed to show up at all. This infuriated John, who admired punctuality and order. Once, he and Adelaide were to meet at Pennsylvania Station to take a train to Florida, and when, at the last minute, Adelaide had not appeared, John simply boarded the train and went off to Florida without her.

Adelaide had started consulting a psychiatrist. She had also started drinking heavily. There were terrible scenes. Like many alcoholics, she would not admit that she was one and was very defensive about her drinking. She did, in a sense, try to control it by going for long periods without alcohol. But then she would begin to drink; when drunk, she became assertive and opinionated and would make extravagant statements— praising or detracting another writer's work, for example— that she would then find herself having to defend when sober. The Marquand household, wherever it happened to be, had become one that was hardly ever settled or relaxed. Adelaide had taken to eavesdropping on his telephone calls, and John once discovered that she had been steaming open his letters.

And yet, at the same time, there were moments of tenderness between them, and times when John seemed genuinely to feel guilty about the offhand way he treated Adelaide. One evening, for example, guests at 1 Beekman Place were startled to see the host appear wearing what was for him a very uncharacteristic pink shirt, and the hostess wearing a skirt made of the same pink fabric. It was a rather touching attempt at a show of unity.

John was also a heavy drinker, and had been since the 1930s. But drinking had never managed to affect John's professional or social life. He kept to a very strict working schedule, starting punctually in the morning with his dictation of whatever story or novel was in progress. He would dictate for about four hours, or until lunchtime, and then the tray of martinis would appear. John rather enjoyed it if whichever secretary was working for him joined him in the martinis. He did not enjoy drinking alone and liked to consider the preluncheon cocktail hour as a time for social conversation and, perhaps, discussion of the morning's work. If the secretary declined the drink, this annoyed him, and as a rule that secretary would not remain long in his employ. Then, in the afternoons, he would work over and edit material that had been dictated into the typewriter that morning. Martinis would not reappear until the customary pre-dinner hour. One rarely saw John Marquand drunk. With Adelaide, alas, that was not the case.

And so Carol, who shared John's passion for order and routine, came into his life and helped him make it follow a plan. The little details of living with which, according to himself, he could never quite seem to cope—getting checks cashed, letters mailed, shirts to the laundry, coats back from the dry cleaner—she could, in her smooth and efficient way and with the help of an accomplished secretary, handle for him. Her office could make hotel and plane and rail reservations for him, see that he was met at his destinations by the proper cars, send him reminders for his social calendar, and even do some personal shopping for him. She helped him put together, by remote control, his summer retreat at Kent's Island, and her shopping lists included his linen, towels, china, glass, and electric blankets. All this, since Carol was the methodical person she was, she managed as though by sleight of hand. He gave her credit for performing miracles. Actually, of course, the little services Carol Brandt helped do for him amounted to rather little time or effort on her part. But she, intuitive woman that she was, was wise enough never to let him know it.

"And," as Carol Brandt says, "I amused him. He enjoyed watching the way I worked. I'd be with him, and I'd also be in the process of working out a movie deal—either for him, or for another client. I'd be back and forth with calls to the Coast, bargaining for terms and escalator clauses, and when I'd finished he'd smile at me and shake his head and say, 'It'll be a long time before Buster'—meaning my son—'will be able to do *that!*'"

Adelaide, with her interest in music, had become fascinated with the development of Aspen, Colorado, which was started by Chicago's Walter Paepcke as a center for its music festival long before it became famous as a ski resort. As she usually did when she discovered a spot she liked, she bought a house there. Adelaide fell in love with Aspen. John announced that he detested Aspen. When Adelaide begged to know what it was that he disliked about Aspen, John replied that her Aspen house provided him with no studio in which to work. So Adelaide bought another house in Aspen, to be used as John's studio. This move did nothing to change John's feelings about the Rocky Mountain resort, which he began vociferously referring to as "my Ass-pen." Adelaide continued to try to stimulate John's interest in music; she had even had him placed on the Music Committee of the 1939–40 New York World's Fair—John, who could not sing a note, and whose musical tastes had never gone farther than a handful of rather raffish barroom ballads.

Early in 1941, the director King Vidor purchased *H. M. Pulham, Esquire* for Metro-Goldwyn-Mayer and invited John to come to Hollywood to work on the motion picture script. John accepted without a moment's hesitation; Hollywood would give him a chance to escape the growing disorder of his domestic life. Before starting the film, Vidor wanted to see Boston, and so he came east and Vidor and John went up to Boston, where John gave the director a full day's tour of his beloved city. They visited old houses along the Charles River and on Beacon Hill, and John took Vidor to lunch at the Somerset Club, where Harry Pulham would have lunched, and treated him to the club's sweet martinis and the third-floor sign reading, "This watercloset for emergency use only; other waterclosets available on the second floor." John showed Vidor the house in Louisburg Square where the Pulhams might have lived and pointed out such Bostonian eccentricities as the quaint phraseology of the public notices, including a sign, at the entrance to an alleyway on the Hill, which to this day reads: PRIVATE WAY. PERSONS CAUTIONED NOT TO TRAVEL THEREON. He took Vidor to the Boston Athenaeum, the venerable private library at 10½ Beacon, where share-owning members could, until quite recently, enjoy tea or bouillon with three crackers for three cents; with three crackers and cheese, the price was five cents; with one plain cracker and one sweet, three cents; with one plain and cheese and one sweet, four cents; with extra sweet crackers a penny apiece, and extra plain crackers two for a penny. He also told Vidor that the Athenaeum frowned on popular magazines other than the *Atlantic Monthly*, except, a number of years earlier, when a discreet sign had been posted that read, "Copies of *Cosmopolitan* are available for the duration of the Coolidge articles." Another notice in the reading room advised: "Window sashes should not be raised or lowered without prior consultation with the other members." At the Athenaeum, John introduced Vidor to its imposingly scholarly-looking librarian, Mr. Walter Muir Whitehill (married to a Coolidge) who always liked to remind John of an error he had spotted in *The Late George Apley*. John had had Apley, in a letter to his children written in 1912, point out that an Apley family portrait hung in the Athenaeum's Oval Room. "Highly amusing," Mr. Whitehill had commented, "but I must point out that this room was not built until 1913." He had added hastily, "I yield to no man in my appreciation of the book as satire." In the process of their Boston day, King Vidor and John Marquand became good friends.

Hollywood enthralled him. It was, among other things, so utterly different from Boston. Immediately upon checking into the Beverly Hills Hotel, John realized that his tweedy-seedy Boston-*cum*-London tailoring was all wrong for the film colony, and his first request to Vidor was to get him to a clothing store where he could outfit himself more in the manner of the natives. That done, he went to work on the film script with relish. He was given a large office and a blonde secretary, and he soon found himself falling in love with Hollywood. He was charmed by Hollywood's glittering nuttiness, by the fact that all the living rooms had bars, that life there was as different from Boston as chiffon from sackcloth. He dined out with Dolores Del Rio and Rosalind Russell and Charles Chaplin. At one party, Chaplin spent most of the evening doing hilarious imitations of such people as the King of Denmark and the Lord Chief Justice of the Old Bailey (later John would perfect his own hilarious imitation of Chaplin imitating the King of Denmark and the Lord Chief Justice.) There were meetings and more dinners with Robert Young and Hedy Lamarr, the film's two stars.

John loved the life on the M-G-M lot and was full of eager questions about film-making. It amused him that a great many of the people involved in the film had never read his book and almost certainly never would. At one story conference, copies of the *H. M. Pulham, Esquire* script was passed around the table, and one bemused casting director, after studying the title, asked, "Is this a story about an over-aged destroyer?" John roared with laughter and said, "As a matter of fact, that's not a bad description of it."

Part way through the filming of *Pulham,* King Vidor was called to take over the direction of *The Yearling,* whose director had just quit. John, during the suspension of work on *Pulham,* made himself happily at home in Hollywood. He trotted around in Vidor's wake, collecting bits of film-making lore. One of the problems of *The Yearling* is that the title "character" is a fawn, and, since fawns only appear at a certain season of the year, production of the movie had to keep stopping to wait for a new fawn to be born who would match the fawns used in previous shots. This sort of detail John relished. He also loved a frantic call that came through to Vidor from the art director of the film, who said, "We've got thirty thousand cans of growing corn! What'll we do?" Vidor replied, "Water it." John had admired the Marjorie Kinnan Rawlings novel (which had won the Pulitzer Prize the year following *Apley*), and John one day went with Vidor to the screening room to watch tests that had been made for the young boy who would play the child lead in the movie. A first test was shown, and John was asked what he thought. He announced that he thought the child was entirely "too Hollywood," and this got him off on a long harangue about what was wrong with Hollywood films. A second test was screened, and John said, "No comment." Then a third test was shown, and John leapt to his feet and cried, "That's the one! That boy is absolutely perfect for the part." There was a pause, and then an assistant director said politely, "Mr. Marquand, they're all three the same boy."

For a few days' holiday, John suggested that Vidor and his wife join the Marquands for some trout fishing on the Rogue River in Oregon, where Adelaide had discovered a very much out-of-the-way house. As was her wont, she had bought it. One had to go *up* the rapids to get to it, and the cabin itself was a refreshingly primitive one where you had to fill a basin from an outside spigot to wash your hands, and where there was an outdoor shower. An Indian guide was hired to carry the Marquand party's luggage to this remote spot, and it amused Marquand and Vidor to learn that the Indian suffered from an ulcer, the traditional "Broadway stomach." John loved trout fishing, but he and Vidor did not have much luck. One day, coming home with nothing at all in their creels, the two men met another fisherman with a long string of shiny trout. Marquand and Vidor made a deal to buy half the other man's catch so that they might not be disgraced in front of their wives. But their deception did not work. The two women, it seemed, had watched the entire transaction through field glasses from the cabin above. It was on this trip that John and King Vidor discovered that they were both, semisecretly, Sunday painters. John confessed that he kept his paintings hidden away in a bottom dresser drawer. Back in Hollywood, he bought Vidor a handsome set of oils and gave him the advice, "Always put in the background first."

Vidor paid another visit to the Marquands that was less pleasant. He went to spend a few days at their Aspen house, or houses, and today he recalls only "the terrible sense of turmoil and confusion and dissension" that existed there, the quarrels and the silences and the tensions when John locked himself in one of the houses in order to be alone. He had bitterly explained to Vidor that, back in New York, he had to rent a hotel room in which to work. The atmosphere at home was such that it was impossible to work there.

Late in 1941, work on the *Pulham* film was finished, and there was excited talk of a world premiere in Boston. Marquand, after seeing the final cut, was somewhat disappointed in it and began forewarning friends that he didn't consider it much good and that he had not had much to do with it other than write some of the dialogue. Vidor was much more optimistic about the film, and about John as a screen writer. He had enjoyed working with him so much that he suggested that there might be other projects they could undertake together. There was, for example, a story by Clare Boothe Luce called *Pilot's Wife*. A screen writer was needed. Would John be interested? John came to Carol Brandt with a proposal. She was, after all, herself in the movie business. He had enjoyed Hollywood and the whole style of California life. What, he asked her, if they both moved permanently to the West Coast? They could buy a house in Beverly Hills or in one of the canyons above Sunset Boulevard. He urged this on her as a possible solution to the marital difficulties they were both enduring.

It was during one of Carl's bad periods of drinking, and Carol was at least briefly tempted, though not to the extent that she felt she should mention it to Carl. "It might have been a way to bridge the situation until John could get a divorce," Carol says, "and we toyed with the idea. We toyed with it for quite a while." But would Adelaide, who had refused him a divorce for so long, give him one now? If John had moved to California with Carol Brandt, that might have forced her hand. But would John P. Marquand, the distinguished novelist, winner of the Pulitzer Prize, member of the Somerset and Tavern Clubs of Boston, the Century and Knickerbocker Clubs of New York, a listee in the *Social Register,* have really gone to California to live with a woman not his wife—even in the enlightened air of Beverly Hills?

And Carol, though she loved John, knew that he would never be happy anywhere very far from Boston. No matter where he went, he always went back there. Carol herself was a New York creature, just as Marvin Myles was. Carol knew that she could not endure in Hollywood, just as Marvin Myles had known that she could not have possibly endured in Boston. Carol had seen another side of Hollywood that John had been a bit too dazzled to see, just as Marvin had seen a side of Boston that Henry Pulham had been too close to recognize.

And so "going to live in California" became a kind of charming fantasy, a fiction that diverted and amused them both, and distracted them from the reality and certain anguish of their personal situations. They would chat about it for hours, imagining what it would be like, and when, and how soon, and wherever. Neither of them, Carol now feels, really believed that it would ever happen. "Deep down, I always knew that I could never leave Carl, and Carl knew it, and I'm sure John knew it too," she says. Still, for a moment at least, it was perhaps a possibility, another possibility that was lost.

Chapter Seventeen

*T*he dichotomous nature of his literary output worried John more than most people realized. He was, after all, turning out two different kinds of fiction, and he sometimes wondered if the two were having the effect of canceling each other out. It was not quite as simple as Conney Fiske had made it seem in talking about "serious" novels as opposed to those that were not serious. Both varieties of book took equal time and attention and effort and had to be undertaken with equal seriousness. It was not a case of one kind of writing being easier for him to do than the other. He did seem to be writing for two different kinds of reading audiences, but even that was becoming very difficult to gauge. It was not just his spy and detective novels that were being serialized in the big magazines; his so-called "quality" novels were also being run in places like the *Saturday Evening Post,* though in cut or otherwise speeded-up versions. So the interrelated questions continued to plague him: Did serialization of novels like *Wickford Point* and *Pulham* help him lose serious readers, and did the fact that his Mr. Moto stories appeared in the same periodicals damage him with critics? It was certainly true that those critics whom John sneeringly characterized as "the deep thinkers," who wrote for the highbrow literary quarterlies, had very little that was kind to say about John P. Marquand, whom they tended to regard as a successful hack. "Don't take yourself too seriously, and don't worry too much about your art," he would say to beginning novelists who sought him out for encouragement or advice. "Write the way you feel and what you want to write. Writing is the loneliest occupation in the world because it is entirely up to you." But these calm sentiments were only part of his façade. He took himself quite seriously, and he worried a great deal about his art.

These questions were very much on his mind during the early months of World War II because he had, after publishing *Pulham,* turned to another Mr. Moto novel. It was an idea that automatically had a certain amount of box-office appeal. Mr. Moto was a Japanese. America was now at war with the Empire of Japan. If John Marquand involved Moto in a yarn concerning Germans, Japanese Intelligence, stolen aircraft parts, and the American Navy, in which Moto was outwitted in the end, both the story and the character immediately became more exciting. John thought the idea had merit, but there were difficulties with Adelaide. Adelaide had very little use for Mr. Moto in any of his incarnations, and said so. She considered John's return to Mr. Moto a regression, and said that also. She was more ambitious for her husband. And so now, for John, there was no longer the problem of writing "something nice" for Uncle Ellery Sedgwick, but instead the more galling one of having to write something nice for Adelaide, whose name appeared next to his own as joint copyright holder of his books.

Carl Brandt, in the meantime, had been urging John to write another Mr. Moto. There was always a ready market for Mr. Moto books, and Carl knew how much John enjoyed doing them. Plotting a spy-detective story was a thing John liked to do almost as a form of mental exercise. Adelaide had no appreciation of this, and also tended to take a disparaging view of Carl Brandt's efforts as her husband's agent. Perhaps she regarded Carl as a bit too moneygrubbing. In any case, in her letters to Alfred McIntyre, Adelaide had begun inserting small snide references to the Brandts, as well as to Bernice Baumgarten.

With the sort of tug-of-war that was going on over his talent and the direction that his career should be taking, it is perhaps surprising that the new Mr. Moto novel should have got written at all. But it did, and, late in 1941, as the serialization started in *Collier's* under the title *Mercator Island,* John told Alfred McIntyre that no matter what inducements Carl Brandt and Bernice Baumgarten might try to press upon him he had no intention of permitting the new serial to be published in hard covers; he considered it a trivial piece of work, done mostly, he said, because Carl needed the money and, with the income tax the way it was, he himself now found himself with less reason to make money. To hell, in other words, with the financial pressures that had driven him. He would stick to writing the things he wanted to write, and he intended to make that crystal clear to Carl. From now on it was to be all for Art.

One of the financial pressures that may have impelled the new Mr. Moto may have been the fact that John's and Adelaide's second child was to be born that year, a son whom they named Timothy Fuller Marquand. Behind John's determined words we can almost hear the voice of Adelaide Marquand dictating these ultimata. And, almost needless to say, because Carl Brandt could persuade John and could convince him, the serial—retitled *Last Laugh, Mr. Moto*—was published in book form by Little, Brown in 1942. The story suspends from one of John's most complex spy plots, and as a result it is almost compulsively readable. It is hardly a perfunctory piece of work but is instead a highly competent thriller in which, almost literally to the last sentence, the reader cannot guess whether Mr. Moto will succeed in his mission or fail, and it sold considerably more copies than Marquand's other Mr. Moto titles.

Adelaide had been urging John to write a novel that dealt with the Second World War, or events leading up to the Second World War, in some important way, not in terms of a Mr. Moto character. John, in his late forties, was too old to get into this war, though he had, through his friend George Merck, volunteered to take on a stint of civilian work with the Federal Security Agency in Washington. John and Adelaide had taken a big house in the capital where Adelaide, with her customary zeal, had set about to become a Washington Hostess, giving "interesting little dinners" for prominent government and military people. Among the friends invited down were the Fiskes from Boston, to whom Adelaide confided that she was entertaining a "very top-secret V.I.P."—so important that Adelaide would not even reveal his name in advance. It turned out to be New Englander (and Harvard man) Vannevar Bush, an old friend of Conney's. As Conney put it, "And so the little Boston mouse ended up cornering the guest of honor—Adelaide was simply furious."

Meanwhile, John's son, John, Jr., would soon be of military age. Young John and his sister Tina lived officially with their mother in Boston, in her house at 2 Mount Vernon Square, but they often visited their father and Adelaide.

John had a tendency to let their respective mothers raise his children; having sired them, and having been willing to pay his share of their expenses, he seemed to feel that he had done enough. He either didn't much care for, or couldn't understand, children; they made only fleeting appearances in his novels, and he seemed deliberately to be shying away from using them as characters. He had dealt mostly at a distance with his children by Christina, and, as for his children by Adelaide, there was such a difference between his age and theirs that the gap was more than generational; he felt more like a grandfather toward these little things. Seeing his oldest child approach young manhood amid the threats of another war may have made John realize that he had been a somewhat indifferent father.

John had never liked to talk much about his own war experiences. Battery A had been clubby and fun, and he was always full of border anecdotes. The war was something else again. He did not like to remember it, had pushed it far back in his mind, and when other men begun recounting their war experiences John would become silent. There was nothing about the war he had fought in that he found either special or worthwhile, though of course one could not forget it, no matter how one tried. He had used certain of his experiences in several short stories, such as "Good Morning, Major." But he had never put the war or his feelings about it, and what it meant to him to see the world rushing headlong into another conflict, in a book.

By the end of 1942, Marquand—feeling middle-aged, even old—was in one of his "low" periods, moods of depression and discontent that would, with increasing frequency, assail him, and which even his love affair with Carol could not really comfort or bring him out of. The East Coast was under a black-out. Adelaide was shedding no joy into his life. The world was at war, and the past, even the years with Christina, had become suffused with an aura of bittersweet nostalgia. He had taken to musing about the happy times—even though they had not really been quite that—with Christina, who was about to remarry. More than half his life was over, and what seemed like the best of it was through.

It was the early winter of 1943, not one of the brightest moments of the world's history. His son John had got his orders to report to Fort Devens for military service. John senior had known this was coming, but the actuality of it made him, as he used to say, "very low in my mind." He often said that he thought a boy should at least be permitted to finish college before going into the Army. "But then," as he said to Conney Fiske, "this is a tough war, and we all have to take it."

It sounded very much like the theme for a novel. Or Novel.

Chapter Eighteen

*I*t was, on the surface, an odd collaborative team—John P. Marquand and George S. Kaufman, the Protestant novelist of New England manners and the Jewish ex-shoe salesman, turned successful playwright, from Pittsburgh. But from the moment they were brought together—by Harold Freedman, who headed the Brandt & Brandt Dramatic Department—they got along swimmingly and became close friends. George Kaufman once commented that he liked John because "He's the only person in the world who can make worse faces than I can." Their collaboration was to prepare *The Late George Apley* for Broadway.

Working with Kaufman, every trace of Marquand's decided attitude of social anti-Semitism (which was more a part of his upbringing than anything else, in a world where most Jews were considered not "attractive" and were not admitted into the best clubs) evaporated. On the other hand, George Kaufman, as his daughter, Anne Kaufman Schneider, has pointed out, was a Jew but not very Jewish. The Kaufman household was not at all religious, and the only time a rabbi was ever called was "when someone got married, or someone died."

Neither Kaufman nor any of his family were synagogue-going Jews, not even on the High Holy Days. He even wrote as a Christian. Plays like *You Can't Take It with You,* and *The Man Who Came to Dinner* can hardly be said to contain any remotely Jewish themes, and when Jewish characters entered his work it was always in a minor way—a comedy producer, for example, or Hollywood agent. As a person, Kaufman was a reserved, almost austere man with an Old World manner, and Harold Freedman had been right in suspecting that they would get along.

The Kaufmans had a large and comfortable country house in Holicong, Pennsylvania, in Bucks County, and during the summer of 1943 Marquand spent long periods there, working on the play adaptation with Kaufman. "I write the dialogue and he puts in the punches," Marquand used to say, which was more or less the case. But it was a true collaboration in which the two men talked out the story line—to overcome the most obvious difficulty, which was to turn a novel composed of a series of letters, with very little dialogue, into a play in which people moved about rooms and talked—then discussed scenes, wrote dialogue, analyzed it, rewrote. Kaufman, of course, was a master at providing "punches" and getting laughs. The summer of 1943, in fact, was not only one of the pleasantest but one of the most interesting of Marquand's life, for he had become fascinated with the theater and the people who worked in it.

The Bucks County days passed virtually without disagreement or disruption until one week end when Adelaide Marquand arrived to join the little group at the farmhouse. Adelaide took a Friday afternoon train to New Hope, and the Kaufmans met her there. The four had a pleasant dinner.

Beatrice Kaufman, George Kaufman's wife, liked to sleep late, and on Saturday morning she rang for her maid at around ten thirty and was presently delivered her breakfast tray, the newspapers, and the morning mail. Before arising, Mrs. Kaufman liked to apprise herself of the situation in her household, and she asked her maid if there had been any telephone calls. "Yes," her maid said in somewhat awed tones, "Mrs. Charles Lindbergh telephoned for Mrs. Marquand." "I see," said Beatrice Kaufman. "Have you given her the message?" "Not yet," said the maid. "Then don't give it to her," her mistress instructed. "*I* will give it to her."

Adelaide's friendship with Anne Morrow Lindbergh went back to their girlhood days when Anne Lindbergh's family, the Morrows, had an apartment in the same building as Adelaide's parents, the Hookers. Adelaide's sister Helen and Anne Morrow had been classmates at Miss Chapin's School, the Morrows had visited the Hookers frequently at their summer place in Greenwich, and both families' backgrounds were similarly New York and moneyed. It was through her old friendship with Mrs. Lindbergh that Adelaide had first become involved with Charles Lindbergh and his America First Committee, and after that committee's collapse with Pearl Harbor the two women had remained good friends—Anne Lindbergh admiring Adelaide's hail-fellow-well-met quality, her bluster and exuberance and cheerfulness, and also what Mrs. Lindbergh recalls as Adelaide's "sense of mission." Adelaide had, Mrs. Lindbergh feels, "The deepest respect, almost reverence, for John and his talent, and she wanted to be one of those women, those heroines, who nourish artists and feel that theirs is the highest of callings." And Adelaide, no doubt, admired Anne Lindbergh's delicacy of manner, her gentle and shy nature, so unlike Adelaide's, and perhaps even envied the Lindberghs' quite obvious devotion to each other. But in the summer of 1943, with war raging in Europe, the Lindbergh name had become anathema to millions of Americans. He had publicly defamed the Jews, had been associated with Goering, and had been labeled as a Nazi.

At around eleven thirty, when everyone had gathered downstairs in the living room, Beatrice Kaufman spoke up in her clearest and coolest voice. "Adelaide," she said, "while you were asleep this morning, Mrs. Lindbergh telephoned you here." "Oh," said Adelaide, "I'll ring her back." "You may call her back if you wish," Beatrice Kaufman said, "but you may not do so from this house." There was an awful moment, and then Adelaide burst into tears and ran out of the room.

A few minutes later she was back, dressed and carrying her suitcase. "John," she said, "I want you to drive me to the station." Without a word, John rose and did as she had asked him.

Later in the afternoon, after John had returned to the house, the two men were standing on the front porch of the house. There had been no discussion of the scene that had occurred, and quite obviously both men were somewhat embarrassed by their respective wives' behavior, Kaufman for his wife's insulting a guest and John for Adelaide's poor taste in leaving the Kaufmans' telephone number as one where the Lindberghs could reach her. It seemed a rather poor show for both women, and it was hard to see how anyone could come out any the better for what had happened. At the same time, the collaboration had to continue, and the two men could not let their wives' hostility affect either their work or their friendship. The two stood in silence for a while, and finally Kaufman said, "John, why do you associate yourself with people like the Lindberghs?" Marquand thought a moment and replied, "George, you've got to remember that all heroes are horses' asses."

The novel, meanwhile, that John Marquand had been working on was one that had found him in a new and different mood. The Second World War, as a fact, had affected him profoundly and seemed to fill him with a sense of futility and loss over the fighting and bloodshed he had experienced himself in the first war, barely twenty years earlier. He had trouble accepting this second war, grasping its whole point, or even the whole point of his life. In 1943 he entered his fifties, and with it came a deep sense that there was no way to alter or reshape the past. His marriage to Adelaide had become both a private trial and a public embarrassment, and there was comfort to be found only in brief affairs and in the solidity of his love for Carol, upon whom, as she had hoped he would, he had become dependent. Not only could he call her up at odd hours of the day and night and be certain of finding a sympathetic ear to listen to the details of his latest domestic ordeal, she could do other things. "We could completely level with each other," Carol says. "There was complete honesty between us. He knew he wasn't the only man in my life, and he never asked to be. I assumed there were other women in his life and wouldn't have dreamed of raising an objection. For instance a woman he knew needed an abortion. John knew I knew how to cope with problems like that, and so he came to me, and I arranged it."

But all the same, the center of his life had become wistful, clouded. There was a line he claimed to have once encountered in James Russell Lowell that he had begun to quote frequently: "The leaves are falling fast that hide our generation from the sky." And the novel that came from these days would wear a wistful title, *So Little Time*. In Marquand's fictive view of himself, he was always two characters—the New England aristocrat, with ancient and distinguished lineage entitling him to membership in the best clubs, and, at the same time, the self-made *arriviste* who had struggled up from early poverty, through public school in a small town. He could play either role. In his new novel he chose the latter character as his hero, whom Marquand named Jeffrey Wilson. Marquand was also, with this book, flexing his muscles again and attempting still another kind of fiction—fiction on a more serious and therefore perhaps more important level. Books, after all, such as *Apley* and *Wickford Point* and *Pulham* seemed to have achieved their popularity by virtue of their broad comic strokes, and now, in the 1940s, it irked Marquand to realize that whereas once he had been dismissed as a writer of slick detective stories he was now being treated by critics as a writer of light social satire. John Marquand always insisted that he paid no attention to the critics, but he could not help taking in what they said. And *So Little Time* was in many ways his bid to be placed in the topmost drawer of American novelists, to go beyond, in a sense, the Pulitzer Prize.

Also, Alfred McIntyre and others at Little, Brown had for a long time been urging John to get away from Boston as a locale, to be less parochial and take in a larger landscape. In this sense too he was in danger of becoming type-cast. *So Little Time* was to be definitely non–New England; to emphasize this point the novel opens with a number of strongly descriptive phrases taking in the vastness of the New York skyline. Also, from very early on the novel announces its mighty theme:

America in the twenty months before Pearl Harbor—the world, really, moving inevitably toward war.

Jeffrey Wilson was brought up, and went to public school, in the very small town of Bragg, Massachusetts, a place that sounds very much like the Newburyport of Marquand's youth, and his growing-up years were spent in a run-down old house full of elderly and eccentric relatives who bear distinct resemblances to the elderly and eccentric relatives in *Wickford Point*. Jeffrey has worked his way to considerable riches and some celebrity as a sort of literary hack—a play doctor who can turn a Broadway dud into a hit by sleight of hand but who himself cannot do a sustained piece of creative work. Jeffrey has an intelligent and insightful but tiresomely complaining wife, Madge—"You never tell me anything," she keeps saying—who bears no small resemblance to Adelaide. He is romantically drawn to the beautiful, tough, and brittle actress, Marianna Miller—Carol Brandt—who moves with catlike grace through the ego-ridden jungle of artists, writers, and theater people. Jeffrey also looks wistfully back to the bittersweet days of his youth, and to the golden girl whose presence filled them, his first love from high school, Louella Barnes, for whom it is possible to read Christina Sedgwick. A desperate sense of lost youth, lost time, fills Jeffrey Wilson.

In the background of his domestic malaise—of his marriage, Jeffrey Wilson comments, "No one is exactly right for anyone, not ever"—is the war in Europe, the reports of buzz bombs and blitzkriegs, and a radio announcer who with gonglike regularity intones, from the crackling set, 'This—is London." Jeff Wilson also desperately wants to understand the war, what is happening over there and why. He has a son who, if America gets into the war, will surely have to go. His wife loves Jeffrey more than he loves her; for him, their love has become perfunctory routine. She suddenly asks him, "You're not sorry, are you? I mean, you've liked it, haven't you? The children and the country and being here in the winter. You *have* liked it, haven't you?" His answer, Pulham-like, is, "Why, of course. . . ." She also urges him, "Don't worry about the war. You can't do anything about it." And there is the subtheme of the novel: a man's helplessness in the face of the inevitability of history, the onrush of events, old age, with time running out.

For all its seriousness of theme and general pessimism of tone, Marquand could not resist adding comic strokes to *So Little Time,* and some of them are not a little broad. There is, for example, the character of Walter Newcombe, war correspondent and buffoon. Walter has written a book with the weighty title of *World Assignment,* which, as the title suggests, attempts to explain the world. *World Assignment* has been taken with enormous seriousness by the deep-thinking critics and with the as-easily-gulled reading public, and as a result Walter has become in great demand on the lecture circuit for his analyses of the European Situation. But Walter quickly reveals that he has no more grasp of the European Situation than the average tourist of thirty years earlier, and when asked his views of individuals or events connected with the war he has a catch phrase to cover up the vastness of his ignorance: "Don't get me started on that!"

Walter Newcombe was Marquand's way of getting back both at war correspondents, most of whom he either regarded as muddleheads or outright liars, and at the literary critics who gave the words of these men prominence. If Walter has one redeeming characteristic it is that in his secret heart he knows he is a fool—he has become a celebrity by sheer dumb luck— and he confesses this to his old friend Jeff Wilson; with child-like wonderment Walter asks Jeff if Jeff realizes that he and Walter are the only two boys from Bragg to have made the pages of *Who's Who.* Sometimes, to make Walter seem ridiculous, Marquand goes a little far—such as in the scene where Walter tells Jeff how, by sheerest accident, Walter stumbled upon a book in a Liggett's Drug Store which, when he read it, impressed him deeply. The book is a little on the long side, Walter warns, but it is really well-written: "Every thoughtful American ought to read it." Walter, furthermore, intends to tell his lecture audiences about this book to help lift it out of obscurity. The book is called *War and Peace.* It is a funny scene, yes, but, as Marquand himself knew, satire loses its bite when the scale tips toward slapstick.

Walter Newcombe, incidentally, has also gone to a "wrong" Ivy League college, Dartmouth, though Jeff Wilson went to

Harvard. And in *So Little Time* Marquand managed to take a sly poke at Adelaide and her America First Committee by having Jeff's Cousin Ethel, from the decidedly "wrong" town of West Springfield (the fashionable side of Springfield is the southeast, as "everybody knows"), be an American Firster.

To readers more than a generation later, *So Little Time* may seem an excessively slow-paced novel which takes far too many pages to reach its scattered climaxes. And indeed it was by far the longest novel John had written, nearly six hundred tightly packed pages in the cloth-cover edition, more than a quarter of a million words. In its original state the novel was much longer, and the Marquand device of repeating sentences and key phrases was indulged in to the point of tediousness. Halfway through the manuscript, Marquand himself became very depressed and discouraged about it, and by the time the final page was typed he was not sure what could be done with the bulky pile of typescript. It was at this point that Adelaide, forceful woman that she was, took over.

Adelaide was determined that a successful novel could be brought out of the manuscript. Working with John, the two cut some three hundred pages out of the vitals of the script, reducing it by nearly a third. It was hard and unpleasant work, for such major surgery to a book is always painful, and there were, needless to say, many and vociferous disagreements between the author and his editor wife over what should be allowed to fall on the cutting-room floor.

Adelaide objected to John's habit of repeating certain catch phrases; John insisted that his readers enjoyed this device and expected to encounter it in his books. Adelaide found the first thirty pages of the new novel unduly verbose, creating a top-heaviness at the beginning; John at last agreed to cut in this section. Adelaide found the last twelve pages anticlimactic, but John—backed by the Brandts—insisted she was wrong. There were a few episodes, early in the book, that John had cut out. Adelaide wanted these restored but placed later in the story. And so it went.

Whether John, even begrudgingly, would admit it or not, Adelaide Marquand must be given some credit for salvaging *So Little Time* and helping it become a publishable book. But in the process the personal relationship between John and Adelaide did not improve. Adelaide had discovered that she was pregnant with a third child, and John was appalled. It seemed to him grotesque to become a father again at fifty, and he told friends that he had begged Adelaide to get an abortion, which she refused, as was certainly her right. As soon as the baby was born, he announced that he was taking off for Hot Springs, Virginia, for a two-week holiday with Carl and Carol Brandt. Elon Huntington Hooker Marquand—whose name encompassed a number of his mother's New England ancestors— was left with his mother at Harkness Pavilion. John announced that he did not even intend to telephone New York to see how mother and child were faring. Carol Brandt, insisting that he could not treat his wife so cruelly, finally was told she could write Adelaide a newsy letter about the trip if she wished. She did, but her letter was not well received.

There was the usual struggle for a title of the new novel. John had been fascinated by the lyric of an old drinking song that went:

> ". . . . Looking for a happy land
> Where everything is bright,
> Where the highballs grow on bushes
> And we stay out every night."

Americans in 1940 and 1941 were, he thought, looking for just such a worry-free place, and for a long time he fought for "Looking for a Happy Land" as the book's title. Throughout, Alfred McIntyre was steadily pressing for "So Little Time." John then suggested "The Fifes Will Play" and "Young Men for War" (from the proverb, "Old men for council, young men for war"). Little, Brown cared for neither of these. Coming down on the train from Boston, John had another idea—"Time and Jeffrey Wilson," which he proposed as a short title, easy to remember, and better than "So Little Time" or "In That Last Year." It seemed to him admirably lacking in melodrama and fancy thinking. It was the "melodrama" of the words "So Little Time" that he objected to the most.

But Little, Brown, gently but firmly reminding him that they had chosen the successful titles of his last three books, pressed for their title and John gave in. By the time of the book's publication, in fact, he had become quite excited about it and was eagerly editing the publicity release about the book that his publisher was sending out to booksellers. Where the release said that this was to be John's longest book, John penned in the added phrase, "on the broadest canvas he has so far used," and where the copywriter had said, "perhaps his finest," John wrote: "We believe it will be considered by many critics his finest." So much for a man who insisted he never worried about critics. He also wrote a dedication for the book which, perhaps, should have been for Adelaide but instead was for "Alfred McIntyre, in memory of all the trips we have taken together over the rough roads of fiction."

For all its length, its leisured rhythms, and its generally melancholy tone, something about *So Little Time* caught and matched the mood of American readers in the autumn of 1943, with war raging, it seemed, all over the world, and the future dark and uncertain. *So Little Time* became John Marquand's first big success; it quickly climbed to the top of the best-seller list and stayed there. Critically, the novel didn't do exactly what Marquand had hoped it would. The critics did not hail it as a novel of world-shattering importance, though the reviews were good. But the public loved it, and the book made its author a considerable sum of money. Eventually 787,000 copies were sold. That year, his income from royalties nearly doubled, to $74,300, and the next year—as royalties continued to pour in—he earned $92,000. And so now, having survived two labels, first as a writer of potboiler detective stories, second as a writer of light social satire, he would now have to endure the curse of a third: as a writer of immensely popular books.

It was, very oddly, like a three-act play.

Chapter Nineteen

*M*arquand was not much of a letter writer. His letters for the most part were hastily dashed-off affairs, written in his tiny, slanted, almost illegible hand. But he loved, wherever he happened to be, to receive letters from his friends; their letters comforted him and reassured him. And so, before leaving alone for Kent's Island—and after begging Carol to accompany him, though she could not—he said to her, "Please write to me—just a letter." And so Carol wrote to him in Newburyport. It was not strictly speaking a love letter, but it was full of affection, telling him how much she missed him, how she was certain that in time their various problems would resolve themselves. But in telling her to write to him in Newburyport, John had forgotten that the Newburyport Post Office had been instructed to forward all mail to the New York apartment, 1 Beekman Place, where Adelaide was. The letter may not have been a love letter, but it contained enough, when she had steamed it open and read it, for Adelaide to infer exactly what her husband's relationship was with Carol Brandt, and that it had been this way for some time.

Actually, Adelaide had long suspected this. Like many

women, Carol Brandt had a favorite scent that she always used—in those days it was the distinctively Oriental and musky perfume called Shalimar. Once, after meeting with Carol, John had come home to Adelaide with the scent still clinging to him. Adelaide had accused him then of having a love affair with Carol, but John had denied it. Now Adelaide possessed what she considered conclusive proof of his infidelity.

She immediately telephoned her psychiatrist and asked to see him. She had grown increasingly reliant on psychiatrists and was of that generation of Americans who first discovered Freudian psychoanalysis. Adelaide often said that she was attracted to Freud primarily because Freud believed in monogamy at all costs. And Adelaide wanted desperately to salvage what seemed to be becoming, on her husband's part, a loveless marriage, just as she wanted to continue to enjoy the honor—and share the spotlight—of being Mrs. John P. Marquand, Wife of the Novelist.

After several sessions with her doctor, Adelaide decided— whether or not on his suggestion, she never said—to confront John with what she knew. She had, after all, been married to John for more than ten years. She also demanded a meeting with Carol. The Brandts were then living at the St. Regis, and the three corners of the romantic triangle met there on a sunny morning. Adelaide opened the proceedings by demanding that John and Carol promise never to see each other again, that this was a terrible thing that they had done. John replied that he would promise no such thing. Carol, cast in the role of peace saver, explained that Carl was aware of John's and her relationship, and that, though he did not approve of it exactly, he had accepted it for what it was and understood what it meant to both Carol and John. Carol said that, after all, they were all mature men and women in their forties who should be able to approach situations such as this in a civilized fashion, that the clock could not be turned back, and that screaming or recriminations or histrionics could not possibly help or change things. "After all," Carol said, "people have affairs all over the world, for better or for worse. Why can't we behave like sophisticated adults? Why can't we all live pleasantly with this?" Then she said, "Let's all calm down, and have a drink, and then some lunch." John said that he thought that a splendid idea. Adelaide, however, rose a little stiffly from Carol's sofa and said that she had said all that she intended to say. She would now excuse herself.

Carol and John fixed drinks for themselves. Perhaps fifteen minutes later, the telephone rang in the suite. It was Adelaide. She was waiting in the lobby. Where was John? John said, "I'm staying for lunch. I told you so," and hung up the phone. And that was that. Adelaide's reaction was not recorded.

In an effort to keep matters sane and civilized at all costs, John and Carol suggested that the two couples—the Brandts and the Marquands—should all sit down and have dinner together and make peace, if possible. And a few weeks later the four met at the Plaza. John was in his best form, and Carl and Carol Brandt did their best to keep up their end of things. But Adelaide sulked through dinner and would not speak, and the evening was a pronounced failure. At last the Marquands left, and Carl and Carol were left alone.

Carol's love for Carl was and always would be very strong, and she considers him today the most important man—indeed the most important figure—in her life. "It was Carl Brandt who created me," she has said. The couple lingered over coffee and then ordered champagne. There was an orchestra in the Persian Room, and a dance floor, and they drank champagne and danced to the Plaza's stately dinner music, and it was as though they were two dear friends, once lovers, tied together by bonds stronger than love. Both wanted to keep the "trio," as Carl expressed it, intact and, most of all, civilized and forgiving, remembering that at each point of the triangle there were children involved, John's five, Carl and Carol's two. Dancing with her husband, Carol said, "And so I guess that's the last we will ever see of Adelaide."

"It had become, in a very real sense, a *ménage à trois,*" Carol Brandt says. "John was wonderful company. When Carl was sober, we had marvelous trips together. John would make us laugh and laugh. My children loved him too, and they had no trouble seeing how happy John could make both Carl and me. Vicki, who was younger, never thought a thing about what was going on. Carl junior, being a boy and older, I'm

sure was aware of the state of affairs. But it didn't bother him
in the slightest. It was a relationship, you see, that's very common, very much an accepted thing in England, though Americans have difficulty understanding how rewarding such a
relationship can be."

Adelaide certainly did not understand it. Nor would she
give up. There were nights when she had had too much to
drink that she would call up Carol Brandt and scream at her
over the telephone. She began a long personal campaign to
discredit both Brandts—Carol in particular—with anyone who
would listen to her. And so, at last, John was forced to telephone Carol and say, "Look, there's nothing I can say or do.
She's my wife; she feels this way; you and I must not see or
speak to each other again. I'm sorry." Sadly, Carol admitted
he was right.

When John Marquand was asked to be a judge for the Book-
of-the-Month Club, that vast organization that caters to and
in some ways dictates the literary taste of America, he was
delighted to accept for a variety of reasons. To begin with,
Book-of-the-Month Club judgeships are not dealt out lightly,
and the position carried with it considerable prestige. Such
imposing figures as Dorothy Canfield, Christopher Morley,
William Allen White, Clifton Fadiman, and Henry Seidel
Canby have all been Book-of-the-Month Club judges. The job
carried with it, furthermore, a salary of $20,000 a year, which
Marquand really didn't need but which was a sum worth
adding to his already comfortable earnings as a writer. With
his parsimonious and definitely acquisitive nature, he always
seemed to be filling storehouses against the possibility of some
future state of poverty. He was the same way with bank
accounts from which, having filled them, he hated having to
withdraw. But best of all, perhaps, was the fact that the
Book-of-the-Month Club gave John a valid reason and excuse
to disappear from Adelaide's side, wherever she might be—in
Aspen, Florida, or Newburyport—and go to New York for
the club's monthly meetings. The highbrow side of Adelaide,
of course, regarded the club with a certain disdain, since she
felt it pandered to the reading needs of the uncultivated

masses. But John immediately saw how the club would open up his life, free him a bit more from the assertive woman who, on week ends, would scurry about the house saying, "Where's my Sunday *Times?* Has anyone seen my Sunday *Times?*" Copies of the Sunday *Times* always eluded her, even though, as was her habit when she purchased anything, she often bought as many as ten copies of a single issue so that the Sunday *Times* would be close at hand.

And the Book-of-the-Month Club put John in the delightful position of playing critic. Throughout his career John had been the victim of literary judges of one sort or another. Now he was able to mete out justice of his own and to get back at certain of his enemies. Like many writers, John did not enjoy the company of other writers. He shunned literary "sets" and circles, and parties where gatherings of authors were likely to occur. Once, in Italy, his friend Henry James Forman introduced John to a cadaverous man with flaming hair and bloodshot eyes, who Marquand was told was D. H. Lawrence. Afterward, Marquand was asked what he thought of Lawrence. John said, "I think he is a nut." (Lawrence, meanwhile, asked what he thought of Marquand, said, "I think he is quite mad.") After meeting Somerset Maugham, who was one of Carol Brandt's friends, John reported to Carol, "I saw your old pansy, Maugham, in Venice. K-rist!"

He was no more charitable in his appraisal of authors whose works came to the attention of the Book-of-the-Month Club. Though by no means a prude, John Marquand was generally uneasy when he encountered fiction that dealt explicitly with sex—particularly when he felt that sex was handled obviously or tastelessly. Of one well-known writer's latest novel, he reported to the club:

> He writes with his genitals and all his characters can scarce keep their minds off theirs for a single moment. His women are nymphomaniacs. All his men seem to take two tablespoonful of Spanish Fly before breakfast. There is more dirty talk in this book about private parts and fornication than almost any I have been privileged to read while a member of the Book-of-the-Month-Club board. However this is what we now term "lusty" and maybe I am undersexed. At any rate the characters

are convincing when they can get their minds above their waistlines, which they contrive to do occasionally.

On the other hand, he was a good enough judge of what it took to sell popular fiction to see that the particular novel under consideration would make a strong selection for the club, and his letter concludes, "Take the book. My objections are old-fashioned and maybe all this thrown-away potency makes me jealous."

Clearly he relished the role of critic. His appraisal of another novel was:

> Here we have a saga of the dear, quaint South, from the turn of the century to the present, full of hillbillies, fiddlers and Bible-thumpers. The first half of it, though it tickled my throat, did not make me vomit. It sounded like a pretty good soap opera that I had heard many times. The second half, when we move forward into radio and into a narrowness less comprehensible than that of the old Scopes trial in Tennessee, made me lose my interest in the whole work. I won't go further with the plot and characters. American readers are too familiar with them both. In spite of its cleanliness and quaintness, it has not the drama, the skill, nor the conviction of the Warren book. I do not think we should take it.

He found the works of William Faulkner unreadable and Hemingway "flat and boring, all on one key." He did not care much for Robert Penn Warren, John Hersey, or James Michener —particularly Michener. He considered Michener a journalistic show-off and self-promoter who, with no credentials or literary qualifications to speak of, had appropriated as his fictional bailiwick a whole quarter of the globe—the South Pacific, an area about which John felt he knew just as much, if not more. He frequently compared Michener's grasp of the Pacific with that of Joseph Conrad, Robert Louis Stevenson, and the "old pansy," Maugham, all of whom John felt had better command of their territory and material than Michener. When Michener's panoramic—and in John's view, pretentious —novel *Hawaii* was submitted to the Book-of-the-Month Club in 1959, John Marquand was vociferously against it. He knew, though, that Michener enjoyed a vast popularity, had also won a Pulitzer Prize, and that the whole subject of Hawaii—

which had recently become the fiftieth state—virtually guaranteed the novel a huge success. John was certain that he would be out-voted on the board, and he was. But he could not accept his defeat, and the Club's selection of *Hawaii* as a choice, without complaining that the Club was simply pandering to public taste and the box office.

As for writers whom he admired, he often said that *Madame Bovary* was the greatest novel ever written, and he once privately admitted that his one secret dream in life was to equal, if not surpass, Flaubert's achievement with that book. Once, to a questionnaire, he replied that the "prose author" he admired the most was Fielding, that his favorite poet was Milton, and his favorite painter Botticelli. But he may not have been entirely serious, because in the same questionnaire he also replied that his idea of unhappiness was "being constantly occupied" and that his favorite hero in life was "the inventor of the safety razor." He had great affection for the novels of Jane Austen, and once, on a crowded train in Havana, full of people and cocks heading for the cock fights, he was observed thumbing through a copy of *Pride and Prejudice*. But nobody meant more to John Marquand than Flaubert. And when Francis Steegmuller completed his superb translation of *Madame Bovary* in 1958, John was influential in getting the Book-of-the-Month Club to make that work its selection for June–July of that year. Although he was not, as a rule, enthusiastic about living American authors, there were a few that genuinely excited him. He very much admired James Jones's novel *From Here to Eternity*, writing in the Book-of-the-Month Club News that Jones's book had a "whole greater than any of its parts. And the whole rises from depths to magnificent heights with a sweep very often approaching greatness. *From Here to Eternity* is so good that it is in the realm of the impregnable." He also praised, though more faintly, Herman Wouk's *The Caine Mutiny*, saying, "Unlike so many other contemporary novelists, Mr. Wouk prefers to entertain rather than to advance an ideology, and believes that the best way to bring home a point is by holding his readers' attention. That he succeeds will be quickly apparent to anyone caught up in this rousing tale."

One of John's greatest joys in terms of the Book-of-the-Month Club, however, was the opportunity it gave him to indulge in his particular style of invective. As he wrote in a memorandum to the club, about Messrs. Swanberg, Thurber, and an author whose name John preferred to forget:

> I have spent quite a while with "Jim Fiske" by W. A. Swanberg. The subtitle, "An Improbable Rascal," strikes me as improbable and also too disagreeable for my taste and perhaps for that of the ordinary reader. The amorality, the greed, and the venality of Fiske, I think, would finally turn anyone's stomach. I can hardly see the value in a number of hundreds of pages that go into great details regarding his thefts and regarding his horrible associates. I can only feel that in every way the world is getting better and better. When I was a child, Mr. Jay Gould's grandson, Edwin, who went to school with me in New York, asked me to spend a day on the Gould yacht. When my grandfather, who was Mr. Gould's contemporary, heard of it he refused to let me accept the invitation, saying that he would not allow a relative of his to set foot on anything bought by the money of that thieving rascal.
>
> If I had my way, I would not allow anyone to read this book. . . .

> I finished the Ross book on the plane and feel more violently against it than before. It seems to me unduly long and painfully provincial and I thank God I never met Ross if he is like the Thurber profile.
>
> The book will of course be read on Park Avenue, around the Algonquin and in Westport, but I really don't think many people elsewhere will be as fascinated with the New Yorker, interesting and sometimes beguiling though it may be.
>
> Let us face it. The Algonquin Round Table and the whole New Yorker Galerie are a lot of conceited log rollers. Woollcott was second rate and so was Gibbs. I'd put Thurber a little higher, and possibly "Andy" White—but not such a hell of a lot. In their proudest days this band of heroes and heroines—including Dorothy Parker—have always stuck in my craw—with their attitudes and silly pranks and their sickening feeling of intellectual superiority.
>
> Actually the New Yorker with its editing and formulas has hurt American letters greatly—and established an intellectual

mediocrity worse than the Sat Eve Post. For my money there was only one man in that group who is worth this sort of adulation and that is Bob Benchley. Why in hell not write about him?

To hell with it all. I vote against it—and if my colleagues take it my resignation—long overdue at any rate—is figuratively on the table. . . .

When I get these photostat manuscripts that smell of ammonia, in order to keep me from dying of asphyxiation, I throw them away page by page. Consequently, to my great joy, I cannot remember the name of the author of the last manuscript you sent me, or even the title of it. This will not be too difficult, however, because it is a short something in epistolary form, dealing with letters written and received by a West Coast— presumably Berkeley or Palo Alto—professor, who previously was a pugilist and now is a teacher of English who has written a play. This, I trust, will identify it for you.

Now I am as aware as you that I am becoming senile. My mind, I am sure, is somewhere in the Victorian era. I have this scholastic feeling that there should be form, content, and grammar in a piece of so-called literary work. Nonetheless I try to be broad-minded, God knows I try. I try as hard as I can to like young people and the things they do and write. I have a sneaking feeling that this work that I have perused is what may be called hilarious and zany and that beneath its good, clean fun there may be an undercurrent of truth, although I don't know what in hell it is. The only thing I can say for it is that it is short. It could be a part of a dual, but I hope that we have no part of any of it. It is the story of a confused young professor who feels that he is a genius. So, to my amazement, do his friends and associates, and even his wife. Do I give a damn? I do not. Personally I feel that the whole thing is a gross piece of balderdash.

My only reason for going into the thing at such length is that I find myself at the present time being exposed to the West. This epistolary novel is a California western piece of work. Westerners, I discover, are becoming arrogant. When in the West you have to wear Pendleton Round-up shirts, and high-heel boots, so that you may look like a Texas ranger. We must even understand the culture of the U.C.L.A. We must be patient with them, because the West is the growing part of our community, and, with the oil wells, they get 27 per cent off their income tax. Therefore, they are superior to all of us, and now they know it. This piece of work is a complete example of this. It is hideous, and they should all be put in their place. . . .

He was frequently sarcastic about the works of Sinclair Lewis, whose *Main Street* had been cited by critics as the perhaps-model for *The Late George Apley*. But when John finally met Lewis, he rather liked him—particularly the madcap and unpredictable behavior that often overcame Lewis when he was in his cups. The two men had first met at Carol Brandt's apartment, on a night when Lewis was on his way to the film premiere of *Arrowsmith,* and when he was already far from sober. He demanded Scotch, and when Carol handed him a glass he shouted, "Do you call *that* a drink?" and, with a few profanities, seized the bottle and poured himself a tumblerful. Immediately Lewis put himself and John on a first-name basis, Red and John, and, though there were editors and publishers and agents in the room, Lewis launched into a violent tirade against the publishing profession, clutching Marquand by the lapels and saying, "Come on, John, I want to talk to you, let's get away from these lousy bloodsuckers, these goddamn hucksters, these fucking exploiters." For several alcoholic hours—the premiere had long since started— the two were inseparable; whenever anyone suggested that he should be at the theater, Lewis would shout, "Let me alone, let me alone, I want to talk to John here. John and I understand each other, we know what a writer is. Keep these goddamn bloodsuckers away from me, will you?" And then, "Come on, John, I want to talk to you, I want to talk to you about your writing, John. Listen, come to Detroit with me! We'll disguise ourselves as waiters and get jobs in some joint. Will you, John? What do you say? Detroit! Waiters! How about it?" Presently Lewis was singing John a selection of Methodist hymns.

John P. Marquand and Sinclair Lewis never got to Detroit disguised as waiters, but this sort of thing vastly entertained John. It appealed to his sense of the grotesque in life, and he and Lewis became friends, though he could not abide Lewis's wife, Dorothy Thompson, who, whenever she was around, insisted on doing all the talking and would never let her husband say a word. Lewis's erratic behavior helped John understand another situation in which a fellow writer, who had been an alcoholic, reformed and went on the wagon, at which point his wife, who had seldom taken a drink before, suddenly became a hopeless drunk. "After all," Marquand commented at the news, "you can't live with all that excitement going on around you and then all at once start spending a series of evenings playing crokinole." Sinclair Lewis—who genuinely admired Marquand's work—also, in a more rational moment, suggested to John that his three big New England novels, *Apley*, *Wickford Point*, and *Pulham*, should be published in a single volume called *North of Grand Central*, for which he, Lewis, would write an introduction. (At the time, Little, Brown was not interested in the idea, but the book was later published in 1956—after Lewis's death—with an introduction by Kenneth Roberts.)

John's work with the Book-of-the-Month Club took him regularly away from Adelaide, but it did nothing to improve their relationship. And so, one day in her office, Carol was surprised to hear John's voice on the telephone. Their separation, John said—it had gone on for nearly two years—made no sense. He begged to see her again.

"Of course I agreed," Carol Brandt says. "I only insisted that this time he must tell Adelaide what was going on. I didn't want there to be any more lies. If John was going to be with me at my apartment, I wanted her to know it. I was determined to have us behave as much like adults as possible. Ending the separation was a great relief for *all* of us. Being apart and unable to communicate with each other had been terribly painful for both John and me, and it was also ridiculous —having Carl, who would see John on business, come home to me and say, 'John sends you his love,' and so forth. Carl had thoroughly disapproved of the separation and thought John was being stupid to let his wife lead him around by the nose like that. When John and I became lovers again, everybody was happier for it. My children were overjoyed to have John back. It was as though he had rejoined the family."

Everyone was happier except Adelaide. Though John had asked her several times for a divorce, and she had refused to grant him one, she responded to the new development with hysteria. Once more she took up her verbal attacks against the Brandts, this time concentrating her comments on her own growing children. To them she depicted Carol Brandt as a brazen harlot, a home wrecker, a whore. She was so successful in her characterization that when John took one of the children to the Brandts' house for dinner, the child was astonished to find not the scarlet creature their mother had depicted but a tall, elegant, handsome woman who wore well-made dresses, who combed her waving and graying hair gently back in a simple style, and who entertained graciously in an antique-filled Fifth Avenue apartment. Their father's mistress, his children were amazed to learn, was a lady.

Adelaide did hold one trump card, a small one perhaps, but one she decided to use. It was the joint-copyright arrangement—worked out by lawyers for tax purposes—under which John received, starting with *Pulham*, 75 per cent of the royalties and Adelaide 25 per cent. She would not, she announced, have her royalties paid or her contracts negotiated by the Brandt agency. Her refusal presented something of a dilemma, but Carl was quick to see the way out of it. He suggested that John, in his book contracts, deal directly with Little, Brown; the Brandt office could continue to handle magazine serialization and motion-picture rights. The change was a wrench for both men. As Carl Brandt wrote to John, "Even if I suggested this break in our business relationship, it makes me very sad that something which had endured so long should end. . . . It is my hope, and a sincere one, that you will find this a happier condition of affairs."

There was nothing more that Adelaide could do.

John began to play the role of Carol's literary mentor, and he was forever suggesting good books for her to read. "I remember one winter when he was snowed in at Kent's Island," she recalls, "and could only get in and out on snowshoes. He told me that he had this fantasy of the two of us going off to live in some cabin in the north for perhaps six months,

John Marquand as a child.

John Marquand at nineteen.

Photographed in the house at Newburyport.

The 1913 staff of the *Harvard Lampoon*. Marquand is second from the right in the next to the last row, with Edward Streeter on his right. (Christian Herter stands next to Streeter.) Gardiner Fiske is seated on the floor at left.

Christina Sedgwick, photographed a few days before her marriage to John Marquand in 1922.

John Marquand, sketched at about the same time.

Adelaide Ferry Hooker Will Become Bride Of John Phillips Marquand, Noted Author

Miss Adelaide Ferry Hooker

Dexter Studio Photo.

The announcement of Adelaide Hooker's engagement in the February 26, 1937, *New York Times*.

John Marquand in his early forties.

Mr. and Mrs. Elon Huntington Hooker of 620 Park Avenue and Chelmsford, Greenwich, Conn., announced the engagement of their daughter, Miss Adelaide Ferry Hooker, to John Phillips Marquand, author, son of Philip Marquand of Curzon's Mill, Newburyport, Mass., and the late Mrs. Margaret Fuller Marquand.

Miss Hooker is a descendant of Thomas Hooker, who founded Hartford, Conn., in the early part of the seventeenth century and drafted the Constitution of the State of Connecticut. Her paternal grandparents were Horace B. Hooker and Mrs. Susan Huntington Hooker of Rochester, N. Y.

Her father is president of the Hooker Electrochemical Company, chairman of the Research Corporation and of the executive committee of the National Industrial Conference Board, and a director of the American Association of Manufacturers. He was Deputy Superintendent of Public Works under Governor Theodore Roosevelt.

Through her mother, the former Miss Blanche Ferry, Miss Hooker is a granddaughter of the late Mr. and Mrs. Dexter Mason Ferry of Detroit. Mrs. Hooker was a founder of the Women's University Club, and, with her sister, Mrs. Avery Coonley, gave to Vassar College the Alumnae House on the campus. Miss Hooker is the sister of Mrs. John D. Rockefeller 3d, Mrs. Ernest O'Malley of Dublin, Ireland, and Miss Barbara Ferry Hooker.

She was graduated from the Spence School and Vassar College, and received her Master of Arts degree at the Eastman School of Music of the University of Rochester. For several years she studied singing in Germany as a pupil of Lilli Lehmann. Miss Hooker writes the program notes for the Women's Symphony Orchestra and has written music criticism and travel articles for various periodicals. She is a member of the Cosmopolitan Club and the Junior League.

Mr. Marquand was graduated from Harvard University in 1915 and served overseas with the A. E. F. during the World War. He is widely known as a contributor of fiction to popular magazines, particularly The Saturday Evening Post. His latest novel, "The Late George Apley," is at present on the national list of best sellers.

Miss Hooker's fiancé is a member of the University Club and the Coffee House Club of New York, and of the Tavern and Union Boat Clubs of Boston. In 1922 Mr. Marquand married Miss Christina Davenport Sedgwick of Stockbridge. They were divorced in 1935.

Adelaide and John Marquand at the Brandts' house in New Jersey, 1937.

Carol Brandt, 1940.

Carl and Carol Brandt.

The Kent's Island house before, during, and after the many additions
to the original cottage.

Carol Brandt, 1944.
Halsman

Hedy Lamarr (with Robert Young) in the film role of Marvin Myles.

Chester T. Holbrook

John Marquand in the country.

Marquand with the Fiskes at Kent's Island, 1948.

The Mill House at Curzon's Mill, where
The Late George Apley was written.
Robert W. Kelley, LIFE Magazine © Time Inc.

The Hale cousins visit "Wickford Point."

Robert W. Kelley, LIFE Magazine © Time Inc.

The Hale cousins discussing the upcoming lawsuit. The beautiful Renée Oakman is on the left.

The Yellow House
Curzon's Mill.

Phil Marquand before the trial.

Robert W. Kelley, LIFE Magazine © *Time Inc.*

John Marquand before the trial.

Robert W. Kelley, LIFE Magazine © *Time Inc.*

High jinks with chums at Pinehurst.

A Book-of-the-Month Club meeting in the early 1940s, painted
by Joseph Hirsch. Left to right: Henry Seidel Canby,
Harry Scherman, Dorothy Canfield Fisher, John P. Marquand,
Clifton Fadiman, Christopher Morley, Meredith Wood.

The Apleys of Boston as conceived by Hollywood. Ronald
Coleman, seated, left, played the title role.

Leo G. Carroll as Apley on Broadway.

John Marquand during his last years.

completely cut off from everybody and from the outside world. The cabin would be equipped with certain luxuries, of course. John liked comfort. And I remember that among the luxuries he would have brought along were certain books, and I was to read them aloud to him by the Primus stove while he fixed the rabbit snares or jerked the venison, or whatever one does in a cabin in the north woods. He used to refer to me as the literary huckster, and the books were to be read primarily for my profit in addition to my enjoyment. I remember the books were to be primarily Shakespeare, the Bible, an early translation of Tacitus, a good Thucydides, Plato's *Republic,* some Fielding, some Jane Austen, Thoreau, Emerson, but not a single one of what he used to refer to as 'the goddamned Russians.' All this was intended to be literary therapy for me, to give me something to read other than what he considered the generally lowly output of my clients, including Willie Maugham, and to give me the basis of some solid literary opinions. Needless to say, we never it made it to our cabin, but it was a wonderful fantasy."

While John Marquand was snowed in alone in Newburyport, Adelaide and the children were off in Hobe Sound. In Hobe Sound there was another problem, another embarrassment. The Marquands had had a small house there for several years which John had christened "Nervana." Nearby were John's friends the George Mercks, and Philip Barry, the playwright, lived down the road. The president of Du Pont lived on one side of the Marquands, and the president of Morton Salt lived on the other, and little Ferry once asked, "Daddy, are you the poorest man in Hobe Sound?" But the resort—developed by Adelaide's friend from Greenwich, Mrs. Joseph Verner Reed—had a definitely anti-Semitic cast, and there had been an episode involving Mr. and Mrs. Arthur Hays Sulzberger of New York, the distinguished publisher of the *New York Times,* when the Sulzbergers had been politely told that they would be welcome at Hobe Sound but that they could not bring any guests. In the hubbub that ensued over this, John and Adelaide Marquand drew criticism for staying at Hobe Sound, and the whole business of the Lindberghs and America First came back under attack. John had at first enjoyed Hobe Sound, despite the fact

that Adelaide had somewhat whimsically decided to furnish
the place with some maids' furniture she had found on sale,
and which she thought an amusing touch. But after the Sulzberger incident, John confided to his friend and Hobe Sound
neighbor, George Merck, that he could no longer live there
comfortably. After all, he pointed out, he had to deal professionally with a number of Jews, including the Sulzbergers,
Max Gordon, the producer, and his fellow Book-of-the-Month
Club judges, Clifton Fadiman and Amy Loveman, and the
Club's head, Harry Scherman. He could not face any of these
friends and associates if he continued to keep a house at Hobe
Sound.

Chapter Twenty

*T*he *Late George Apley* opened on Broadway in November, 1944, with the beetle-browed Leo G. Carroll in the title role, and was an immediate critical and popular success. It would run two years and would earn John Marquand an additional $30,000 a year in play royalties. At that point, at the peak of his powers and career, he was very likely the highest paid novelist in the world.

During the out-of-town tryouts of the play, John had been eager to have the Fiskes—particularly Conney—see it in performance, since Conney had been so important in encouraging, and in some ways even inspiring, *Apley* as a book. Conney admired the play—Gardi still felt somewhat dubious about the whole *Apley* business—but she had several specific suggestions to make. Nobody knew her Boston better than Conney, and when on opening night she spotted a French brocade sofa in the set of what was supposed to represent the Apley's Beacon Hill drawing room she protested that such a stylish piece of furniture would never be placed in a proper Boston house. It was all wrong. The play's producer, Max Gordon, took her at her word and had the sofa replaced with

a more genteelly shabby piece. She also said that she did not
feel that the Boston accent of the English-born Mr. Carroll
rang true. When this was presented to Carroll, he protested,
"I've already been taught fourteen different Boston accents!"
But he did spend some time talking with Conney, listening
to her speech and studying the broadness of her A's. After
catching another performance, somewhat later, Conney reported a marked improvement.

John, of course, would never admit it because of Adelaide,
but he had become a writer who could work well with a col-
laborator and who, at times, even needed the help of collaboration. There was the happy experience with George Kaufman,
for instance, and there were the editorial taste and guidance of
Conney Fiske. He had begun the habit of using his friends as
sounding boards for his ideas, buttonholing them with questions about their careers and lives which he would then employ
in his fiction. If a character were to be a bond salesman—as
in *Pulham*—John would huddle for hours with Gardi Fiske,
learning details of a bond salesman's business day. If the character were to be a banker, John would turn to his banker
friend and former Harvard schoolmate, Edward Streeter, of
the Fifth Avenue Bank.

Then there were the professional editors with whom John
discussed his story ideas and who frequently came to him with
ideas of their own. First and most important had been George
Horace Lorimer of the *Post*. After Lorimer's death, the editor
in New York whom John had come to respect the most was
Herbert R. Mayes, who for many years headed two large
Hearst magazines, *Cosmopolitan* and *Good Housekeeping*.
Mayes, seven years younger than Marquand, came, like George
Kaufman, from a background quite alien to John's—New York
City-born, Jewish, educated at city public schools, a self-made
success. And yet the two men, though they never became close
friends, had early established a strong and productive author-
editor relationship, and each had great respect for the other's
views.

Although John disliked Maugham personally, he found Herb
Mayes's working arrangements with him fascinating. John
tended to regard Maugham as his literary counterpart in

England—Maugham was also vastly successful, a man whose books and short stories became lucrative plays and movies— and saw him, somewhat warily, as his chief competition in the marketplace of American fiction. John, for example, was always trying to find out how much Mayes paid Maugham for his stories—and Mayes was always careful to keep this figure a secret, since he often paid Maugham as much as $10,000 for a short story, while he paid John Marquand about half this amount. John, having written a story, disliked making revisions. So do all writers, but John was particularly stubborn about it. John and Mayes had disagreed about a story of John's called "Sun, Sea, and Sand"—the same story in which Conney Fiske had taken exception to the dress with the printed cocktail glasses. When the story came to Mayes's desk he sent it back, saying that he thought the story took too long to get under way and that he thought the name of the leading character, Epsom Felch, was absurd. He asked John to change it, but John refused. Mayes then told John about the trouble he had had with a Somerset Maugham story called "A Woman of Fifty." Mayes had told Maugham that he would not accept the story unless Maugham eliminated a long section that did not seem to belong, and after a certain amount of grumbling Maugham made the requested cut. John was astonished at this. *Why*, he wanted to know, would Maugham—a man of such stature—agree to this? Herb Mayes shrugged and said that he supposed Maugham needed the money. John shook his head and said, "I could believe that about almost any writer other than Maugham." Yet he still would not cut "Sun, Sea, and Sand."

John was also interested in Mayes's relationship with Sinclair Lewis, and in what Mayes thought of Lewis as a writer. John found Lewis's antics amusing; Herb Mayes found them appalling. John was shocked to hear how Lewis had disrupted a dinner party at Herbert and Grace Mayes's house by picking a fight with Lester Markel, editor of the Sunday *New York Times*, and of how dreadfully Lewis treated his agent, Edith Haggard. Mayes had also been with Lewis one evening at the Stork Club when Lewis, in anger at a waiter, had picked up a knife and smashed a glass with it. John found it hard to believe that his friend could be capable of such behavior. At the same time, John could not understand why Mayes published the works of Booth Tarkington, a writer whom John actively disliked. John considered Tarkington a literary traitor since Tarkington had written—and Mayes had published—a short story in which, very thinly disguised, John's friend George Horace Lorimer, Lorimer's wife, and Lorimer's secretary appeared as the central characters.

Sometimes the story ideas the two men discussed—usually over chatty lunches in the then all-male Oak Room of the Plaza—ended up being written by John, and sometimes the ideas came to nothing at all. Other ideas John mentally filed away and did not use until years later. One idea that Mayes was particularly fond of involved a railroad man who begins as a laborer and works himself up over the years to the presidency of the line, becoming a magnate. But the time comes when he decides that there are more important things in life than money and success, and he will put it all aside and devote himself to art, music, literature, and travel. The kernel of the idea, however, is the hero's discovery of all the things that make his retirement from business impossible—the banks that have placed their confidence in him by making huge loans which are likely to be called if the hero leaves his job; the inept son and son-in-law whom he has brought into the business with him, and who are earning their livelihoods only by virtue of his support; the numerous people at the executive level and all the way down who trust him, whom he has brought along with him up the ladder of success, and who will be likely candidates for removal once he departs. It was a story, in other words, which with Marquandian irony would tell of a man trapped by his possessions, whose very success resulted in his failure to achieve his ultimate objective, which was freedom from responsibility, and who, having gotten everything he wanted, had also lost everything. It did sound like a Marquand theme. But, after Mayes had finished reciting the idea, John thought a moment and then said, "Sounds like a good idea. Why don't *you* write it?" Mayes said, "I'm not a writer." John said, "Well, I'm not a railroad man." "It doesn't *have* to be a railroad," Mayes persisted, "it could be any sort of big company." But still John shook his head, and that, for the time being, was that.

One day at another of their lunches Mayes asked John whether he played chess. John said that he did, a little, and Mayes asked him if he would consider an idea Mayes had for a story about a chess player. John did not seem immediately enthusiastic, but he said, "Okay, let's hear the idea." Mayes's idea was to make the hero one of the men who make a living of sorts playing chess and checkers in booths at Coney Island. It was to make this man the son of a West Point family, a family in which all the boys, from the moment they were able to toddle, were taught to play chess, and in which this had been going on for generations and in which ultimately all the men grew up to be generals or at the very least colonels. The hero, however, would be an escapee from this super-regimented, Army-oriented family, who hated West Point and, finally disowned by his family, had wound up playing chess in a booth at Coney Island.

John, mildly interested in the idea, said that he had never been to Coney Island and had never realized that there were chess players there who played games for a fee. Mayes said that John didn't have to go as far as Coney Island to find such men, and that, if John liked, they could wander after lunch to the vicinity of Eighth Avenue and 42nd Street, where chess partners were for hire in various penny arcades as well as in unoccupied store fronts. John agreed, and after lunch the two men set off for this fairly rough part of Manhattan and spent the better part of an hour watching the chess players there.

Months went by, and Mayes heard nothing from John until one day when Mayes happened to be lunching at the St. Regis with someone else, and John Marquand came into the dining room with a group of people. John stopped at Mayes's table and, after greeting him, said, "Oh, by the way, I've finished that chess story. I'm checking on a few final details in it, but you'll have it within the next few days."

The story, when it arrived, was called "The End Game," and when Mayes had read it he was overwhelmed and immediately bought it. It is very likely the best short story John ever wrote. And it is also a John Marquand novel in almost

perfect microcosm. In it can be seen, in a kind of miniature
view, nearly all the elements of the Marquand craft, the fictional devices that made him, if nothing else, a superb techni-
cian, particularly in his handling of time. Henry Ide, the story's
narrator and main point-of-view character, muses at one point
about "the task of piecing together out of allusions and in-
directions the details of someone's life." This is precisely what
the story sets out to do in eight distinct episodes, each set at a
different point in time and each of about equal length, in the
life of a seedy-looking and tough-talking chess player who
sits in a Sixth Avenue penny arcade playing chess for twenty-
five cents a game.

The story opens in the fictional present—it was written in
1943—at a New York cocktail party where a number of the
guests, including Henry Ide, had had professional or military
experience in China before the war. At the party, Henry meets
a Colonel Blair, also an Old China Hand and soon due to head
back there, and the two men admire an antique ivory chess
set in their host's apartment and sit down to play. Rather
arbitrarily, the name of a Chinese General Wu is mentioned,
and established as a name that will have some significance in
the story later on, and as the two men talk Henry keeps
thinking that Colonel Blair reminds him of someone else, and
the details of the Colonel's life that he reveals seem strangely
familiar. At last Henry realizes what it is: The Colonel must
be the brother of Joe, the chess player Henry met and played
with months ago in the Sixth Avenue arcade. Colonel Blair
is stunned; the family has not seen his brother Joe for years.
Henry Ide offers to take the Colonel to the penny arcade and
find him, much as Herbert Mayes offered to show the chess
players to John Marquand.

The story now moves smoothly, in a flashback, to the moment
when Henry Ide first encountered Joe, when Henry, lonely
and late at night, wandered into the neighborhood of the
penny arcade and sat down at one of the chess tables for a
game. During the course of the evening that followed, Henry
learned a few tantalizing details of Joe, his opponent's life.
It became the first of many evenings, during which Henry

learned more and more about Joe—of his childhood spent in a series of military posts, of his father, known as "the C.O.," or commanding officer, of Joe's uncles, all Army men, and of Joe's father's determination that all of his four sons will enter West Point and become career Army men. The C.O.'s household, wherever it was, was always run with heel-clicking salutes and discipline, and as a young man Joe tried to be like his brothers and live by the rules of the Army Training Manual, but Joe was different, a dreamer and a romantic who, as John Marquand had done as a youth, took long walks in the woods and by the rivers and the sea.

"While Joe was talking, Henry Ide was able to see it all as though he had been part of it," Marquand wrote. And in this effortless and quite artless way, about one third of the distance through the story, the reader is whisked as if by magic out of the consciousness of Henry Ide and into that of young Joe Blair, and we are in Hawaii in the midst of smells of tar and surf, sugar cane and ginger flowers. It is an almost breathtaking transition, and presently we are not too surprised to discover that Joe Blair is in love with a beautiful girl named Ruth Postley. Marquand was not quite courageous enough to make her a native girl, but she is definitely from the wrong side of the tracks and otherwise unsuitable. Her father sweats and wears wrinkled linen suits and her mother sits on her front porch with her feet pushed into dirty bedroom slippers, while inside the house is full of beach sand and dirty plates sit on the table. Mrs. Postley calls people "dearie." But the Postleys, though common, are kindhearted and gentle people who like Joe Blair and approve of him for their Ruthy. Joe, of course, cannot tell his father of Ruth's existence, and so we have again Marquand's recurring theme of the insurmountable barrier between social classes.

The love story develops tenderly, and at the same time with great suspense toward the inevitable moment when the C.O. learns about Ruthy and charges into the Postleys' house to remove his son and order the two never to see each other again. Joe goes with his overpowering parent meekly, but returns secretly to Ruthy's house at night and tells her that he

is running away from home. Her father offers to help him
arrange passage on a ship out of Honolulu, and Joe promises
to come back to Ruthy some day.

The story then shifts back to the present time and to the
consciousness of Henry Ide, who is riding in a taxi with Joe's
brother, Colonel Johnny Blair, headed for Sixth Avenue. There
is a reunion scene between the two men, and in it Joe tells
Johnny that he did go back to Hawaii and marry Ruthy; that
they are indeed still married, and very happily. It is difficult
for Colonel Johnny to understand how this could be, how
anyone could have a satisfying life outside the Army, much
less as a chess player playing for twenty-five cents a game.

It was at this point that Herbert Mayes would have had
the story end, but John was not satisfied with this ending. He
felt that the story did not yet have sufficient shape, that it
needed just one more twist or turn of the screw to bring the
curtain down on his characters. And so he added a page in
which Joe Blair makes one more revelation to his colonel
brother, Johnny. Joe has had, it seems, a career in the Army
also—the Chinese Republican Army. He has become, in fact,
a general in this army. He outranks his brother, and, furthermore, it is to General Joe that Colonel Johnny will soon be
reporting on his upcoming assignment in China, where Joe has
been called back to the staff of General Wu. Chess playing has
been little more than a pastime.

The ending, which is a jolting surprise, does indeed tie together all the scattered threads of the story in one tidy
package. It makes it clear, too, that the mention of General
Wu in the opening was a conscious plant. But it also in some
ways undoes the character of Joe Blair to have it turn out that
he has had a military career after all, that he ended up doing
more or less what his father wanted, even while, at the same
time, doing what his father didn't want. So, in the end, with
this final move of the chess piece, Joe turns out to have won,
but also lost, and is suddenly somewhat less interesting than
when the reader thought of him as the romantic defier of
tradition.

"The End Game," which Herbert Mayes published in *Good
Housekeeping* in March, 1944, was widely discussed and later

became included in numerous anthologies. Though it was admired, several critics pointed out the artificiality of the surprise O. Henry-esque ending—the end a kind of "game" in itself—and John became quite sensitive about this. He began, in fact, to talk about the story, saying that he himself liked it "in spite of a tricked-up ending being tacked on by Herb Mayes." Herb Mayes did not mind, particularly, being handed the blame for John's ending. But he did mind, several years later, when in an anthology of John's short pieces called *Thirty Years* John wrote in a short preface to "The End Game":

> Mr. Herbert Mayes, who, next to George H. Lorimer and Maxwell Perkins, is the best editor I have ever met, once thought highly of this story, and I hope he still does. He may have been partial to it because he gave me the idea of a chess player in a Sixth Avenue (I mean Avenue of the Americas) [Mr. Mayes recalls Eighth Avenue] Arcade. I recall that Mr. Mayes personally took me to see one of these places, but aside from this the machinery of the story was my own—and so was the motivation, except, naturally, that I wanted Mr. Mayes to buy it.

In his preface, John went on to explain that in writing "The End Game" he had drawn on his experiences in the Orient and in Hawaii, that he knew well the military mind, that he was a fair chess player, and that "These facts all form essential parts in the story." John, like a number of other writers, was not overgenerous when it came to giving credit to others for his story ideas. But in reading this preface Herbert Mayes felt quite definitely slighted; he thought he had been responsible for a great deal more detail in the story than John had admitted. The matter rankles with Herbert Mayes—retired now and living in London—even today.

John had begun to think of his novels in groups of threes. Having done a neat threesome of New England novels, he now decided to do the same with World War II as a background. *So Little Time* had been set in the months preceding the war. Next, he explained to Alfred McIntyre, he would do two more war novels—one set during the war, and the other during the months just afterward. McIntyre was enthusiastic about this double-barreled idea, but the results were two of

Marquand's least interesting novels, *Repent in Haste* and
B. F.'s Daughter.

Repent in Haste, which appeared in the fall of 1945, the
shorter of the two, is a slight affair in which, when reading it,
one can almost sense the haste with which it was put together.
Marquand had made a short trip earlier that year to the West
Pacific under the auspices of the United States Navy, and the
book, which attempts to take in the whole Pacific War as a
background, was the result of these Navy-supervised travels.
The theme of the novel, as it keeps recurring to its protagonist,
Lieutenant Jimmy Boyden, is "It's funny the way things happen, isn't it, when there's a war on?"—which seems an obvious
and not very stimulating observation. The plot is a simple
affair, too simple perhaps to hold even a short novel together.
It is the story of how William Briggs, a middle-aged war
correspondent and the point-of-view character, comes back
from the Pacific theater and calls on Daisy Boyden, the "cute
little trick" Jimmy Boyden married—in haste—just before he
shipped out. Daisy, meanwhile, has repented the marriage;
when Briggs comes to see her she tells him this, and also that
she has another lover. It is then Briggs's job to take back this
bad news to his friend Jimmy on his next trip to the Orient—
and in the process to discover how heroically Jimmy, the war
hero, will bear up under this emotional blow.

For the middle-aged war correspondent, of course, one can
easily read the middle-aged John Marquand, and William
Briggs is a convincing character. But Jimmy Boyden is thin and
unclear. One reason for his failure to come to life on the page
is probably the background Marquand chose to give him. Marquand was attempting to answer the question of how it is that
extraordinary men, heroes capable of performing extraordinary
feats in time of war, can emerge from very ordinary and un-
exceptional surroundings, but in sketching the youthful environment of Jimmy Boyden Marquand was a bit out of his
depth. Jimmy Boyden, we learn, is from East Orange—not
West Orange—New Jersey, and East Orange, as everyone
knows, is the wrong one of the Oranges to come from. That
this should matter in time of war is questionable, but it is still
another example of Marquand's fascination with social divi-

sions. Jimmy's father is a minor executive "with an annual income of perhaps eight thousand dollars," and their house, in a middle-class neighborhood, has its "antimacassars on the parlor chairs," a radio with "Jacobean legs and an inlaid front," a kitchen with a "breakfast nook" and various small appliances, plus a gas stove that will "cook without watching." Marquand was familiar with the houses of the very rich and also with those of the genteelly poor, as in *Wickford Point*. He could even write with authority about the ramshackle beach houses in the back streets of Hawaii, where he had visited. But he had certainly spent very little time in homes of the middle American mediocrity, either in East Orange or in any other part of New Jersey. His description of Jimmy Boyden's family and home and home life is not only unreal but quite unpleasant, since it is quite clear that Marquand has nothing but disdain for Jacobean radios, antimacassars, and breakfast nooks. By surrounding his protagonist with so much dullness and bad taste, some of it cannot help but rub off on Jimmy Boyden himself. One has trouble really caring about him or his problems.

Still another reason why *Repent in Haste* fails is probably that Marquand, though he prided himself on understanding "the military mind," really understood best the military mind of an earlier war. His short stories set in World War I are all convincing, and he could also vividly evoke the Civil War, and did, in a long series of short stories. But World War II was something else, something Marquand could never really grasp and put together or get into focus—best summed up for him in the baffled observation that it was, indeed, "funny the way things happen . . . when there's a war on." His best evocation of the war years remains in *So Little Time*, where he could define the mood of uncertainty and impending doom that settled across America in the last few months of unsteady peace when the lights were going out all over Europe.

Marquand himself was nervous about *Repent in Haste*, not really certain that it was up to several of his previous books, and for a while toyed with the idea of having the novel published as a serial only, not as a hard-cover book. But Alfred McIntyre, who was hoping for another profitable property for

Little, Brown, was a persuasive editor, and John agreed to let
Little, Brown have it. Even so, John insisted on having the
manuscript read by two Navy experts in Washington, who
were instructed to look for flaws, but when Carl Brandt wrote
to John that the book might require fixing here and there,
John became quite testy about it and suggested that Carl was
overstepping his capacity as a literary agent.

Repent in Haste was also the first of John's novels for which
he wrote his own blurb for the book jacket. His view of what
elements in the book would help its sale is interesting. Saying
to McIntyre that there was "nothing like writing fulsome
praise about one's own efforts," he wrote of his book:

> The natural simplicity of the plot and the writer's delicately
> detached method of treatment make this tale highly poignant
> and convincingly real. The short flashes of the Pacific life that
> run through it—the transport planes, Pearl, Guam, the smoking
> Japanese island, the transport bringing back the wounded, and
> the give-and-take of every-day war life—are all selected with an
> artistic skill which gives this small book both depth and stature.
> It is a mingling of love and war and peace and home, and a
> preview, perhaps, of the world of tomorrow, and no one who
> reads it can fail to gain a new insight into the thoughts and the
> environment of fighting men.

B. F.'s Daughter, the third of what Marquand thought as
his "war trilogy," is both a more successful and a more ambitious novel. It is also the first of his novels to have a woman
as protagonist. It contains two familiar Marquand elements,
the long central flashback and the double hero—solid, respectable, perfect-gentleman Bob Tasmin, whom Polly Fulton
loves, and brash, erratic, *arriviste* Tom Brett, whom Polly
Fulton marries, both these men reflecting Marquand's twin
views of himself. There is also a marvelously realized character
in Mr. B. F. Fulton, Polly's rich and overpowering industrialist
father, whose only standard in judging a man is whether or not
he would hire him for his company. And in Polly Fulton herself there is Marquand's first full-length portrait of Adelaide.

Polly Fulton insists that she is nothing like her father and
then spends the book discovering that she is his perfect mirror
image. She marries Tom Brett and not Bob Tasmin because

she is a woman who must dominate, just as her father dominated everyone and everything in her life, and her troubles with Tom stem from the enormity and relentlessness of her ambitions for him. Bob Tasmin tells her, "I'm sorry for him with you running his life. Of course that is why you married him." She is a dangerous woman, Tasmin tells her, because she doesn't really know what she is doing or why she does it. "You have to run things, like B. F.," he tells her. "It's all right as long as you know you're doing it, but you don't know."

Her husband has a mistress, and Polly discovers it, and there is a confrontation scene between the two women not unlike the scene that had occurred, not many years earlier, between John, Adelaide and Carol that morning in the civilized ambience of the St. Regis. Tom Brett's mistress, a beautiful divorcée named Winifred James, a career girl who works as a secretary in Tom's office, understands both Tom and Polly perfectly. In addition to her central problem—that Polly always had much more money than was good for her—Winifred tells Polly that her husband " 'needs someone he doesn't have to compete with. You're so brilliant, so charming, such a rare and lovely person, Mrs. Brett. I think you're too good for him really. I know I'm saying this badly, but he needs someone who loves everything he does without so many perfect standards. I do hope you know what I mean.' " Winifred tries to spell it out to Polly: Tom needs someone " 'who doesn't—well, keep him stirred up. Someone not quite as lovely—without as many definite ambitions for him. I mean someone common. That is what he needs.' She raised her hands and dropped them gently on the table. 'Like me.' "

In the novel Marquand punishes Polly—and, in the process, Adelaide—by having her demand, and then beg, Bob Tasmin to go to bed with her, and having Bob refuse. Bob is a gentleman, and much as he loves Polly and desires her he cannot betray his code. The novel ends on a familiar Marquand note, with Polly realizing that, in the last, it is always necessary to lower one's sights a little, to surrender a portion of the dream, to compromise.

Both *Repent in Haste* and *B. F.'s Daughter* sold well. John Marquand had reached the point of popularity where his name

alone sold books, regardless of their content, and he had a
loyal band of readers across America who made his novels
almost unfailingly best sellers. *B. F.'s Daughter* was by far the
more successful of the two titles, and between its publication
in the fall of 1946 through June of the following year the book
sold over 170,000 copies, an extraordinary figure for any novel.
A less expensive edition offered by the Literary Guild (John's
membership on the board of the Book-of-the-Month Club
precluded any of his books being Book-of-the-Month selections) sold nearly 700,000 copies. The novel was also sold to
the films, and *B. F.'s Daughter* became a big starring vehicle
for Barbara Stanwyck. For Adelaide, who was no Stanwyck, this
may have been some consolation—but not much. Adelaide disliked the film version of *B. F.'s Daughter* and said so vociferously. To Adelaide, the intellectual snob, films were an inferior
art form in the first place, and she very nearly succeeded in
convincing John of this as well. After the picture's release he
told Carl Brandt that he would have liked it better if the
movie rights had not been sold at all and said he considered
the treatment of *The Late George Apley* even worse. The
present story he was writing, he said, did not contain any
motion picture possibilities. He even suggested a stipulation in
his contract that no future book of his could ever be turned into
a film. But he could, in the face of upcoming six-figure movie
contracts, be persuaded to change his mind.

Book reviewers were harsh on both *B. F.'s Daughter* and
Repent in Haste—particularly the former, since it was the
bigger and, in John's mind, the more important book. John
complained that the critics had "missed the point" of *B. F.'s
Daughter*. The point, in John's view, was the mood of the
period that was reflected in the novel, the sad, frustrated,
uneasy mood of the war years, the war that from the home
front was so difficult for Americans to understand, and yet the
war that reached out and touched and changed every life and
every aspect of life irreparably. It is the mood which Polly
sums up when she thinks back nostalgically to the years before
the war, when life was predictable and clear-cut, "before the
war fixed it so that no one had time for anything." It was very

like the mood the same critics had found admirable and telling in *So Little Time.*

Marquand had begun to speak bitterly about the critics of his novels, whereas a few years earlier he had insisted that he never even read, much less paid attention, to their views. When *B. F.'s Daughter* was published—a week from his birthday—he was fifty-three. He had reached that point in life, which every man who works hard at anything reaches, when he had begun to wonder whether perhaps his best work was behind him. In his flying trips to the West Pacific a phrase had caught his ear which navy pilots and navigators used when they passed the mid-point of their flights between the California coast and the Hawaiian Islands and, again, between Hawaii and the coast of Japan. This point was called the "point of no return." It meant that, no matter what happened now, there was no going back; one could only go on. It was a haunting phrase that might have come right out of the ending of a Marquand novel. It somehow summed up John's bitter-sad feeling about his own life, the direction his career had taken, his endless ordeal with Adelaide, his lack of connection with his children. It was also a phrase, as he suggested to Alfred McIntyre, that would make an absolutely smashing title for a book.

Chapter Twenty-one

*T*he novel that would become *Point of No Return* was long a-borning. It would mark, in fact, the longest gap in time between any of Marquand's books—nearly three years, since he had been producing a novel a year with almost clocklike regularity. John had decided, as a result of the fun he had had creating B. F. Fulton—who bore no small resemblance to the late Mr. Elon Huntington Hooker of New York and Greenwich, Connecticut—to leave the war and write a book with a businessman hero. Business was something John admittedly knew almost nothing about, though he did have several businessman friends such as Gardi Fiske and George Merck. But for his new novel he had decided on a banker hero, and the obvious person to turn to for advice on banking was Edward Streeter, who had been one year ahead of John at Harvard. Streeter was a vice-president of the Fifth Avenue Bank (later the Bank of New York), had worked previously with the Bankers Trust, and also had a lively career outside banking as a writer of light novels—*Dere Mabel, Daily Except Sunday,* and others. Streeter seemed an ideal choice, not for collaboration, really, but for editorial help and information. Marquand approached him about this one afternoon in the Century Club, and Streeter agreed that he would be happy to assist in any way he could.

Streeter, now retired from banking, recalls vividly the summer of 1947 when John Marquand arrived at their vacation house at Martha's Vineyard wearing a long raincoat and carrying an armful of typescript. Streeter read it that evening and was shocked by what he read. "The book was in ridiculous shape," he says. "He'd done no research. He was naïve as well as cynical. He said ridiculous things. He wrote that the vice-president of a bank spent his time selling Wyoming sporting ranches, camps in the Adirondacks, and estates on Long Island. I asked him, 'What do you think bankers run—a real estate operation?' After a moment, John rather sulkily replied, 'Well, what the hell *do* they do?'"

Streeter recalls that John was almost childish in the way he reacted to criticism. John had written a scene, in the first draft of the novel, in which the directors of the fictional bank were holding a board meeting in the basement of the bank, near the vault. Streeter said to him, "John, boards don't meet in the cellar. They meet in paneled rooms on the top floor." But John had been intrigued with the fact that banana oil was used to polish the prisonlike steel bars on the doors of bank vaults and said, "You've got to admit, Ed, that the way I've described the smell of that banana oil is pretty good writing. Couldn't we keep the scene the way it is, and just add a couple of sentences saying that the board room upstairs was being painted so they're using the cellar temporarily?" At another point in the story, as Streeter recalls from the original manuscript, John had Charles Gray, the hero of the novel, say to an associate something like, "Well, I've got to get back to work. Let's meet tonight for a drink at the bar of the Harvard Club, where it'll be quiet and there'll be no people and we can really talk." Later on, John had the two men meet in the quiet, uncrowded bar. Streeter asked John if he had ever been to the bar at the Harvard Club, and John admitted that he had not; the Harvard was not one of the clubs he cared much for. Streeter pointed out that the Harvard Club bar was not only an extremely popular but extremely noisy place, and that on most afternoons it is packed to the walls with bodies. John said, "*Really?* You mean that? To me, that's shocking!"

The two men worked on John's manuscript until two o'clock in the following morning, and Streeter gave John over three hundred specific suggestions. Rather typically, Streeter recalls, John did not ever really thank him for what he had done. Streeter had not expected payment for the work he had done for his friend and would not have accepted it if John had offered it. But when *Point of No Return* was published—two years later—Streeter remembers, "This is a mean-spirited thought, but he never even sent me a copy of the book."

But John could be generous in a perhaps more meaningful way. Edward Streeter had been working on a book called *Father of the Bride,* and John offered to read that manuscript. The next day—he was an extremely fast reader—John said, "I'm only one voice in five at the Book-of-the-Month Club, but I'll back this book if you can put it in shape in forty-eight hours." Streeter telephoned Cass Canfield, his editor at Harper, the book was typed within the required time for the meeting, and, with John's backing, *Father of the Bride* became the Club's dual selection, along with Arthur Miller's *Death of a Salesman.*

There were personal difficulties, meanwhile, in John's life that were slowing up production of *Point of No Return.* Early in 1948, John's Aunt Greta—Margaret Marquand Hale Oakman —died. ("Suppose . . . she dies," Jim Calder had suggested of Cousin Clothilde, the bulwark of Wickford Point.) She had owned a 40 per cent undivided interest in the houses and property of Curzon's Mill, and in her will this property was bequeathed to her six children by Herbert Dudley Hale and their half sister, Renée, her daughter by John Oakman. John Marquand had already inherited another 40 per cent interest, and his aging father, Phil Marquand, owned the remaining 20 per cent. John, meanwhile, had been appointed his father's sole conservator, which gave him control of 60 per cent of the Curzon's Mill property.

Adelaide, with her passion for houses, had long had her eye on Curzon's Mill. In particular, she coveted the lovely old Yellow House, the best house on the property—John once commented that every woman he had ever known had wanted to own the Yellow House—but over the years Adelaide had begun to have grandiose plans that involved the entire property, including the Red Brick House and the Mill. All three buildings had become even more run down than they had been in John's youth, and Adelaide envisioned remodeling and restoring them completely. John, too, had a deep sentimental attachment to Curzon's Mill and its houses, and soon after his Aunt Greta's death he approached his Hale cousins with a proposition: Since, in a situation of property division such as this one, it was impossible to say which 60 per cent was in John's hands and which 40 per cent belonged to the Hales, John offered to buy out the Hales' share of the estate. His offering price was a fair one—$21,500, along with a certain amount of land across the road from the houses. The entire Curzon's Mill property had been appraised at $33,000, so John was offering two thirds for a two-fifths share.

The Hales politely but firmly declined the offer. At least one Hale already lived at Curzon's Mill and looked on it as her home. Her brothers and sister, along with their wives and children, were always coming and going and regarded the place as their summer residence. Nearly ten years had passed since the publication of *Wickford Point*, but the Hales had not forgotten it, and relations between John and the Hales had remained cool. For this reason, John had turned down a number of offers from motion picture companies to produce *Wickford Point* as a film, not wanting to open up the whole family controversy all over again. The Hales resented John and Adelaide's way of appearing at Curzon's Mill and cavalierly carrying off pictures and pieces of furniture for the Marquands' Kent's Island house, and the Hales were also well aware that John and his lawyers had been pressing their mother, long before her death, to make a settlement with John on her share of the property. Certain of the Hales even suggested that John's legal pestering had shortened their mother's life, though this was probably an exaggeration. Aunt Greta was a doughty Yankee and a fair match for John Marquand, even when she was old and ill. In a letter to "Dear Aunt Greta" written in March of the previous year, John had pleaded for the property, saying, "I have lived on it, off and on, since I was two years old, and I believe I have been there for a longer period than any of your own children. Furthermore, I feel a deep sense of personal responsibility regarding the future of the place as Aunt Bessie and Aunt Mollie both asked me, in the last years of their lives, to take care of it and not let it go to pieces, as it is in the process of doing now."

John went on to talk about the happiness it would give to his old father, who was Aunt Greta's brother, to live on the old family place knowing that it was all, once again, in a Marquand's hands. He offered Aunt Greta the Mill as a residence —he would completely refurbish it for her—for the rest of her life, and enough land for her heirs to build a new house of their own, in return for her share. In her no-nonsense reply to John—which she never got to mail before she died—Aunt Greta said, "Here is a letter to you. Now why don't you stop all this damn law stuff and just take the Mill as a share of your share and use it for whatever purpose you can use it and do anything you want to do about making it more attractive for you and later on if you still want to arrange things differently, take the matter up with whoever I leave my share of the place to." John and Adelaide had also gone through all the houses at Curzon's Mill, placing tags marked "J.P.M." on various pieces that John considered his. The tags soon fell off, but nonetheless this sort of behavior from their celebrity cousin quite annoyed the Hales.

The Hales rejected John's offer through their lawyer, Thomas Shaw Hale, another cousin, of the New York law firm of Hale, Grant, Myerson, O'Brien & McCormick. There followed several long talks between Thomas Shaw Hale and John, during which John increased the size of his offer. Still the Hales were adamant. Legally, the term "undivided interest" means that the people who own a piece of property must agree on its use; otherwise, it must be turned over to the courts, who will then rule how the property should be divided, or whether it should be sold and the proceeds of the sale divided proportionately among the owners. In a case such as this one, the judge usually finds it simpler to rule that the property be sold, rather than attempt to divide it physically, and the Hales were aware of this. They also knew that if the property were sold, John, since he outweighed them financially, would buy it. So Thomas Hale approached John with an offer. John could have both the Yellow House and the Mill, and the Hales could keep the Red Brick House and a parcel of land across the road. John agreed to this but said that he would have to ask Adelaide about it.

The next day, Thomas Hale had a telephone call from Adelaide Marquand, who wished to see him. When Hale got to the apartment, Adelaide explained that she would agree to no arrangement that gave the Hales anything but money. She increased the offer to $40,000. She explained that she felt strongly that Curzon's Mill had to be treated as an entity. If it were going to restored, it made no sense to restore it in bits and pieces; it had to be restored in its entirety. During the course of the conversation, Thomas Hale got the distinct impression that Adelaide didn't think much of the Hales as neighbors, that she regarded them as eccentric nuisances and would really prefer to get them off the property altogether. Faced with this, there was nothing for the Hales to do but let the matter go to court and hope that the judge might be prevailed upon to divide the property, even though to do so would be highly unusual since most pieces of property cannot really be divided.

During the summer weeks that followed, as word got out that the famous novelist had become involved in an intrafamily legal battle, with lawyers on both sides furiously preparing briefs, the press descended. *Life* magazine sent reporters and photographers to Newburyport, and Murray Davis of the *New York World-Telegram* began gathering material for a series of dispatches centered on the fascinating fact that here, at last, were characters from a popular novel stepping out into real life. Soon readers were devouring John's and Aunt Greta's exchange of letters throughout the entire Scripps-Howard chain. Thomas Hale had, in his youth, worked for a while as a newspaper reporter, and he offered his cousin clients a piece of advice: Be nice to the press. The Hales decided to be more than nice; they decided to be utterly charming.

"After lampooning us as characters in his book he now wants

to boot us out," declared Robert B. Hale to one reporter. "He is using the proceeds of 'Wickford Point,' indirectly perhaps, to put us out as characters. We are going to ask John if he isn't using the proceeds of the book to kick out his cousins. We spent all our childhood summers at the Mill—John and the rest of us. And we've always liked John. We still do. He has as much right there now as we have. He has relatives buried up on the hill. We have a right to be there too. We have relatives buried up on the same hill. When he offered money I countered with an offer to take one of the houses. His answer to that was just to offer more money. We judge everything on the heart, John on the dollar. If we thought of it from a financial standpoint we'd take his offer, for it was much more than our share was worth. But we weren't thinking of that. We were thinking of the place. It is beautiful beyond description. You get a feeling of it in the novel. John wrote it at the mill."

The Hales proved to be a newspaper interviewer's dream. As for *Wickford Point,* Robert Hale went on, "John combined some of us with other people he knew, but we were pretty easily identified. I'm Sidney in the novel—a bad character. Mother was a pretty clear picture, although done a little bit on the dirty side. We thought about a suit, but only casually, for we liked John. We still like John. Mother held the place together. She was fond of John and he was fond of her, but even before she died John began trying to get the property. She wanted us all to have it. Now she's gone. Her passing is what brought this action." Robert Hale pleaded his case to the delighted reporter. "We'll take any one of the buildings— we just want a foothold," he said. "If mother had died last we'd have given John a house. Now he has us absolutely. If he can throw the place up for auction he has the money to buy it in. We can't compete with him. We want it because it has been a part of us for so long. And when you get old you want to go back to the beginning. You want security—the security that we have in the mill. The family has always lived there. The weddings are always there. The family has always gone back there to die—and be buried on the hill."

Next H. Dudley Hale, Robert Hale's brother, came forth with a lengthy interview. "We all dislike the idea staring us in the face of having our old home shot out from under us by force. It seems wrong that, because of death, nineteen people may have no roof over their heads while fate, through wills, can give that property to someone who already is land poor." Dudley Hale announced that he was Harry Brill, the social climber in *Wickford Point*. "I'd say I was Harry, physically," Mr. Hale explained, "but heaven knows I was no social leader at Harvard."

Laura Hale, one of Robert and Dudley's two sisters, who had married a man named Patterson Hale (no relation), revealed that she was the novel's Mary Brill, poor Mary who always loses her men to beautiful Bella. "John is fond of my husband, Pat," Laura Hale said. "But I'm afraid this legal thing will end everything. John says this will not make any difference, that he'll still drop by and see us. I don't think so, and I told him that."

"I'm Bella the Bitch," announced Renée Oakman Bradbury, then thirty-seven and at that point four times married and living in Long Island, who allowed herself to be photographed in a low-cut dress cuddling three of her large collection of dogs and other pets, which included five birds, among them a talking blue jay. "He really talks," she explained, speaking in a style very similar to that which Marquand had given Bella in the book. "He imitates things. He's a very, very strange bird. He fell out of a nest, you see. We took care of him. But that Bella business—I even named my little Crosley Bella the Bitch. It burned up about a month ago right in front of the gas station. The talk at Curzon's Mill is bad enough, but it is nothing compared to what happens around here. Nothing good seems ever to happen!" Of John's lawsuit, Renée said, "I see no reason why John should have the whole hog. There's no reason why he should have the entire family place. I don't know why he must be so possessive. We've always been fond of John and he liked us. He was always fond of me. Whenever it was necessary for someone to go down to his place at Kent's Island to bring back some old family portrait that he had stolen out of the mill, it was always little old Renée who had to do it. But honestly, I didn't like his making Mother's last days so difficult, trying to get the place, and I told him so. Even so, he has always been very fond of me. I went to Kent's Island and asked him to leave my mother alone, that she didn't want to divide up the place or sell it to him. It was rather hopeless, though." As the date of the trial approached, Renée announced to the press, "I'll be there! I promised Greta I'd fight to the last ditch to keep our part of the place, for that was what she wanted. John should have his share and we should have ours. I'm going to get a black hat for the hearing."

On and on the Hales talked, with the press loving and recording every word they said. John and Adelaide and the three children, meanwhile, had disappeared to their house, or rather houses, in Aspen. John, when reached there by telephone, behaved somewhat oddly. He had once worked as a newspaper reporter, just as had Thomas Hale, and should have known, too, the value of establishing good press relations. But when the reporter asked him his feelings in the case, he replied somewhat stiffly and stuffily, "I am not accustomed to try legal cases in newspapers." That was his only quote. Beyond that, he had no comment.

The result of all this was that as the case moved toward trial the Hales had built up a considerable body of sympathy behind them, and public feeling was running strong in their favor and against John. Much was made in the press of the disparity between the Hales' economic situation and John's, in which the tables had been oddly turned since the days of John's boyhood, when he had come to think of himself as a poor relation compared with the "rich" Hales. The Hales were portrayed as gentle, sweet innocents—and the underdogs— while John was depicted as a selfish bully who, very likely, had an exaggerated opinion of his own importance due to the fame of his books, and who, though he already had a number of houses and apartments—in New York, Newburyport, Hobe Sound, Aspen—wanted more, including everything that belonged to his poor cousins. It was in this highly charged atmosphere that the case came to the Salem, Massachusetts, Probate Court on October 21, 1948, Judge Phelan—a Boston Irishman—presiding.

Here again, John seems to have been somewhat naïve in his approach to the case. His attorney was a Mr. F. Murray

Forbes, Jr., of the distinguished Boston firm of Welch, Brown, Forbes and Welch. Thomas Hale, though masterminding the proceedings for his cousins from New York, kept his own name —and that of his Manhattan firm—completely out of the case and, instead, engaged a young lawyer from Salem named James J. Connelly to try the case. Connelly, representing the Hales, had the appeal of a local boy on his way up; he was also a relative and attended the same church as the judge. John's lawyer, on the other hand, came down to little Salem from the big city wearing a cutaway and a silk hat. Before the proceedings got under way, everybody had been wondering what old Phil Marquand felt about it. When the little group gathered in the courthouse it was noticed that Phil was sitting on the Hales' side of the room. Outside, John Marquand was being photographed by *Life* on the courthouse steps looking handsome, prosperous, and confident.

From the outset it was clear that young Jim Connelly was conducting the hearing beautifully. He pulled out all the stops, and his rich Irish voice quavered with emotion as he described how the powerful rich man was trying to take away his cousins' property. Quietly he reminded the Court that these gentlefolk, the Hales, were the descendants of Edward Everett Hale, the great author. "And today," Connelly intoned, "we are witnessing Mr. John P. Marquand trying to make these people men without a country." There was hardly a dry eye in the courtroom, while the color rose on the back of John's neck.

John did not make a particularly good witness when he got to the stand. His usually resonant voice failed him, as did his own theatrical ability. He muttered and mumbled replies to questions. His heart seemed to have gone out of it, and in all likelihood it had. It was, after all, not he but Adelaide who had got them all into this position; just as he had defended her during the America First period, he stood by her through this. On November third, after hearing just a little over a week of testimony, Judge Phelan decided the case. Curzon's Mill should be divided, he declared "in metes and bounds"—into appropriate divisions, to be determined by the land commission, between the opposing parties. The Hales had won.

Adelaide was furious. So were John's Boston lawyers. At first the land commission gave the mill to the Hales—the Mill House that John himself had wanted most of all—along with some land. John's lawyers took an immediate appeal on the technicality that the place split was not worth as much as the place whole. Finally an agreement was reached; John was given the Yellow House, which Adelaide wanted, and the Mill House, which he wanted, while the Hales were given the Red Brick House and the parcel of property across the road. It was, of course, exactly the division which had been suggested to John, and which he had agreed to, in the first place, before Adelaide had begun insisting that Curzon's Mill not be divided. It was like the neat and ironic denouement of a John Marquand novel. And once the case was settled there was no more dropping in, or even any speaking, between John Marquand and the Hales. Cousin Laura Hale had been right.

All this litigation had seriously interrupted John's work on the new novel he was trying to write about a banker. During the ordeal, he made frequent trips back to New York, where he would arrive unannounced at Carol Brandt's office at Metro-Goldwyn-Mayer. She would turn off the telephone except for West Coast calls, fix him a drink, and listen to him as he paced up and down her office, complaining that he could not understand his cousins, why they were putting him through all this. Now John and Adelaide were off for Europe—to London, Rome, and Athens. Adelaide wanted the trip, she said, to "heal some of the wounds" their marriage had suffered. John just wanted to get away. Adelaide was hopeless when it came to details and planning, and so John had asked Carol to wire ahead to London to reserve a car and a suite at Claridge's. John and Adelaide were seated on deck chairs on the high seas bound for England when a cablegram was delivered from the manager of Claridge's, saying that all arrangements had been made for the arriving Marquands according to Mrs. Brandt's instructions. John started to crumple up the cable and toss it over the rail, but Adelaide snatched it from him. There followed a stormy shipboard scene. As John told Carol later, it was one instance where Carol's famous efficiency had backfired on them.

Chapter Twenty-two

"The typical Marquand hero reaches the point of no return when he draws his first breath," wrote a reviewer in *Time* in a survey of John's work. Marquand heroes are always looking back, wondering where it all went wrong, what turn, if taken, might have changed the course of everything. They are always trying to go home again, back to where it all began, and, when they arrive at that polarizing place, they discover that, even though things did not turn out quite the way they dreamed they would, there is little chance that anything could have turned out differently, and that is that. A settlement is reached, a compromise; that is the best a man can hope for. John Marquand himself was just this sort of man. He had wanted to go home again, to Curzon's Mill, and yet he knew—must have known—that he couldn't really. Had he let Adelaide push him into a court battle with the cousins he had grown up with, roomed at college with, just to watch a Marquand fictive situation spin itself out in real life? Perhaps, and now he was faced with the inevitable bitter result: Curzon's Mill was divided, an armed camp, with a family, once close, no longer on speaking terms with one another. And yet—in the Marquand novels,

at least—this sort of thing *had* to happen from the moment
one passed the point of no return, which in this particular case
might have been that moment when John Marquand encountered the Hooker sisters on the beach at the edge of the
Yellow Sea. If he had turned and walked the other way, would
it all have been different? Perhaps, but it was too late to wonder now. "In the end . . . you always drove alone."

There is a great deal of this feeling of futility and fatalism
in John's "banking" novel, *Point of No Return*, which was published in the year following the trial and which, at the time,
was greeted by many critics as John's finest work. The book is,
indeed, much more than a book about a banker and banking.
It is a book about love and marriage, about the nature of success and the American dream. The banking details are rich and,
with Ed Streeter's help, convincing: "The depositors' room off
the vaults had just been refinished and redecorated and Tony
Burton had called the conference there because he wanted to
see how everything looked," John had written. ". . . There was
an efficient smell of oil on all the glittering steelwork." But
the problem that besets Charles Gray could find him in any
career. He has reached the point of no return in life where he
cannot turn back, where he *must*, even though he no longer
has any real taste for it, compete against his colleague, Roger
Blakesley, for the vice-presidency of the staid old Stuyvesant
Bank in New York, a position that is about to become vacant.
He must compete because that is what he started out doing.
Having set his course, Charles Gray must complete the journey,
end as it may, as it was charted.

In this enterprise, Charles is aided, or rather pushed force-
fully along, by his determined and ambitious wife, another
Polly Fulton—and another Adelaide. The way Nancy and
Charles Gray go at each other in the novel is a disturbing reminder of what John and Adelaide Marquand's married life
had become by 1949, just as Gray's disillusion with the considerable success and money he has achieved already is a comment on John's feelings about his own success and reputation.
Charles Gray "felt contented and at peace doing nothing but
raking leaves on the lawn, he and his two children." All the
rest is as dust in the mouth. And where did the long journey

all begin? Why, in Clyde, of course, the pretty little New England seaport town with its white picket fences, green lawns, and fine old Federalist houses where Charles Gray was born, and born not on Johnson Street, where the best people like the Lovells lived, but on Spruce Street where the might-have-beens like Charles's father lived—the father for whom nothing ever turned out quite right, the father who should, by rights and heritage, have been successful, but who let every opportunity slip from his hands and whose baffled excuse is that "we can't help how we're made, can we?"

John, by 1949, had lost Christina Sedgwick more thoroughly than ever—not only through the divorce, but now she was happily remarried to a man named Harford Powel. Perhaps this fact added special poignancy to the love story in *Point of No Return* between the young Charles Gray and the beautiful Christina-like Jessica Lovell, whose family owns the finest house on Johnson Street. And it all comes back to Charles when he is called, by the Stuyvesant Bank, to go up to Clyde on business and to revisit the old streets where he had wandered as a boy and where he had wanted to marry Jessica.

In many ways, of course, John's decision to make Charles Gray a banker was both a brilliant and a revealing one, because in *Point of No Return* the importance of money as a theme announces itself more honestly than in any of the previous Marquand novels, where money had been a more muted subtheme. Not only does money drive Charles Gray the banker (as money drives every other upwardly mobile American, Marquand seems to say) and his ambitious wife—money to pay the taxes and the mortgage, to pay the children's school tuition and the dues at the country club—but money and the lack of it were right there at the beginning, back in Clyde. It was money that separated Spruce Street from Johnson, and the Lovells from the Grays. Young Charles Gray had seen this and had made $50,000 from shrewd investments in the stock market, thinking that this would impress Jessica's father and let Charles have his daughter's hand. Not so. "Money is one thing," Mr. Lovell says, "and stock-market money is another." Mr. Lovell also remarks that it is "too bad" Charles went to Dartmouth and not Harvard. And so there is the crucial difference

separating Charles and Jessica. No amount of money Charles
might *make* would ever be good enough for the Lovells, whose
money was old, inherited. Furthermore, as far as the town of
Clyde was concerned, the Lovells would always be better than
the Grays because the Lovells had been shipowners but the
Grays had only been ship captains, and there was that world
of social difference between the ruling and the working classes.

To further emphasize the money theme, Marquand added a
character named Francis Stanley, who has more position and
money than the Lovells, to show how even people as secure
as the Lovells care dreadfully what people like the Stanleys
think and are saying about them, and when the Stanleys comment to the Lovells that there seems to be something going on
between young Charles and Jessica there is cause for genuine
alarm. It is clear from the outset that by the immutable laws
of American social nature Charles and Jessica cannot marry,
just as surely as oil and water won't mix and cream rises to the
top. And there is never the slightest suggestion that Jessica
will rebel and marry Charles against her father's wishes, because she is a girl who by breeding and tradition will not only
always be a dutiful daughter but who also could not bear to
be married to a man her father did not like and who did not
like her father. It is the doomed love story—with the sexes
reversed, more fully developed, and perhaps more movingly
presented—of George Apley and Mary Monahan, and, just as
theirs was, the love story in *Point of No Return* is one of the
strongest hinges in the novel.

A particular delight of *Point of No Return* is its suspenseful-
ness. The reader is kept dangling for over five hundred pages
and does not know until virtually the last few paragraphs
whether Charles Gray will or will not be handed the vice-
presidency. For a while, John considered ending the book with
the question still unanswered. This indefinite ending had been
the idea of Conney Fiske, who had read what he had written
while he was in New York for the Book-of-the-Month Club
meeting. She said she thought that the ending was implicit,
and it would not make any difference whether the reader was
told whether Charles Gray got the job at the bank or not. But
John was meticulous about tidiness of construction, and so,

though Conney's notion was tempting to him, he eventually settled for an ending that wrapped up everything neatly. The ending may have a touch of theatricality to it—in real life, of course, matters seldom come to such clean conclusions—but it is probably the most reader-satisfying close the book could have.

For the most part, critics were ecstatic about the new novel. Charles A. Brady, in *Fifty Years of the American Novel,* published two years later, wrote, "More than ever in this volume is Mr. Marquand the Thackerayan novelist of personal memory, the laureate of the sick, throat-filling, despairing ecstasy of first love. He understands the mystery and magic of the human personality with a mellower comprehension than before." Reviewers in the daily newspapers were for the most part equally enthusiastic, with one notable exception—Maxwell Geismar in the *New York Times.* Geismar, while conceding that John Marquand, like Willa Cather, was one of the American "conservators of heritage," went on to complain that Marquand ought not to have had to "sacrifice, as he does here, everything he knows about American life and expresses so well, to the demands of a sentimental and romantic tale. True enough, Charles accepts his advancement with acrid knowledge that he has lost freedom forever, and this takes character. But it is character that lacks the real courage to make the break, whose virtue is compromise, and whose discipline is the discipline of submission." Geismar also took exception to Marquand's "oblique attack" on his subject and situation.

John was furious, and so were his friends, including Charles Morton of the *Atlantic Monthly* who wrote to John's publisher about the review, labeling it "patronizing comment by a Deep Thinker—and a nonentity to boot" and adding:

> Here we have Marquand writing about the direction or misdirection of a man's life, his marriage, his work and his place in the world, and I have a great itch to learn what are the "larger questions" which the reviewer thinks Marquand has avoided. What is the objection to "an oblique attack"? Are the bludgeonings by Thomas Mann necessarily better than a more civilized technique? It seems to me that Geismar is an innocent pedant who believes in black and white: to satisfy him, one

supposes a main character would have to wind up hanging himself or else by "living happily ever after."

Indeed, it had been John's whole point, in the novel, that acceptance was enforced upon Americans and that, within the strictures of the American "game," there was no real way to "make the break." The novel ends with Charles Gray, having taken the job, reflecting, "Nancy would understand. Nancy had more ambition for him than he had for himself. Nancy would be very proud. They would sell the house at Sycamore Park and get a larger place. They would resign from the Oak Knoll Club [in favor of a "better" club, more befitting bank vice-presidents]. And then there was the sailboat. It had its compensations but it was not what he had dreamed." John considered this a realistic, almost grim, ending, the opposite of "sentimental and romantic." Paul Osborn, meanwhile, given the job of adapting *Point of No Return* for Broadway, felt that theater audiences would simply not accept such a downbeat ending and gave the hero a redeeming bit of spunk by having him refuse to join the better club—Hawthorn Hill—that his boss suggests. At the time, John commented to an interviewer, "Charles Gray sees he has passed the point of no return and might as well accept it, and that 'The game in many ways is not worth the candle.' But evidently the producers found the audiences wouldn't take to such a pessimistic result. This makes the play seem to mean, 'The game may be worth the candle if you learn to walk erect.'" Marquand disapproved of Osborn's ending, which he felt did not ring true, but agreed to it on the grounds that a play was not a novel and that the ending of a play often had to be "souped up." Osborn was apparently right, for *Point of No Return* became an immediate Broadway hit, starring Henry Fonda.

Throughout *Point of No Return*, Marquand managed to skirt sentimentality with remarkable success. Consider this passage, in which Charles Gray muses about the past:

> If there were anything in the theory that the past remained intact, he and Jessica Lovell must still have been somewhere, with the other ghosts of Clyde. Perhaps all of that summer might have returned to him again if he had stayed in Clyde.

If he had never seen Jessica Lovell again except in the distance, he would have seen the shadows of Jessica and himself around every corner and on every country road. If he walked down Dock Street, he and Jessica might still have been standing in front of the window of Stowell's furniture store, talking of living room curtains. She had wanted green monk's cloth curtains.

As Marquand goes from the soft and whispery "other ghosts of Clyde" in the course of one short paragraph to a furniture store and monk's cloth curtains, it is possible to see the author almost physically reining himself in, resisting an impulse to wax poetic, and pulling himself back to hard and plain reality of living room curtains—real things, tangible things. And so the Geismar charge of romance and sentiment does seem, in the context of this book, oddly misplaced. Suppose, John used to ask his friends, Charles Gray *had* had the "real courage to make the break," and instead of taking the proffered job had been last seen sailing off into the sunset to make a new life for himself in Tahiti. Would not *that* have made it a sentimental and romantic novel?

The theme of going home again, of trying to find one's youth again, is a familiar one in American fiction. One thinks immediately of Willa Cather's lost lady and Thomas Wolfe's Eugene Gant. But John Marquand, by marrying this theme with the theme of the search for meaning in love and marriage, and placing these against the background of American success and money competition, opened up a whole new territory and tradition. The novel set a definite precedent, and in the years that followed a number of *Point of No Return*-type books appeared, among them John C. Keats's *The Crack in the Picture Window*, William H. Whyte's *The Organization Man*, David Riesman's *The Lonely Crowd*, Sloan Wilson's *The Man in the Gray Flannel Suit*, Cameron Hawley's *Executive Suite*, and Hamilton Basso's *The View from Pompey's Head*. After reading the last novel, in fact, John muttered that it seemed more than a case of Basso's having been influenced by *Point of No Return*. It was more like stealing.

Chapter Twenty-three

*T*he success of *Point of No Return* gave John Marquand what is often regarded as the highest accolade America can give to a man: his face on the cover of *Time*. It also gave him new confidence in himself and in his craft, and for the first time in his life he began to relax the frantic pace of his living and his production. He had, after all, produced seven of his "serious" novels in a little more than ten years, and between these had turned out four full-length Mr. Moto books plus numberless other serials, short stories, articles, and reviews for the Book-of-the-Month Club *News*. He had become not only one of the most successful American writers, with an income of $100,000 a year from his writing alone, but also one of the most prolific.

John had been given an even more unusual accolade. His friend and fellow Boston clubman, Bayard Tuckerman (Harvard, 1911), had named one of his racehorses "J. P. Marquand." The horse, as John had predicted, had had an undistinguished career marked primarily by an ability to lose races, but the idea of having a horse named after him amused him. One evening, when he and the Fiskes were dining together at the

Somerset Club, they found themselves confronted with three exceptionally tough sirloin steaks. John summoned Joseph, the head waiter, and ruefully inquired, "Would this by any chance be J. P. Marquand?"

At about this time, he had begun to worry about his health. Though Marquands had generally been a healthy and long-lived lot—John's father would live to be nearly ninety—John had always been something of a hypochondriac, and now he had become convinced he had an ulcer, even though none of the doctors he consulted could detect anything. All the doctors could suggest was rest, a holiday. And so, the winter after the publication of *Point of No Return,* John and Adelaide Marquand rented Treasure Island in the Bahamas, a narrow strip of land just four miles long, an hour's sail from Nassau. Here, away from it all, there would be peace. And there was, of a sort.

Treasure Island had no electricity, no telephone, and no water other than some very dubious-looking rainwater gathered in mossy cisterns. Bottled water for drinking and cooking had to be imported from Nassau. Treasure Island was ringed by tall coral cliffs, with white sand beaches on all sides, and toward the west a watch tower known as the Custom House faced Nassau. It was said that beacon fires could be lighted at the top of the tower in case of disaster. A steep flight of white stone steps led up to the tower from the water, and to a primitive drawbridge that could be lowered for landing parties who arrived from tenders anchored off the shore. A huge black sting ray habitually floated nearby, just below the surface of the turquoise water, and the natives claimed that he was the island's guardian. All these details John relished, and he approached his proprietorship of Treasure Island as though he were another Robinson Crusoe.

The "Great House" at Treasure Island stood at the end of a palm-shaded walk about a quarter of a mile away from the Custom House Tower. It was low, sprawling, shuttered, and cool, with one high terrace overlooking the sea and, on the inland side, a vine-covered, sheltered terrace with swinging ships' lanterns overhead and a long refectory table where meals were served. There was a living room which John quickly established as his winter study, and the round mahogany table at the center of the room was soon covered with books, magazines, and undulating mounds of Book-of-the-Month Club galleys, along with a sturdy liquor supply (the Scotch, John used to point out, had been an admirable bargain due to the recent devaluation of the pound). The living room walls were decorated with shells, bits of coral, dried starfish, and sea fans. Beyond stretched dark bedrooms, an ancient bath and water closet, storage rooms, and a kitchen with a gas-run refrigerator, the most important appliance on the island since it was the only source of ice cubes.

Treasure Island required a good-sized staff. There were Captain Sweeting of the boat *Windrift* and two sailors; there were Josephas, the caretaker, and his wife Lineth; also Josephas's brother-in-law, Richard; Corinne, a waitress, her husband Eric, and Myrtis, a cook. There were also his own secretary, an ex-WAC named Marjorie Davis, who was placed in a tent called "the collapsible house" nearby, and the shy English lady schoolmistress who appeared on week ends to tutor the three children. Still another member of the Marquand household was Myrtis's baby, who required its own ragged nine-year-old baby sitter. All these people immediately began referring to John Marquand as "the Boss," which delighted him. Never in his life, he claimed, had be attained such an exalted position.

As he did with most things, John romanticized and exoticized Treasure Island, turning it into something it never was and never could be, a kind of Eden. There were always guests, some of them famous, like the Lindberghs. others just old friends, like the Fiskes, who arrived by boat from Nassau, entering the pretty lagoon that was the island's only harbor through a narrow, wind-swept cut in the coral rock that was passable only at high tide, making their way across the unsteady drawbridge, then up the cliff and down the path to the Great House. There were luncheon parties and dinner parties and fishing parties and cocktail parties. John would dictate for several hours each morning to Marjorie Davis, then join the party, and the rest of the day would be devoted to pleasure. There was swimming at one or the other of the two beaches, one for morning and one for afternoon—though John enjoyed reversing things by going to the morning beach in the afternoon, and vice versa. There were long walks to the far tip of the island, and fishing expeditions, and trips to nearby Rose Island where English friends had a luxurious beach house with fresh-water showers. But overnight stops in such comfortable oases were prohibited, since John felt that this would be disloyal to the spirit of Treasure Island.

John invented elaborate games and contests to amuse his guests that were devised exclusively for Treasure Island. He would paint numbers on the backs of land crabs and, with each guest assigned a number and a beast, there would be crab races. There were shelling contests for which John and Henry Seidel Canby, another frequent guest, drew up complicated rules with prizes for such categories as the "Most Worthy Sea Fan," the "Best All-Round Coral," the "Most Unusual and Desirable Shell," and the "Shell Most Likely to Succeed." The most ironclad rule of all was that no shell was to have been purchased in one of the shell shops in Nassau. The servants, perhaps because they could not read or write, tended to overlook some of the strictures of the contests and, since they made the daily shopping trips to Nassau, won most of the prizes, to the disappointment of the children, who had spent hours walking the beaches with bowed heads looking for rarities.

Toward evening, the cocktail hour became a ritual with strong drinks John had concocted out of rum and Falernian, and a mysterious and particularly potent secret recipe he christened "Island Magic." It cast its spell efficiently, and, on the lamplit, sheltered terrace, with just the trace of a soft tropic breeze, John would tell his famous stories seated in a chair beneath an ancient wooden sign which proclaimed, "I am Monarch of All I Survey." Some of John's favorite stories were about his friend Gene Tunney who, for all the roughness of his trade as a prize fighter, had an elegant, almost mincing speaking style of which John was an excellent mimic. "Charming" was a word Tunney used frequently, and John loved to tell of Tunney's account of lunching in Havana one day with Ernest Hemingway, whom Tunney pronounced as "perfectly charming." Hemingway had served, according to Tunney, some "charming martinis," and then, after a "charming" lunch, a great many more "charming martinis" which, as Hemingway downed them, had the effect of making the author somewhat less charming. He became, in fact, quite belligerent. John's version of what happened then went like this:

"Gene told me that Hemingway had these Siamese cats, and that even the cats were drinking martinis. Hemingway would kick off his slippers and scratch the cats' backs, and then he began talking about foul blows in boxing and began to demonstrate them on Gene. Gene said, 'Ernest knows a lot about boxing, but perhaps I know a bit more about it than Ernest. Ed Fink, who was Al Capone's bodyguard, was my teacher. And all of a sudden Ernest came at me and started swinging. He came up and cut me across the lips, and there was blood, and then he jabbed me in the left elbow. I said to Ernest, "Do stop it, please, Ernest," but he kept right on punching. I didn't want to get on the outside—I really pride myself on my infighting—and I thought to myself: what Ernest needs is a good little liver punch. There's a little liver punch, and it has to be timed exactly, and when I saw the moment I let him have it. I was a little alarmed, if I do say so! His knees buckled, his face went gray, and I thought he was going to go down. But he didn't, and for the next few hours Ernest was perfectly charming.' "

John was the master of stories like that, stories which involved not only imitations and gestures—he told this story on his feet, dancing about with his impressions of the two pugilists—but which rambled along in that fashion and, as Charles Lindbergh describes them, "Stories that had no real point or punch line, but which were amusing all the way. He was a teller of tales."

Those were happy days. Anne Lindbergh also remembers Adelaide's humor blossoming at Treasure Island. "Because at the end she was such a tragic and distraught figure, one tends to forget her 'all-fellows-well-met' gaiety. The over-all impression was of exuberant good spirits. Her particular brand of free-wheeling extravagant humor—often directed against herself—was the perfect foil for John's dry, urbane satire. And there is no doubt she intentionally played up to him and his stories, and that he responded enthusiastically, and their friends or guests were marvelously entertained and amused, and a splendid evening resulted for all concerned. It was a marvelous show that was put on by both of them, in collaboration, and one had the impression that no one enjoyed it more than the two actors themselves."

No one troubled to dress up at Treasure Island in anything more than an open-collared shirt and khaki shorts or slacks, and after a leisurely dinner on the terrace there were more stories, more talk, or perhaps John would read aloud to his guests in his big voice. Of course one of his favorite readings was from Stevenson's *Treasure Island,* savoring such celebrated lines as Ben Gunn's "many's the long night I've dreamed of cheese—toasted, mostly—" and

> *Fifteen men on the dead man's chest—*
> *Yo-ho-ho, and a bottle of rum!*
> *Drink and the devil had done for the rest—*
> *Yo-ho-ho, and a bottle of rum!*

Then, as coffee was being served, Josephas, the caretaker, would silently enter the room with his guitar, and he would sit and sing island songs. Some of the songs were bawdy, some sentimental; Josephas had the calypso singer's gift of taking the names of the guests around the room and weaving them into the verses of his songs. "He picks the songs up in Bay Street," John would murmur fondly. Josephas's last song of the evening, inevitably, was "I love you but Jesus loves you best, Bid you good night, good night, good night," naming each guest in turn. It was a signal that the evening was over, that it was time for bed in the Great House and the guest house and for sleep with sounds no more disturbing than the noise of land crabs scuttling for each other's shells along the dark paths, a noise like the quiet grinding of teeth, and the rustling of the furry coconut rats that lived high in the crowns of the palm trees, the clicking of palm leaves in the breeze, and the distant repeated rush of the sea across the sand.

Gardi and Conney Fiske spent three months with John and Adelaide at Treasure Island during that first winter there, in 1950, and remembered it afterward as one of the happiest times of their lives. They were given a one-room shuttered house with lumpy iron beds a few minutes' walk from the Great House, where they shared outdoor plumbing—marked by a sign reading "El Retiro"—with secretary Marjorie Davis. The two families seldom met before lunchtime cocktails, with John working diligently through the morning on a new novel, and there were a few upheavals between John and Adelaide, but not many, and none of such importance as to make the guests feel uncomfortable. There were exciting moments, such as the night when Josephas's brother-in-law, Richard, who drank, nearly burned down Josephas's house, and John Marquand, shouting commands in the manner of a wartime general, organized guests and staff into a bucket brigade to save the building. Once, puzzled by the increased nuisance of flies in the kitchen, John announced that he and Gardi were organizing an expedition "to investigate conditions in the interior" of Treasure Island, where many of the native staff lived and where, John was certain, no white man had ventured. They came back, several hours later, muttering and shaking their heads sadly. "Worse than the jungle," was all John would say.

The Fiskes had brought with them a battery-powered radio which, when he heard of it, thoroughly irked John. The whole point of Treasure Island, he explained, was to get away from the reach of the outside world. He spent an entire evening inveighing against radios and communications in general, and there was a terrible scene when another guest revealed that Josephas himself had a powerful radio receiver and that it was from this that he picked up the latest songs, not "in Bay Street" at all. He could not believe it, John said, it was so incompatible with his dream. But it was not long before John was making daily trips to Josephas's house to catch the B.B.C. newscasts.

There was excitement when John's friend from Hollywood, Cedric Gibbons, art director for Metro-Goldwyn-Mayer, arrived on a luxurious chartered yacht. Gibbons had once been married to Dolores Del Rio, and his wife of the moment was a starlet named Hazel Brooks. The Gibbons party and crew came ashore, and there was a bibulous evening—the crew, it turned out, had brought their own rum—which ended with Marjorie Davis having to flee her tent and seek protection in the Fiskes' cottage from an overamorous sailor. In the morning, Eric's hands shook visibly while serving breakfast, and Richard did not reappear for over twenty-four hours. John labeled it another "Night of Horror," and, as always, these episodes became the topics of dinner-table conversations for nights to come and of stories that always ended in laughter. But for all the comings and goings, their happiest times seemed to be when a "dry rage" set in, with high tropical winds that made the sea too heavy for the *Windrift*, the yawl that went with the island, to enter or leave the lagoon, and when the four friends could enjoy perfect isolation, with no visitors and no way to escape. They picnicked on the special island chowder John had discovered, a spicy stew made with fish, Tabasco, Worcestershire sauce, and Bourbon whiskey. At times like these, John seemed most at peace.

At last, when it was time for the Fiskes to leave—a few days before the Marquands—everyone gathered at the drawbridge to say good-by, grasping their hands and begging them to return. Conney Fiske wept a little as Josephas, guitar in hand, sang his farewell song to her and altered the lyric to "good-by, Mistress Fiske" instead of "good night," as he had done so many evenings past. As she stepped into the *Windrift*, Josephas handed her a polished pink conch shell, telling her to keep it and "put it to your ear and you can always hear the island's waves."

John had urged the Fiskes to come back to Treasure Island the following winter, and they had agreed to come. They had been planning on it, in fact, when Adelaide wrote Conney a stiff and rather chilly letter, mentioning, as Conney recollects it, something about "the necessity of our privacy" and rescinding the invitation. Conney was both disappointed and hurt by Adelaide's letter. She had long suspected that Adelaide didn't really like her; Adelaide, after all, didn't like any of John's women friends, all of whom she assumed without question were having love affairs with him. Conney was also certain that John was unaware of the letter and would be furious if he knew about it. But Conney was too much a lady to make an issue of it or mention it to John.

John invited the Fiskes a third time, the next winter. But

by then Gardi Fiske had developed emphysema, as Carl Brandt had, and his health had begun to fail, and his doctors told him he could not go to such a remote place. And so the winter of 1950, like all the happiest and sunniest moments in life and in books, would never happen again.

Chapter Twenty-four

*T*hat winter of 1950 at Treasure Island, John had been working on another Army novel. He had never lost his interest in what he called "the military mind," and now there was a new war, in Korea, which caused John to suspect that there was box-office appeal again in military themes. Ironically, of course, the book that was to become *Melville Goodwin, U.S.A.* was written during a period of great personal serenity in John's life, and perhaps that is why, for a military novel, it seems uncommonly tempered and peaceful. There are few scenes of violence in the novel, and even the conflicts between the characters are muted and civilized. *Melville Goodwin, U.S.A.* is, after all, a novel written by a man who had reached his peak, and knew it, and who had learned to relax and enjoy the quite pleasant life which the years of hard work had earned him. *Melville Goodwin* appears to be a novel written without effort and without pretension, with no bid in it for literary greatness, or even much importance other than to tell a good yarn. With this book, Marquand seems to be saying, "Look, I can do it with no hands!"

There was still another reason why the book was written.

John Marquand's writing career spanned the great years of American magazines, before competition with television caused so many magazine titles that used to dot the newsstands to disappear from the scene. *Collier's, Woman's Home Companion,* and the old *Saturday Evening Post* are only a few of the now extinct magazines which provided writers with their daily bread; in those golden days these magazines paid out huge sums of money to writers like Marquand, Edna Ferber, and Somerset Maugham for serialized fiction. Editors like Ben Hibbs at the *Post,* Herbert Mayes at *Good Housekeeping,* and Bruce and Beatrice Gould of the *Ladies' Home Journal* were given—and spent—huge budgets by their publishers to collect "big" writers' names with which to decorate their covers, and which were intended to spur newsstand and subscription sales. Such expenditures were considered justified as a way to combat the threat of postwar television. At the same time, such furious spending as magazines did in the late 1940s and early 1950s may have helped speed along their demise.

After the publication of *Point of No Return,* Carl Brandt's office had concluded an arrangement with the Goulds and with Hugh McNair Kahler, the *Journal's* fiction editor, whereby John was paid $80,000 for the serial rights to his next and at the time still-unwritten novel. It was a five-figure pig in a poke, but the Goulds must have figured that this investment in the unknown was worth it because they both expressed themselves ecstatic when the deal was closed. John could have copied the alphabet five thousand times and the Goulds, under the terms of the contract, would have had to pay him the money, but of course John was not writing the alphabet, he was writing *Melville Goodwin, U.S.A.* Herbert Mayes had also advanced John a sizable sum of money for a clutch of promised short stories. Though he had become a rich man—John once told Carol about his surprise, on totting things up, at discovering that he had become a millionaire—the fact that he had received a nonrefundable advance of $80,000 on an unwritten book, a sum the book might never approach earning in hard cover, must have made the writing of *Melville Goodwin, U.S.A.* a particularly pleasant and easy-seeming task, or so the book reads.

The book has a bland, straightforward, mature hero, a two-star general who all his life wanted to be a soldier and went into an army career the way his friends went into business, medicine, or law. Once again, his was a small-town boyhood, and, once again, Melville Goodwin fell in love with a beautiful, restless, ambitious, clever, and sophisticated woman who has since married a wealthy publisher, become a widow, and now runs his publishing house. (Carol Brandt had not yet joined her husband's literary agency, but there had been talk, due to Carl's illness, of her doing so.) But Goodwin did not marry the glamorous Dottie Peale (Carol Brandt argued vehemently against naming her Dottie, which she felt sounded all wrong for the character, but John was adamant). Instead, he married Muriel, the Adelaide figure who does her limited best to help plan and run her husband's life. Because he is fifty, General Mel Goodwin is about to be elevated to a solid but unexciting post in the Pentagon, which pleases Muriel but discourages the general. He loves action. And, in Washington, he re-encounters Dottie Peale, falls in love with her all over again, and considers divorcing Muriel, quitting the service, and going off with Dottie to live in Carmel, California.

Thus the triangle and the conflict are set up, and any number of scenes spring to mind which could ensue. Dottie, we assume, will have a confrontation scene with Muriel, Muriel and Mel Goodwin must face each other for a showdown in the arena of love and marriage, and surely some sort of climactic moment is called for when Mel Goodwin and Dottie Peale face the future and each other and decide which way to turn. Alas, John wrote none of these in his novel. Having drawn his battle line clearly in the story, he backed off from it and wound up the narrative in three pallid scenes: one between Goodwin's best friend (the narrator) and Muriel, one between the friend and Dottie, and a final one between the friend and Mel Goodwin himself. There is an unconvincing scene in which Dottie comes to Connecticut to see Goodwin's friend and to tell him tearfully that she never expected the general to marry her anyway, that she doesn't want to marry him either, or anyone else as stuffy and dull as he is, and that she never did have any taste for moving to Carmel. Hard on the heels of this comes a *deus ex machina* in the person of General Douglas MacArthur, who sends orders for Mel Goodwin to join him at his headquarters in Japan—with Korea just across the water—so that Mel Goodwin will have the action he so craved. This, it turns out, is something that Muriel and his friends have been trying to negotiate for him, to keep him happy. There the book ends.

Despite the disappointing conclusion to what might have been a dramatic tale, *Melville Goodwin, U.S.A.* is full of interesting fictional details—details about Army life, the Pentagon, military intrigue, and amusing moments describing Goodwin's best friend's life in a suburban-chic part of lower Connecticut where, by the freakish chance of a resonant speaking voice, the man's enormously successful career as a radio announcer has landed him, almost against his wishes and against his better judgment. And, though its hero is not as interesting as many other Marquand men, the book is never boring. It is also a book which, in writing, as Marquand realized, required the help of an outside researcher, or authority, to bring its author up to date on what had happened to the military life and mind since he had been separated from the Army more than thirty years before. Little, Brown also realized John's need for an editor-collaborator on *Melville Goodwin, U.S.A.*, and for this Stanley Salmen—who had become John's new editor in Boston following the death of Alfred McIntyre—put him in touch with Joseph I. Greene, Colonel, Infantry, Retired, in Washington.

Joe Greene played an important part in the production of *Melville Goodwin, U.S.A.*, but not as important a part as he could have. When he had read the first draft of the book in manuscript, Greene felt that Marquand's main trouble was his depiction of the Pentagon. "Marquand," Greene wrote to Stanley Salmen, "has created a Pentagon that simply never existed. He has somehow carried up into the postwar years a Washington brass and headquarters attitude which has not existed since the Twenties." John had filled his fictional Pentagon with military theoreticians and strategists, men more experienced in desk and laboratory work than in battle, even though, as Greene pointed out, "Hardly anyone has held a high Army office in the Pentagon since 1943 or 1944 who doesn't have a whole chestful of battle ribbons." Marquand had also, Greene felt, made the Pentagon much too stiff and formal, with Army officers calling each other "sir" or using military titles, and he had created a vast social difference between two-, three-, and four-star generals. None of this resembled the real Pentagon, where officers of all rank called each other by their first names and where any general had as much social standing as another.

Marquand was interested in how social divisions are created and maintained and as a young lieutenant in World War I had detected nuances that put officers who were West Point graduates in one class and those who had received their commissions at Officer Training School, or in the field, in another. This degree of difference, which might have existed in 1917, had disappeared long before 1950, Greene pointed out, and non-West Pointers now so heavily outnumbered West Pointers in the United States Army that if any officer tried to high-hat another, on the basis that one had been to the "Academy" and the other had not, he would find himself in serious difficulty. Greene even produced Department of the Army statistics: in 1916, West Pointers outnumbered non-West Pointers by eight to one; by 1945, non-West Point men outnumbered Academy men by fifty to one. John, however, had made nearly every officer in the book a West Point man and had imbued these characters with a strong sense of superiority in both background and performance.

John also had made Melville Goodwin such a thoroughly Army-oriented man that Goodwin hardly ever appeared out of uniform. He wore a full-dress uniform to visit friends in the country and even to call on beautiful Dottie Peale. Joe Greene pointed out that most officers eagerly get into civilian clothes as soon as duty hours are over, and that to behave otherwise made Goodwin look ridiculous. He suggested that John supply Goodwin with some decent civilian suits, cut by the same tailor who would have done Goodwin's uniforms —Brooks Brothers, Morry Luxemburg, or Wilner's in Washington. Joe Greene went on to point out what he felt were flaws in the development of John's characters. "The sexual attraction of Dottie and the (possible) lack of it in Muriel are never sharpened up," he wrote. "In fact, I don't recall much expression or depiction of fondness between Muriel and Mel [a lack of fondness between John and Adelaide might be offered as a reason]. If such attraction didn't exist in Muriel for Mel, a forthright character of his type would very likely have been attracted by other women in the 1920's." Green found it "hard to keep a visualization of Dottie in mind"—a good point, for in this novel particularly John lets his people emerge more through what they say than by descriptions of how they look. And of Muriel he wrote, "She is not direct and overt enough. She is too 'special' in an Army sense that began to disappear 30 years and more ago." The same thing he found true of Mel Goodwin, who "acts too much like a general of 1925." But it was the "illogicalities of background" that he found to be the book's greatest shortcoming, and added, "I would hate to see such a good novel by a first-rate writer appear with unreal people and places in it."

John Marquand, though he needed this sort of detailed criticism—with *Melville Goodwin* in particular—did not always react positively to it. Of Colonel Greene's long memorandum, six pages of tightly single-spaced notes, John told Stanley Salmen that he wasn't much worried by Colonel Greene's comments. John said that he figured he knew the Pentagon pretty well and that it pretty much existed as he said it did; he had been at Washington parties where three- and four-star generals mixed and had observed how, though they might be on a first-name basis, each was careful to pay attention to the other's rank. As for some of the Colonel's other points, those could be fixed without much difficulty. Because John wanted Mel Goodwin in uniform for those specific scenes, he would add a sentence or two explaining that Muriel had given away all Mel's suits while he was overseas; that he had had several nice suits made for himself in Germany, but—in the rush of departure to the States—he had left these suits behind in his quarters in Frankfurt; these suits were being shipped but had not arrived yet. John would also make it clear that with a wife and two growing children Mel Goodwin had never been able to afford suits made up by fancy tailors. Thus, with the flick of his novelist's wrist, did John Marquand cover himself against any sartorial objections that might come from military readers.

As for Colonel Greene's character points, John had no comment. His characters, after all, were his personal property. He would sooner let a stranger look through his bank book than let anyone change a character. For Colonel Greene's trouble, a check went out for $250.

John may have occasionally been careless about detail—or at least stubborn about altering a detail he particularly liked —but he was meticulous about matters that affected his style or the rhythm of his prose. And when the first installments of *Melville Goodwin, U.S.A.* appeared in *Ladies' Home Journal*, John looked them over carefully. Cuts—often quite deep ones —are always made in magazine serialization, but usually novels are pruned by omitting certain scenes or even certain characters from the story. In this case John noticed to his horror that his novel had been cut by having the "he saids" and "she saids" removed from the dialogue. He complained bitterly to Bruce Gould, saying that he had no objection to deep cutting in his manuscripts, even to the elimination of whole scenes or whole characters in order to make a story fit the available space, but that the snipping out of the "saids" ruined the rhythm of his dialogue and made his speech read "like bad Dumas." In future installments would the "saids" please be restored? Bruce Gould apologized, and the "saids" reappeared.

John, in the meantime, was heading for a fracas with another magazine, *Holiday*. *Holiday*'s editors, the late Ted Patrick and Harry Sions, had been making approaches to John for some time about John's writing an article for them. Their approaches had been tentative, and made through delicate feelers to the Brandt office, because John had gained the reputation of having an easily roused temper and a certain amount of artistic temperament. He had become known, in fact, as a writer who was often "crotchety," and what *Holiday* wanted from John was a great deal—for which, due to a smaller budget than the mass-circulation magazines, they were prepared to pay rather little. They wanted a long, definitive article on the city of

Boston, and they felt that no other author in America had made Boston his literary bailiwick more thoroughly than John P. Marquand. From John the *Holiday* editors wanted a piece of journalism that would evoke Boston's special flavor and the special cast of the Bostonian mind, an article that would make readers see, feel, and smell the mustiness of the tufted horsehair sofas in the Somerset Club, hear the sound of the click of teacups on Beacon Hill, the mousy beauty and the haughty pride of the old town. John would furthermore, as they say in show business, have two tough acts to follow. *Holiday* had already published two beautifully written pieces that had become, in a sense, American classics of journalism—William Faulkner's "Mississippi" and E. B. White's haunting evocation of New York City, written from his window on the garden and the sturdy willow tree in Turtle Bay. John's would be a third of these great "place" pieces.

John, though he had pretty much given up writing short stories and articles for magazines, was flattered and intrigued by the idea, and after not too much coaxing from *Holiday* he agreed to write the article. *Holiday* gave him an extremely generous deadline, and after a few months of silence from John on the project, Carl Brandt was able to write Harry Sions, enclosing the manuscript, "Have no worry, pal, it's fine or so I think. And I'm not wish-fulfilling either!" Carl did, however, hedge somewhat by referring to the manuscript of the Boston article as a "first draft." And John had told Carl privately that he had had some difficulty with the article, and some uncertainty about its structure. He had in the beginning used a different lead, then shuffled the pages about and placed the lead, instead, on page ten, adding a new lead to introduce the material that followed. In an uncharacteristically anxious tone, he told Carl that he hoped *Holiday* would like the piece.

Harry Sions, a man known in the publishing world as one not easily satisfied, read John Marquand's Boston and finished it with a sense of bitter disappointment. It seemed to him, frankly, dull, and yet one could not tell a writer of Marquand's stature that his work was dull—not in so many words. Something had to be done to salvage John Marquand's Boston, not only for *Holiday*'s sake, Sions and Patrick agreed, but for the sake of John Marquand's reputation as a writer. Round one had begun.

Cautiously, Harry Sions wrote to Carl that he thought John's article had "the makings of a first-rate story—in fact, a great story, but it will need some fresh material and some changes, especially in the lead." A few days later, he wrote in greater detail:

> We feel that the lead is too slow, too topical and, frankly, too journalistic. . . . One suggestion might be to use the theme of the piece, indicated on page 10, as an idea for a lead—the line that begins with "Boston has been shaken by impacts that may well make strong men weep . . . but it is curious to discover that nothing of its personality has been basically altered yet. It still remains one of the few cities in America with an individuality and flavor entirely its own." We think a lead along those lines would be more effective. . . . In addition, we would like some more intimate material, some more feeling of Mr. Marquand's Boston than now appears in the piece. Perhaps one way of giving the reader this feeling would be to bring people into the piece, people whom Mr. Marquand knows and who would be able to talk about Boston in the language of Boston, the language which Mr. Marquand has been able to interpret with such superb skill. We hesitate to suggest specific types. . . .

John took the piece back—it was sent down to him at Treasure Island—with relatively little grumbling. He had, after all, agreed to revise "within reason." And, within a very short space of time—barely a week, in fact—the Boston article was back on Carl's desk ready to be returned to the *Holiday* people, which Carl did with a note that said, "I think it's much better. Hope you do too."

But Harry Sions did not think it much better. A little better, perhaps, but not much. It was strange; perhaps John was too close to his subject, perhaps too far away—the article had been written, after all, in the gentle breezes of the tropics, a long way from Beacon Hill. The tone of the article was oddly limp and flaccid, leisurely and almost disinterested; the author seemed to be yawning all the way through his subject. And the lead was hardly an exciting stimulus to read on: "Though a large city," the article began, "Boston has many small-town attributes. Everyone seems to know a little about everyone else there, and all good Bostonians are partial to local gossip and anecdote." When compared with the onrush of emotion with which E. B. White opened his New York piece, "On any person who desires such queer prizes, New York will bestow the gift of loneliness and the gift of privacy," Marquand's opening sentences seem very bland.

John knew some wonderful Boston stories and could tell them at a dinner table at the drop of a hat—such as the tale of the proper Boston businessman who, after many long years of toil at the most uninteresting of desk jobs, was about to be retired and was asked by his company what he would like as a gift to compensate him for all his years of loyal service. He could conceivably have asked for a reasonably luxurious gift. The gentleman thought about this for several days and then said that he would like a raincoat. He was given a raincoat. And there was a story John told on himself of how, many years later, he had been asked back to a reunion of former *Boston Transcript* employees. A retired composing-room veteran approached John and reminded him that thirty years earlier, when John had worked at the *Transcript* when just out of Harvard, John had talked of becoming a serious writer. "And what have you been up to since then, Johnny?" the old man asked with a friendly curiosity. John replied that he had been here and there and had also been doing some writing. The old printer clapped the Pulitzer Prize-winning author on the back and said, "Good for you, Johnny! Keep it up!"

But John had used none of this rich Boston material in his article. It greatly lacked personal material that would have brought it—and Boston—to life. From *Holiday*'s standpoint, the article was a great disappointment, and yet to ask an author of Marquand's stature to rewrite *twice* was a thing few editors would dare do. Harry Sions, however, determined to push on undaunted. Writing to Carl, he said that he thought John's revisions had "improved it enormously," but he asked for two things:

We are just a little concerned, in the first half of the piece, whether Mr. Marquand's viewing-with-alarm of the Irish and Italians and other encroaching influences is ironic or real . . . we do think it needs a little more qualification—perhaps a joke or an anecdote or some kind of qualifying paragraph that would avoid the impression that Mr. Marquand is sounding too much like a member of the Somerset Club talking about Curley and Dever. . . . The only other addition we'd like is some kind of reference, spelling out in more detail, the association between Harvard and Boston.

But John replied that he had revised his article as much as he intended.

Holiday now returned to its corner, and all was quiet for several months until the publication date for the article approached. Once again, using Carl Brandt as referee—Sions and Marquand never met, never communicated directly with one another—Harry Sions made a last-ditch attempt to get the kind of story he wanted. In a long teletyped message to Carl from his Philadelphia office, Sions explained his objections. The article, for one thing, was too brief. Sions had wanted at least 7,500 words, "the usual length for our major articles," but John had given him only about 5,000 words. But, said Sions's teletype:

THE CHIEF TROUBLE WITH THE PIECE IS THAT IT SEEMS TO BE WRITTEN OFF THE TOP OF MARQUAND'S HEAD, THAT IT LACKS DEPTH AND PERSPECTIVE. . . . WHAT WE WANT IS MORE DEPTH AND IN-TERPRETATION . . . MATERIAL ON THE CLUBS, LIKE THE ATHENAEUM, THE FAMOUS LIBRARY WHERE YOU CAN ONLY TAKE OUT A BOOK IF YOU ARE A SHAREHOLDER, AND THE SHARES—HANDED DOWN FROM GENERATION TO GENERATION—ARE SOMETIMES SOLD ON MARKET, LATEST PRICE $235 A SHARE. WHAT DO THEY SAY, HOW DO THESE PEOPLE LIVE? HOW HAVE THEY DEVELOPED THE REAL CHARACTER OF BOSTON, PRETTY MUCH THE SAME TODAY, AS MARQUAND POINTS OUT, AS IT WAS IN REVOLUTIONARY TIMES, IN SPITE OF THE IRISH, THE ITALIANS, AND OTHERS WHO HAVE NU-MERICALLY DISPLACED THE BRAHMINS. THAT'S THE REAL STORY OF BOSTON AND WE FEEL IT'S THE STORY OF BOSTON THAT MARQUAND REALLY SHOULD TELL AND KNOWS.

THE PIECE WE HAVE NOW IS A GOOD PIECE BUT HARDLY A DIS-TINGUISHED ONE, AND FRANKLY A SOMEWHAT LAZY ONE. WE KNOW

THAT MARQUAND CAN WRITE A GREAT BOSTON PIECE, EQUAL TO
WHITE ON NEW YORK AND FAULKNER ON MISSISSIPPI, IF HE WILL
TAKE TIME TO THINK IT OUT AND DO SOME MORE REAL DIGGING.

As gently as he could, Carl Brandt sifted these somewhat
harsh comments through his own intelligence and instincts as
an agent and passed a filtered version along to John, saying,
"If you feel you cannot do more to make it better in your eyes,
then that is that. Quite sincerely and although diffidently, they
felt they would be lacking in editorial acumen and good faith
to you and to your and their public if they took the easier
course and did not put to you their conversation. . . . Will you
give it thought? I have a great desire to have the whole profession talk about 'Boston' as they do about 'New York' and
'Mississippi.' "

But John, perhaps feeling that he had earned the right to be
a little lazy, would have no more to do with it, and a few
weeks later Harry Sions wrote to Carl to say, "You have done
everything in your power, both as a good agent and as a good
friend of ours, to try to persuade Mr. Marquand to give us the
great piece on Boston that we feel he can and should write.
However, we have no way of forcing him to make any changes
we suggest, even though we do feel that he is in error."

The Boston article was eventually published, in November,
1953, and created no great stir—not the sort of stir, certainly,
that *Holiday* had hoped for. Most of John's friends in Boston
liked it; perhaps that was why he wrote it the way he did. He
had had enough satiric fun with Boston in *The Late George
Apley* and *H. M. Pulham, Esquire*—the latter of which had
been called a slur on Boston womanhood—so perhaps he felt it
was time to atone for all this with a gentle, noncontroversial,
"nice" little Boston piece. In any case, that was what he had
written. And in the middle of all the commotion that ensued
about it between himself and *Holiday*, he had written to Carl
Brandt to say that never, under any circumstances, was Carl
to agree to have him do an article for *any* magazine, ever again.

He could afford, he felt, to be choosy. With his Little, Brown
royalties being paid on a deferred basis—with a fixed annual
ceiling, for tax purposes—he had amassed quite a sizable

account, something in the neighborhood of $900,000, in Little, Brown's treasury. But no interest was paid on this sum. He brooded about this, until one day Brooks Potter, his lawyer friend, suggested that John might have himself made a director of the publishing house. That way, he could have some say in the company that controlled so much of his funds. John thought that a splendid idea, and at one of the rambling and free-wheeling lunches he liked to have with Arthur Thornhill, Sr., president of the company—lunches sparked with martinis and good cheer—John proposed the directorship possibility to Thornhill. The normally affable face of Arthur Thornhill, a tough-minded, self-made businessman, froze. No mention of that notion was ever made again.

There had, understandably, been few encounters with the Sedgwicks since John's and Christina's 1935 divorce. But when their daughter Christina became engaged to a young history professor named Richard E. Welch, little Tina begged her father to give her away at the wedding, which was to be at the Sedgwick-studded Calvary Church in Stockbridge, hard by the Sedgwick Pie and Sedgwick House, and where Uncle Theodore Sedgwick occasionally preached. Although John liked young Welch—despite the fact that he had committed a much talked about *faux pas* in Boston by showing up at a black-tie dinner at the Somerset Club wearing brown shoes and green socks with his tuxedo—he was reluctant to re-enter the Sedgwick domain and asked Tina please to excuse him. But she persisted, and so he agreed to come to the church services but not to the reception.

After the ceremony—in the same church where he had been married, and where many of the same people who had been at the wedding now sat primly and solemnly in the same pews, looking simply a little older—John tried to slip away. But suddenly there was old Uncle Ellery, of the Magazine, infirm now and walking heavily with a cane, who stepped across the aisle to John and seized his arm. "John," he said, 'Come back to the house with us. I want you to walk with me through the dog cemetery." And so there was nothing to do but go back with the old man into the scented past of the old garden and the little tract set aside for Sedgwick pets, with their tiny stones marked in Latin, animals loved by Sedgwicks for a century and longer. John found himself, after the emotional ordeal of his daughter's wedding, very touched and moved as the two men proceeded slowly among the quiet graves, the older man pointing to this stone, then that, with his cane, commenting on each dog as he went. All at once there was a new grave in front of them, with an American flag implanted next to the headstone, surrounded by a small bed of wax begonias. Uncle Ellery peered at the stone and then read its inscription: "To Tubby, the cutest dog that ever was." Uncle Ellery flung his walking stick at the begonias and cried, "Blasphemy! Blasphemy!"

Chapter Twenty-five

*T*here were more and more long separations from Adelaide —"escapes" he used to call them. John had taken up golf and had been introduced to the golfer's paradise that is Pinehurst, North Carolina. He fell in love with Pinehurst. He loved the loblolly and the longleaf pines that cover the sandhills, and the picturesque little town itself, with its winding, unnamed streets laid out in a pattern deliberately designed to befuddle interlopers who do not belong in this enclave of the secure and wealthy. Pinehurst is cool and green throughout the winter. Camellias blossom in January, and in early spring Pinehurst bursts into riotous color with the blooms of dogwood, azalea, rhododendron, and spring bulbs.

John joined the Pinehurst Country Club, with its famous "ninety holes of golf" on five eighteen-hole courses, and began taking lessons from the club's professional, Harold Callaway. John loved to tell his friends about Callaway's somewhat unorthodox but effective teaching methods, including the Callaway method of mastering the use of the medium iron: "Imagine a fat man bending over in front of you. You've got to swing so the head of the club will go straight up his ass." John commented, "He made it very clear."

John's golf—like his tennis and indeed all his other athletic endeavors—was never very good. He was self-conscious about this and always went out alone, taking with him just a favorite caddy, a venerable black man named Robert Robinson but always called "Hard Rock." Hard Rock would flatter and pamper John and on every shot encourage him with, "Very *good*, Mr. Marquand! Very *good!*" On their walks across the course, Hard Rock would entertain John with tales of how he, in the early days of Fox-Movietone films, had once been a tap dancer, had performed in movies and on radio with the likes of Major Bowes, and had once danced with Gloria Swanson.

Pinehurst had the same appeal for John that Boston had, and for good reason. The resort was developed, in the late nineteenth century, by a Boston millionaire, James W. Tufts, of the same family that donated the land on which Tufts University now stands, and, because of this New England connection, most of the resort's inhabitants have New England roots. The architecture follows suit and is New England in flavor; both the sprawling Carolina Hotel and the Pinehurst Country Club—two of the largest structures in town—might be veranda-ringed hotels on the Maine or New Hampshire coast. Houses are New England Colonial, and modern houses are zoned out. Presently John bought a small Colonial house in Pinehurst called "Nandina Cottage"—too small, really, to accommodate Adelaide and the children (which John considered an important point in his purchase)—just a short distance from the golf course, which had a small apartment for his secretary, Marjorie Davis, above the garage behind the house.

John Marquand the clubman also admired Pinehurst's traditions and institutions, such as the Tin Whistle Club, which he also joined, and which was a men's drinking club so named, according to legend, because a tin whistle had once hung from a tree near the approach to the ninth hole on one of the golf courses. When the whistle was blown, drinks were served. The club's headquarters, aggressively male, were a book-lined room in the one corner of the country club. Then there was a men's bridge club called the Wolves, and John joined that. His bridge was no better than his golf, but he loved to drop over to the little Wolves Clubhouse late in the afternoon to talk to whoever was there and to break up, with his funny and highly gesticulated stories, whatever bridge playing might be going on, just as he could—if not checked—break up Book-of-the-Month Club meetings. At the Wolves Club, the half-joking cry soon came to be, "Well, here comes John Marquand —that's the end of the bridge game." Once when he took young Carl Brandt, Jr., then a student at Harvard, along to the Wolves Club with him, the young man found himself being scrutinized by an elderly and crusty gentleman. "Is it true that they're now letting a lot of Jews into Harvard?" the man wanted to know. (As a resort, Pinehurst has long shown a decidedly anti-Semitic cast.) Carl replied that as far as he knew the old quota system had disappeared from Harvard a long time ago. Muttering, the older man walked away, and John, with a sigh, said to Carl, "Well, you've just cost Harvard twelve million dollars."

But the best thing of all about Pinehurst, perhaps, was that Gardi and Conney Fiske had a house in Southern Pines, less than half a dozen miles away, where Conney wintered her thoroughbred horses.

Adelaide had begun drinking heavily, and when she and John were together there were terrible scenes. When she got drunk at parties, she would come out with vociferous political opinions, loudly stated, and defenses of her position on the America First Committee. When sober, and asked to expand on these opinions—always considerably right of center, po-litically—she could not remember what she had said. There were midnight telephone calls to Carol Brandt when Adelaide would scream at Carol and accuse her of stealing her husband and breaking up her marriage. Although everyone knew of Conney's single-minded devotion to Gardi, Adelaide assumed, as she did of every woman John liked, that Conney Fiske was also having an affair with John and that it had become an accepted thing with the Fiskes just as it had with the Brandts. When John stopped at the Fiskes in Boston to spend an after-noon chatting with Conney and to look in on his ailing old friend, Gardi, who was then gravely ill, under sedation much

of the time, and with round-the-clock nurses, Adelaide said to
John when he came home, "I don't see how you can make
love to your best friend's wife in the drawing room while he is
dying in a bedroom upstairs!" Or so John told Carol Brandt.

Once, when John was staying at the Brandts' Fifth Avenue
apartment, Adelaide telephoned late at night and demanded to
speak to her husband. Carl, who had picked up the phone, explained that John had gone out to walk the Brandts' poodle,
Beau, and would not be back for perhaps fifteen or twenty
minutes. Adelaide said, "Give him just one message. He won't
walk *my* dog, and tell him he can walk that poodle of yours
around and around and around the block until they both drop
dead!"

Marjorie Davis was similarly under suspicion as a love interest. John avoided these confrontations in a characteristic
way, by walking away from them and searching for places
where Adelaide wasn't. "Nandina Cottage"—though John
thought the name ridiculous—became one of these refuges.
Life at Pinehurst settled into a pleasant routine. Day began
with breakfast in bed, served by Floyd Ray, his chauffeur-
houseman who had formerly worked for John's Pinehurst
neighbor, General George Marshall (about whom John was
always asking questions), and whose wife, Julia, had become
John's cook. Then there were a few hours spent dictating to
Marjorie, then down the road to a few holes of golf at the
club with Hard Rock, followed by drinks at the Tin Whistle
and lunch at the club. After lunch, John read and edited what
he had dictated that morning, penciling in corrections before
final-typing, then strolled over to the Wolves for a rubber of
bridge and an afternoon drink. Then, perhaps, dinner with
the Fiskes, in their pleasantly child-free, well-staffed, and well-
run house, or with one or another of the comfortably-off
couples who wintered in Pinehurst, such as the John Tucker-
mans of Boston, the Wallace Simpsons, the George Shearwoods,
the Donald Parsons—he was writing a book on bridge, and
John offered to do an introduction—or the John Ostroms.
John Ostrom's pretty wife, Kitty, was a talented interior decorator, and when John, referring to a previous decorator, wailed
to Kitty Ostrom, "Miss Pleasants has painted me entirely in ice

blue," Kitty Ostrom took on the job of helping him redecorate. From time to time the Brandts, either separately or together, sometimes bringing one or the other of their two children, came down to Pinehurst to visit him.

John was working on another novel. It would be about a businessman again, and it would even return to Charles Gray's fictional home town of Clyde. In an odd way this was to be a return to *Point of No Return*, which so many critics had called his best book. Critical reaction to *Melville Goodwin, U.S.A.* had been cool, led once more by the man who seemed to have become John's chief critical enemy, Maxwell Geismar. (When he could bring himself to mention it, John turned the pronunciation of the word "Geismar" into a hideous snarl.) Geismar had complained:

> The whole point about Melville Goodwin as an angry officer is that his code of behavior is honest. He believes in his career completely and puts it to the test in the field of combat. A good man if kept in his place; but is this the only possible solution for the problem of belief in a commercial society without established forms of tradition? It might have taken more guts, a word which Marquand's General approves of . . . if Melville Goodwin himself had really gone through with his disastrous affair with Dottie Peale. But in the struggle with "authority" that runs through Marquand's work, authority, even if stale or false, always wins. The soldier's code is a logical refuge for his disgruntled bankers and despairing playwrights.

Once more Geismar was asking for a novel different from the one that John had written and had missed the point that lies at the heart of most of John's novels. Geismar wanted Marquand heroes to revolt, to turn their backs on "authority"—or at least the confines of their situations—and emerge, at the end, triumphant over their circumstances. But Marquand wrote novels of defeat and compromise, where the "system" or set of systems is always, in the end, too much for the individual. This is not an unfamiliar point of view in American fiction and can be found in the novels of Hemingway, Fitzgerald, Faulkner, and Wolfe as well. Geismar seemed to feel that the Marquand philosophy of the unbeatable system, expressed in novels of failure or semifailure, was wrong, and therefore faulted the novels for it. Of course Marquand heroes always have something to fall back on, some small thing to shore up against the ruins. In Melville Goodwin's case it was the "soldier's code," which he had believed in since his childhood, along with the belief that the Army might be the last place in America where you could find a gentleman.

Marquand books, however, were by 1951, when *Melville Goodwin, U.S.A.* was published, immune to bad reviews; they were critic-proof. John had a fond and loyal public that had grown with him through the years, and *Melville Goodwin* sold extremely well, boosting his income, in the year following publication, to well over $100,000. There had also been the lucrative magazine serialization, and there was lively interest in Hollywood for a film version of the novel, though no deal had yet been reached. In 1952, Philip Hamburger of *The New Yorker* spent considerable time with John, in New York and in Newburyport, preparing a three-part profile for the magazine, and when it appeared it turned out that Hamburger— who had noticed instantly the fictive quality of John's life, the way he "wrote" scenes and situations and dialogue for himself —had written a parody of a John Marquand novel. Titled *J. P. Marquand, Esquire,* it neatly and gently mocked the celebrated honeyed Marquand style, the satiric touches, the tongue-in-cheek chapter titles, and of course the long central flashback around which every Marquand novel is constructed. John was flattered and delighted with the profile and quickly wrote Hamburger to tell him so. Later published by Bobbs-Merrill as a book, *J. P. Marquand, Esquire* was cheered by critics, one of whom wrote, "Mr. Hamburger's 'novel' bursts into flower as a brilliant piece of biography. The author imitates the Marquandian mood and style so effectively that he gives the impression Marquand might have written the book himself."

Little, Brown, in the meantime, had begun talks with Marquand about a book that might be called *Thirty Years,* a collection of his short stories, articles, and speeches spanning roughly that period of time in his career, interspersed with his own comments on his craft. It was, in other words, a period in John's life when everything seemed to be going well—too well, perhaps, to suit a restless nature that thrived on drama and impending crisis.

One thing that was not going well was the new novel, about the businessman whom John had named Willis Wayde. It was going much too slowly, and John was unhappy with it. Ed Streeter had read portions of the manuscript and had offered suggestions, but in the meantime John's stomach had been troubling him, and once more he was convinced he had an ulcer. In the late spring of 1953 he spent close to two weeks at Presbyterian Hospital in New York, undergoing a series of tests and X rays which revealed an "ulcerous condition" but no frank or apparent ulcer. Somewhat to John's disappointment, his doctor, Dana Atchley, pronounced his problems largely psychosomatic. John blamed them, of course, on Adelaide.

With Carol Brandt he became increasingly reminiscent, liking to dwell on past episodes and pleasures. "We would talk about the old days in Paris and Maule," she recalls, "and the afternoon eating ice cream at Walden Pond, when we discussed our respective marital difficulties and were half in love with each other even then, but would not or could not admit it. What would have happened to us, we used to wonder, if we had said to each other what we really thought of saying, as we ate that wretched ice cream? What if we had admitted that we were both having a rotten time and both had become badly fouled up in our personal problems? What if we had said, 'If things get too bad for either of us let's try to see each other?' Something might have removed that strange repression that used to stand between us. We each might have reached the conclusion that the other might not have minded, and in fact might rather have enjoyed it. As it was, on our way back he never ventured so much as to touch my hand, although I cannot say that the idea did not occur to us in a very forceful way. Perhaps he was afraid that this would have shocked me, which shows how well he used to understand women and himself. In fact he never did do such a thing until some fifteen years later, though through all that lapse of time we increasingly cared for and depended upon each other.

"Of course he was always criticizing me, and reminding me

that there were many things about me which he did not
admire. He didn't think much of my literary taste, or of most
of my clients, or of their output. He thought I was too ma-
terialistic, too concerned with power. He disliked my taste in
furniture, which, he said, was too Chippendale for him. He
claimed to prefer worn carpets and frayed upholstery. He said
I was too concerned with 'gracious living,' and that I put too
much wax on my furniture and too much polish on my silver.
He told me that he didn't much care for my 'fox and mink
and sable jobs' either, although he said that they had 'a definite
comedy value.' He had an aversion to large pieces of costume
jewelry, especially my large bracelets and brooches which he
claimed scratched, and had 'combination locks' on them making them difficult to remove. He complained that I used too
much lipstick and he would speak of my 'long sang de boeuf
fingernails,' and he didn't like girdles either. Of course he used
to admit that I had qualities to offset these 'defects,' but he
would say, 'I haven't time to name them now.' But he also
told me once that I was the only woman who had been completely 'satisfactory' to him in every way. He admitted that
this was not a very poetic way of putting it, that it was rather
like describing an automobile or a washing machine, but he
knew that one of the most precious things about our relationship was that neither of us felt the need to resort to poetry.
He knew that nothing he might say or do would in any great
measure alter the opinion I held for him, and that this was
much the same with me. There was no need to create a good
impression. By the time we came together, neither of us had
many cards left up our sleeves. Most of the deck was face up
on the table, and we were each glad to take a card, any card.
The main thing, he said, was that I was the only person he
could think of who had never let him down."

Carl Brandt went up to Kent's Island to visit John that early
summer of 1953, read 630 pages—tripled-spaced—of the new
novel that was in progress, and wrote to Carol that he thought
it was "swell" and that "He's got revision and cutting to do
but it won't take him long. . . . I think I can get it to 60,000
words of elegant stuff." Carl also noted that Kent's Island con-

tained "less mosquitoes, cool, and much less tension between Adelaide and John." There was a big clambake with a hole dug in the ground, a barrel sunk into it, and fire-heated stones placed in the barrel and covered with wet seaweed. Bushels of clams, corn, sweet potatoes, and halved lobsters in cottonseed sacks were placed on the seaweed, and more seaweed was placed on top of the sacks. John, Adelaide, Carl, and all five of John's children— Johnny, Tina, Ferry, Timmy, and Lonnie —along with Mr. and Mrs. Ricker, John's caretakers at Kent's Island, all had a wonderful party.

On June 11, John went down to Cambridge to receive an honorary degree from Harvard. It amused him, in a grim way, to realize that the universities of Maine and Rochester, Northeastern University, and even Yale had honored him with degrees before his own alma mater got around to it. The possibility of a snub was always there; Harvard's tardiness with a degree reinforced his own sharply divided feelings about the place, and he used the occasion to have a bit of fun at Harvard's expense. Though his acceptance speech at the commencement exercise was an effective one, he drew laughter when he recited the long list of subjects he had diligently studied at Harvard, and about which he had retained no knowledge at all; though he had studied calculus at Harvard he could not answer his thirteen-year-old daughter Ferry's simple question about algebraic fractions, and though he had majored in chemistry he could not help ten-year-old Lonnie assemble his Christmas fun-with-chemistry set. The commencement address was criticized by some Harvardites as being not sufficiently solemn for the occasion.

After the ceremony, there was a procession from the tent to the Widener Library. John, in cap and flowing gown, was walking with Ed Streeter when he suddenly said, "There's Senator Kennedy ahead of us, walking alone," and stepped over to the young John F. Kennedy, leaving Streeter, "Like a flower girl walking behind them, poking my head between the shoulders of the two celebrities."

But through all this John continued to complain that he felt unwell, blaming his condition on "certain environmental stresses," which meant Adelaide. In mid-July, John was suddenly seized with an excruciating pain in his chest. He was rushed to Anna Jacques Hospital in Newburyport, where it was diagnosed that he had suffered a coronary thrombosis. Carl Brandt wired from New York:

JUST HEARD THAT YOU PLAYED TOO MUCH GOLF. HAVEN'T I TOLD YOU THAT WE ARE BOTH IN OUR DECLINING YEARS. WE SHOULD DECLINE SERIOUS ATHLETICS. ASK ADELAIDE OR MISS BAKER TO LET ME KNOW ANYTHING YOU WOULD LIKE OR WANT DONE. HAPPILY COME UP TO SEE YOU SHOULD YOU WISH IT. THREE WEEKS VACATION AWAY FROM THE WORLD SOUNDS WONDERFUL TO ME. KEEP EM FLYING KID. LOVE

CARL

PART THREE

*T*he Ending

Chapter Twenty-six

*N*aturally John held Adelaide fully accountable for the heart attack. There had been no real easing of tensions between the embattled partners in this failing marriage which, at this point, had managed to survive for sixteen years. So bitterly did John feel about Adelaide now that he left instructions that she was under no circumstances to be admitted into his hospital room, and, when it was possible for him to be moved back to the house at Kent's Island, the servants were ordered to keep Adelaide off the property. Adelaide was in the meantime off buying that new house for the family at 1 Reservoir Street in Cambridge. But there had been other "environmental stresses" on John than Adelaide. Just a year earlier, Christina had died of cancer. Though they had been virtually estranged, there was, when John learned of her illness, a tender meeting at her bedside and a reconciliation of sorts.

To ease the tedium of the long recuperative period, Stanley Salmen arranged to have a series of microfilmed books delivered to John's hospital room. These could be projected on the ceiling above the hospital bed, while the patient lay immobile, and the "pages" turned automatically. In this fashion, John caught up with such titles as *Drums Along the Mohawk, The African Queen,* and *Abigail Adams.* After three weeks in the hospital and away from all visitors, John was allowed to get out of bed and walk back and forth across the room three times a day. Adelaide and the two younger boys were returning to Aspen, and John had begun to make plans to return to Kent's Island with Ferry for company. Later in the autumn, if all went well, he wanted to take a short holiday at some quiet place with Carl and Carol Brandt.

Of his five children, John had always got along best with the two girls, Tina and Ferry; with Tina off and married, John had become devoted to little Ferry. He loved to tell stories about her. Once, he told Herb Mayes, Ferry had used a dirty word in front of him and had waited to see what its effect on him would be. John had told her to get a pencil and a piece of paper and said, "I know as many dirty words as you do. I know more of them than you do. In fact, I know *all* of them. Now, I am going to tell you all of them, and you are going to write them down." He then told her all the dirty words, and she wrote them all down. John said, "Now, if I ever hear you use one of those words, you'll wish you'd never been born."

He considered Ferry a particularly bright child and, remembering how his old aunts at Newburyport had drilled the scriptures and the classics into him as a youth, he once said to Ferry, "I'll give you twenty-five dollars if you'll read the Bible, let me ask you ten questions about it, and answer them correctly." Ferry agreed, and some weeks later came to him and told him she had completed her reading and was ready for the questions. John composed ten reasonable questions, and she answered them all correctly. John gave her the money and then said, "Now that you've read it, what did you think of the Bible as a reading experience?" She said, "Daddy, I hate to tell you this, but I think most of it is pretty crappy."

The sheer fact of the heart attack was in itself a terrible shock for John, bringing with it as it did whispers of mortality and reminders that there was, indeed, so little time. But John did his best to face it with good spirit. One of his Newburyport neighbors, calling at Kent's Island soon after John's return home, reported that after a few minutes' talk John had suddenly leapt out of bed and, in his pajamas, had seized an antique sword that hung on his bedroom wall, unsheathed it from its scabbard, and, striking a John Barrymore pose, announced in his booming voice, "Death—thus do I defy you!"

Some months later, when he was able to get down to New York, novelist Louis Auchincloss recalls meeting Marquand at a party at the Thomas K. Finletters'. John was back in his old form, swinging his glass in his hand as he entertained his audience, holding forth on what he called "the lack of taste and reticence" in younger American writers. A few minutes later, he was talking about his weeks in the Newburyport hospital and how, as part of his therapy, an abdominal massage had been prescribed. His nurse, John confided, had whispered to him during the procedure, "How lucky I am to be able to manipulate the lower abdominal muscles of a man like you!" One of the guests at the gathering was the New York *grande dame* Mrs. August Belmont. When Marquand had finished this anecdote, Mrs. Belmont inquired, "And where, Mr. Marquand, was the taste and reticence in that remark?"

Carl and Carol Brandt had, in the meantime, made their autumn trip to see him. They had gone to the Ritz, and the visit had included the memorable guided tour of Adelaide's house in Cambridge, the house John swore he would never inhabit. But Adelaide was stubborn and, perhaps more than anything else, wanted to be Mrs. John P. Marquand. John continued to ask her to give him a divorce, but she would not, and now, after his recovery, there were tearful entreaties and begging letters; they must, she insisted, try to save their marriage. And so John once again relented and moved into 1 Reservoir Street, where life became more chaotic and destructive than ever before. Lillian Hellman recalls one strenuous evening:

"I had gone up to Boston, to lecture as I recall, and there was a party afterward and both John and Adelaide were there. I had met him only once before, a number of years earlier, at the George Kaufmans' house, when the two were working on 'Apley.' I hadn't liked him much that first time. He seemed —I don't know, rather snippy. I had just come back from Russia, and everybody was asking me about my trip, and I felt that Marquand rather liked the center of the stage and this time he wasn't getting it. Anyway, this second time in Boston he made a great fuss over me, and I enjoyed that, and that made me like him better. He insisted that we leave the party and go back to their house in Cambridge, and so I did. It was a hideous house. It completely bewildered me. It was hideous in the most hideous way, as though it had been deliberately made hideous—hideous on purpose, as though the people who lived in it had worked to make it as ugly as possible, and thought that this made it cute, or amusing. It didn't. The living room was like a huge, dark Victorian ballroom. Upstairs, there was a bathroom with a huge sunken bathtub with steps going down into it. John, showing me the house, kept saying wasn't it dreadful, wasn't it awful?—and this disturbed me, puzzled me. The evening left me with so many unpleasant impressions. One of the little boys, I forgot which, was running about. Adelaide was drunk. She seemed just—a slob. John insisted that we go and wake up Ferry, though it was quite late, after midnight. He said that Ferry had just read 'The Children's Hour' and would be so disappointed not to meet me, though I'm not sure I believe that. We went up to Ferry's room, and I remember that Ferry had written on her wall, 'Down with God, Up with Allah!' and that amused me. It was quite clear that John was enchanted with Ferry. She was twelve or thirteen. I kept having the feeling that Ferry was being used somehow in a power struggle between John and Adelaide. It was a very unpleasant evening, and I came away with the impression of terribly unhappy people, leading crazy lives, in that demented house."

It was strange, in the case of the Cambridge house, how as Adelaide herself deteriorated so did her taste in interior decoration. She had taken their first apartment, at 1 Beekman Place, and done it tastefully and beautifully, filling it with fine old English and American antiques, turning it—many of their friends thought—into one of the prettiest apartments in New York. But later had come the Hobe Sound house, furnished with maids' furniture because she thought it was "cute." "Cute" and "cunning" were two of her favorite words. And now there was this monstrosity at 1 Reservoir Street, which, indeed, she did seem to find cute in its monstrousness. Carol had helped John decorate several rooms of the ever-growing Kent's Island house, and Adelaide, on first seeing Carol's touches in the Kent's Island entrance hall, had exclaimed to Mr. Berry, one of the caretakers, "It looks just like the anteroom to a whore house!"

The Book-of-the-Month Club, in the meantime, meant more than an occupation, a salary, and—as he discovered after the heart attack—a welcome source of free medical insurance. It was a consolation in itself, for it helped keep his mind off more depressing matters. John loved to read, and he loved the monthly meetings, which were always stimulating and convivial—bright people, good conversation, in pleasant surroundings, always including drinks and lunch. The meetings were held in the big handsome office of the board chairman, the late Harry Scherman, which overlooked the Hudson River to the west and the towers of Manhattan to the north; oysters on the half shell were served during the "R" months, and there was always a good wine with the meal. The other judges and officers—Dr. Henry Seidel Canby, Clifton Fadiman, Amy Loveman, Christopher Morley, and Meredith Wood, the president of the club—provided a perfect audience for John's mimicry and wit, which ran to the caustic and derisive and was thus at its best when John was decrying a book of which he thought little. He had a particular loathing for costumed or bosomy melodramas, where the men carried flintlocks and the women wore bombazine or poke bonnets, and he detested reading about cheerful peasants and cherub-faced children. "Why, they're all so goddamned healthy it's positively painful!" he would cry, swinging his glass in circles and twisting his face into an expression of utter revulsion. John Mason Brown once described the performances of his fellow judge:

> Others might review a book in reviewers' terms. Not he. His opinions often took the form of snatches from spoken novels, complete with improvised bits of dialogue, in the manner of the writer being discussed, emphasizing his merits or his weaknesses. . . . With John overstatement was a game which all of us at the Book-of-the-Month-Club looked forward to having him play. John would moan with outrage. His right hand would

reach for his chin and swing his head to one side in agony. His blue eyes would freeze with mock anguish. He would howl to the deity. His contempt, part feigned, part real, would erupt into the brief standbys of eloquent dismissal. These outbursts were grand sport and play-acting of which W. C. Fields would have been proud.

Dr. Canby, the chairman of the panel of judges, always tried to lead their discussions, but sometimes it was difficult when John's demonstrations and imitations had the other judges choking on their cutlets and gasping with laughter. "Now, John," the scholarly Dr. Canby would say crisply, "you're being *too* funny."

The Book-of-the-Month Club not only got John away from Adelaide; it got him away from his study and his typewriter and what he always called the writer's "lonely world" of fiction and out into the world of living human beings. There was more to the Book-of-the-Month Club job than reading and attending meetings. The judges also frequently had to deal personally with touchy and temperamental authors, and often these dealings required diplomacy and tact, both of which John was usually capable of summoning. When Allen Drury's first novel, *Advise and Consent,* was submitted, the judges liked the book very much but felt that it was over-long and could be improved by cutting. It fell to John to explain the club's feelings to Drury and to try to get him to do some blue-penciling. John invited Drury to his house in Pinehurst for the week end and, over the course of it, mentioned several places in the novel where the club felt cutting should be done. Drury promised to think this over. A few days later, Drury wrote to John, thanking him for the week end but saying, sadly, that he simply could not cut his book. Nonetheless, he added, it was good to know that his book had come so close to being a Book-of-the-Month Club choice. John loved to tell that story because Drury's book already *was* a Book-of-the-Month Club selection —and would be with or without the cuts—though Drury hadn't realized it.

Not all such encounters had pleasant endings. When Edna Ferber's big novel about Texas, *Giant,* came to the club, the judges admired the book but again felt strongly that it badly needed cutting. Miss Ferber was a novelist who had already gained considerable fame in literary circles for her temper, temperament, and knife-edged tongue, and so it was decided that the two best-looking male judges should arrange to call on Miss Ferber at her Park Avenue apartment to apprise her of the club's views and try to persuade her to the club's position. Without question, the two males would *not* be bearded Morley or stringy Canby. That left Fadiman and Marquand.

The two men made their appointment with Miss Ferber and, after being ushered into the formidable presence of the authoress and spending twenty minutes or so in polite social chitchat, brought up, as delicately as either man knew how, the subject of cutting. Miss Ferber flew into a rage in which she attacked not only the Book-of-the-Month Club but the two men themselves, their talents as writers, their tastes as judges, and their intelligence as people. Finally, after this had gone on for some time, it all became too much for John, who rose, stiffly and formally, and said, "Miss Ferber, I don't see anything to be gained by our staying here any longer. You've been kind to receive us. The only thing I might add is that I, unlike you, in my professional career, have always been grateful, even if I did not accept their advice, to anyone who took the time and the trouble to read my books and give me any comments and criticism when the books were in manuscript form." The two men then departed.

Edna Ferber eventually did make a few cuts in her manuscript, though nowhere near as many as the club wanted, thereby allowing John Marquand, when he told the story, to indulge himself in the quip that "We got just so far and no Ferber."

And of course, at the end of the day, there was always the possibility of dinner with Carol at the St. Regis. "During the years of our affair, I think John and I occupied every civilized suite in that hotel," Carol says now, with a little smile.

Chapter Twenty-seven

*D*uring the months following the heart attack, John devoted himself to the pleasant and not very wearing task of selecting and gathering together certain of his shorter pieces, which Little, Brown wanted to place in a book under the title *Thirty Years* and which were to provide a catholic sampling of an author's work over the span of roughly a generation. Most of these pieces—fiction and nonfiction—had been previously published in a range of magazines, but John also wanted to include some of his unpublished writing—his Harvard commencement address, for example, and one of several papers he had prepared for oral delivery before Newburyport's Tuesday Night Club, a venerable literary institution of that city. John took his membership in the Tuesday Night Club with great seriousness and worked on these papers, for which he was paid nothing, with as much care and diligence as he did on his novels. He also took a certain amount of quiet satisfaction from the fact that the club's meetings were frequently held at the High Street house of old Mr. L. P. Dodge, the Newburyport worthy to whom John had come years ago to plead for—and to be refused—the Harvard Club scholarship. John enjoyed the neatness of such little ironies.

Putting together *Thirty Years* was a somewhat unsettling experience for John Marquand, providing him as it did with the not altogether welcome opportunity to reread a great deal of his own work that had been written almost a generation earlier. He told Stanley Salmen that he honestly believed he had become a better writer and craftsman over the years, and that many of his early stories were "brash and immature." Some of the early material struck him as downright awful. It seemed to him, he told Salmen, that he had written too many stories about Honolulu, about China, and about U.S. Army generals. Perhaps, he suggested, it would be helpful if someone else could write an introduction or foreword to the collection, in which it could be pointed out that this was not intended as a gathering of superb stories and articles but, instead, a roughly chronological depiction of a writer's development and growth. He suggested that his friend and fellow Book-of-the-Month Club judge, Clifton Fadiman, might be willing to write such a preface. To write it himself, Marquand pointed out, seemed a touch "ungraceful."

Salmen approached Fadiman, who was delighted with the idea. He not only agreed to write an introduction, adding, "It can be long or short, casual or friendly or more seriously analytical—whatever you wish. Naturally, one kind of introduction will take more time and effort than another," but he also, as a former editor (at Simon & Schuster and later at *The New Yorker*), had a number of specific criticisms of the various Marquand pieces to offer. One story, for example, he felt was "too forced," another "just a little too slight and, though charming, a bit conventional," and of another he said, "Don't pay any attention to me—stories of Southern honor and chivalry just bore me; I prefer John in his more modern moods." The controversial *Holiday* article on Boston Fadiman was less than sanguine about. But John—perhaps simply to spite Harry Sions—was insistent that it be included; it was his way of asserting that he was proud of the article, regardless of what anyone said.

Perhaps Fadiman's most important contribution was to propose a pattern for the book—that is, a scheme by which the articles and short stories could be arranged that would not be chronological, in terms of when they were written, but instead under categories such as "School and College," "The Wars," and "Local Flavor." This idea was a great help in pulling the book together. Fadiman also wrote an introduction that was both kind and candid, pointing out that many of the stories were "tailored to meet the needs of the market," and that the ending of "The End Game" might be a "secretly ironical bow to the bright tin divinity of the Happy Ending." Fadiman also noted the "laboratory accuracy" with which Marquand's fiction noted "a hundred tiny differences of caste and class," and praised the "absolute rightness" of Marquand's dialogue, asking, ". . . can any contemporary American novelist other than Hemingway touch Marquand for dialogue?" Fadiman was also the first critic to point out that what lay behind the celebrated clear and honeyed and unrushed Marquand style was perhaps what lay at the heart of his great appeal: It was his special way of mixing merriment and melancholy, of taking nostalgia and a bittersweet contemplation of *temps perdu,* and adding grace notes of humor, of being mocking and yet tender toward a past when snows were probably whiter and loves were certainly younger and stronger. This is the particular Marquand emotional stance and the secret of his charm. As Fadiman put it, "He is at once outsider and insider. He is the sympathetic dramatizer of that moment of doubt—the doubt as to whether outer or inner security necessarily coincide—which, though it comes to all of us, is the particular gadfly of the gentility."

Meanwhile, *Sincerely, Willis Wayde,* the businessman-hero novel that John had been writing at the time of the heart attack, continued to move along, but slowly. John told Stanley Salmen that although he had written about 325 pages, his hero was still only in the Harvard Business School. This meant that quite a lot of cutting would have to be done. John had, however, already received another big advance from *Ladies' Home Journal,* on terms much the same as had been offered for *Melville Goodwin, U.S.A.,* so there was no need to apply undue pressure on the manuscript. He had started the book in the summer of 1952, and it was not until November of 1954 that the *Journal* was able to publish the first installment of the serial. It was quickly apparent that John Marquand was once again concerning himself with "differences of caste and class," the unbridgeable social gap between "sincere"—and doggedly ambitious—Willis Wayde, son of a machinist, and the aristocratic Harcourts, leading citizens of Clyde and possessors of ancient wealth whom Willis Wayde aspires to be like; in particular, the difference that separates Willis from old Henry Harcourt's spoiled and beautiful granddaughter, Bess.

Some reviewers had complained that John Marquand never seemed to like his heroes very much—bumbling, hoodwinked, cuckolded Harry Pulham; pompous, provincial George Apley; down-the-line-military, hard-nosed Melville Goodwin. This critical point is acceptable if, to be acceptable, heroes in fiction must also be likable and, if this is the case, *Sincerely, Willis Wayde* must be considered an unsuccessful book. Without doubt, Willis Wayde was John's most dislikable hero yet.

Young Willis Wayde has no taste for sports, for girls, for social life; his push is only for business success, and he goes after this with a single-minded disregard for other people and other things. His father warns him, "You keep on trying to be something you aren't, and you'll end up a son of a bitch. You can't help being, if you live off other people." Keep in your own place, in other words, and stick to your own kind. "People are divided into two parts," his father says, "people who do things and the rest, who live off those who do things. Now I may not amount to much, but . . . I can do anything in that damn mill that anyone else can do, and they all know it, boy. Well, maybe you'll spend your life living off other people's doings, but if you have to, don't fool yourself. Maybe you'll end up like Harcourt. I don't know. But you'll never *be* like Harcourt." Willis Wayde has a carefully cultivated veneer of niceness, and a surface charm. But under the polish that he has acquired solely to help him get ahead, it is difficult to see what sort of a person Willis Wayde is. He is not only a repugnant but a hollow character. When Willis and his wife run into Bess Harcourt and her husband at the same restaurant and Willis extends his hand in cheerful greeting, Bess Harcourt orders him out of her way, and when Willis protests Bess says, "Get out, Uriah Heep."

Another trouble with *Sincerely, Willis Wayde* was that it was impossible not to compare it with the earlier *Point of No Return*. *Point of No Return,* when it appeared in 1949, not only seemed a highly original work but it also had a strong point of departure—a whole generation of bright young men whose lives had been deeply scarred by war and who had returned full of questions and uncertainties and anxieties about the values which, before the war, had seemed so settled and sure. Was success in business worth the candle? The novel's haunting questions and uncertain answers captured the imaginations of young men—and their wives—all over America, giving the book great pertinence and meaning. But now, half a dozen years later, these questions not only seemed not so fresh but not so pressing. Willis Wayde's problems seemed less interesting than had Charles Gray's.

And there was still another problem. *Point of No Return* had, in a very real sense, created a fictional genre, and there had since been a number of imitators. In 1952, Cameron Hawley's *Executive Suite* had appeared, and he had followed this with another businessman novel, *Cash McCall*. Although *Executive Suite* was much less expertly written than *Sincerely, Willis Wayde*, it told a considerably more exciting story, causing Marquand's novel again to suffer by comparison. Hawley's hero's struggles through the jungles of big-company management are accompanied by corporate intrigue, strife, and setbacks, whereas Willis Wayde's journey to the top appears to carry him serenely through an uninterrupted string of successes.

The beautiful and haughty Bess Harcourt, whom Willis loves and loses, seems more a plot device than a character. Willis, according to the Marquand code, *must* lose Bess because of the unalterable difference in their backgrounds, but for the first time in a Marquand novel this necessity rang somewhat false, and it seemed to some readers as though Willis might have won Bess if he had unbent a little, let his hair down just a bit, been a trifle less stiff and humorless. Or was it possible that the social dividing lines John had stressed so often in his novels over the years were beginning to disappear in America, and that *that* was what made the inevitability of Willis's losing Bess a bit difficult to credit? In any case, the character of Sylvia, Willis's wife, is much better drawn. And it is she who by the end of the book—as so many previous Marquand characters had done— realizes that her husband is what he is and she had better accept it. It is she who makes the Marquandian compromise.

As the novel progresses—through, to be sure, some interesting and well-detailed episodes of corporate life—the cold genius of Willis Wayde grows even colder. It is almost as though, in developing his story, John Marquand grew to like Willis less and less. Edward Weeks, whose critical opinions John did not always care for, mentioned this fact to John after the book's hard-cover release in 1955, saying that Willis Wayde "had started out as a rather appealing young man, and wound up as a truly disgusting individual." John's first reaction was surprise, and then, after thinking about it for a moment, he said, "You know, you're right. He turned out to be a real stinker, didn't he?" The book did not achieve a movie sale, though it did become the basis of a television play, several years later.

Meanwhile, negotiations had been going on since 1950 between the Brandt office in New York and Famous Artists, who represented the Brandts in Hollywood, to obtain a motion picture sale on *Melville Goodwin, U.S.A.* John Marquand's career reached its peak not only during the last of the glorious days when mass magazines were paying out huge sums of money for serialized novels but also during the even more glorious days when movie companies were paying even bigger figures for novels to be made into films. Again, the furious movie spending on fiction properties during the postwar decade—also intended to combat television—may have helped motion picture companies into the doleful state they found themselves in by the late 1960s. But in the meantime nearly every one of John's big books—plus the Mr. Moto stories that had become a whole series of movies—had been bought and made into motion pictures, much to the enlargement of John's already large bank account.

Because of the sums he had received for *Apley, Pulham,* and *B. F.'s Daughter,* John had at first set a price on *Melville*

Goodwin that both Carl and Ray Stark, at Famous Artists, considered too high. He wanted $200,000. Also, he hadn't wanted any studio to see the book until it appeared in hard cover, on the theory that the studio should judge the book by its full and final version, not by the cut version that was to be serialized by *Ladies' Home Journal.* But Carl pointed out that as soon as the *Journal* installments began the studios would prepare their own synopses of the book, and that it would be far better if John could have his own synopsis prepared and shipped out to Hollywood as soon as possible. John agreed, and Carl prepared a three-page synopsis—something he was good at—and sent it to Stark.

Stark, who was delighted with the synopsis, then proposed, as he put it, "to cook up a little intrigue with this situation, and have Marquand send a little note saying that under no conditions must any studio see the synopsis, but if Darryl Zanuck saw it personally, but was not given a copy to keep, that John didn't mind Mr. Zanuck reading it in the presence of you or me. I really think this could be an important hunk of strategy, Carl." Stark also suggested that the same bit of strategy—dangling the bait in front of the big producer's nose, yet not letting him keep it for copying and circulation around the studio—could be worked with Stanley Kramer.

But, a few weeks later, it was necessary for Ray Stark to report back to Carl that neither Zanuck nor Kramer had nibbled. There was another problem. Metro-Goldwyn-Mayer had just bought a story titled "The Day the General Returns" ("or something to that effect," as Stark explained to Carl), and it suddenly seemed as though Hollywood had become awash with Army general stories. And so the *Melville Goodwin* synopsis began its long, slow round from studio to studio, with brief flashes of interest here and there—sparks that glimmered for a day or so, then died—and the months turned into years, with still no sale. John became discouraged, then resigned to the fact that this novel would never be a film.

Then all at once, in March of 1955, the man who had produced *Point of No Return* on Broadway wrote to Carl to ask, "Did you ever sell the motion picture rights to MELVILLE GOODWIN, U.S.A.? If not I should very much like to talk to you about it." Carl wired back that the rights were indeed available and that all parties were open for discussion. John, in the intervening four years, had lowered his sights considerably and reported that he would accept any "reasonable" offer, and presently—by June of that year—an agreement had been struck for $46,500. It was not imposing movie money but a fair price for a property that had gone begging this long, and Carl explained as carefully as he could to John that in the Hollywood market place the price for novels seemed to be declining and that "the six-figure deals" of the late 1940s seemed to be getting harder and harder to come by. The movie production, initially, was to be an elaborate one, co-starring the husband and wife team of Humphrey Bogart and Lauren Bacall. But, in the process, the producer's sights also became lowered somewhat, and the result was an indifferent picture called *Top Secret Affair*, with Kirk Douglas playing Melville Goodwin.

It is hard to see why John, now a rich man, married to a richer wife (Adelaide had inherited over $3,000,000 worth of Hooker Electrochemical stock) should have been haunted by the fear of poverty. But he was, and as he told Carol he continued to worry "that I'll have to take my dark glasses, my tin cup and cane, and sit in anterooms for work."

It was not as though he was an extravagant spender. Quite the opposite; when he traveled it was often on an expense account provided by one or another of the big magazines, and in New York he had acquired a certain reputation as a man who often displayed a decided slowness when it came to reaching for a check at one of his clubs, the Harvard, the Century, or the Knickerbocker. Only infrequently, and with great care as to who were the recipients, did he give away copies of his books. He did not even give away photographs of himself, when asked for them by readers. He once received a polite letter from the inmates of a reformatory in New South Wales, telling him that his books were great favorites with the prisoners. Would he be so good as to send a picture of himself to be hung in the prison library? He turned the request over to his publisher.

Chapter Twenty-eight

*E*ver since its publication in 1939 there had been strong movie interest in *Wickford Point,* and a number of producers had sent out feelers through Famous Artists and the Brandt office. But John had become lawsuit-shy about *Wickford Point,* and, since the day he had lost the court battle, he had developed a whole new set of feelings about his cousins and former friends, the Hales. He now claimed that the Hales had brought the whole Curzon's Mill business to court in order to "claim notoriety," by reading themselves into the book as characters. He said they had done this simply to make him look ridiculous, and that there was no—and never had been any—connection or even similarity between the Hales and the Brills. On the other hand, the Hales had publicized their identity as Brills so thoroughly that John was afraid that if a movie about the fictional family was produced, the Hales would sue for libel or invasion of privacy. This possibility did not seem to worry the movie producers (who are always being sued for this or that), who would be the ones the Hales would sue, if they sued. But it worried John. The last thing he wanted was another lawsuit. His life had already had, as it were, its big trial scene.

In 1951, however, a producer named Julian Blaustein had expressed an interest in making a film of *Wickford Point*, and John, with Carl Brandt's persuasion, was quite tempted to pursue the possibility. But there were a few things he insisted on. The price, for one, would have to be high enough to make any further alienation of his family worth his while; he proposed a $15,000 to $20,000 option price against a final price of $150,000 to $200,000. The Hales, furthermore, would have to be "bought off," he said, and that, he estimated, would cost an additional $15,000 or $20,000. Also, he could not approach the Hales personally, nor should it appear that he was paying off the Hales himself even indirectly. After all, if he paid them, it would be tantamount to an admission that he had used them in the book. Carl offered to approach the Hales for him. He also suggested that Blaustein's lawyers could approach the Hales through their lawyers and get them to sign quitclaims, or agreements promising not to sue. But the price John asked was too high for Blaustein, and the deal fell through. In 1955 it revived, briefly, this time with the producer Sol Siegel. But John demanded the same terms: $150,000 for himself with "payments spread out over five years," as Carl outlined it to the Hollywood office, "and it would have to be worked in some way that he would be satisfied that the money was put in such a spot that he'd get it no matter what happened to the film in question." The Hales would also have to sign their quitclaims, and John was certain they would want money for this. Once again, the price he set was too high for the market, and so one of John's finest novels, which, if sensitively done, could have been made into an engrossing film, was never sold.

Today, the Hales laugh at the suggestion that they would have sued over a movie version of *Wickford Point*. "John simply would not understand that we were really very quiet and gentle people," Robert B. Hale said not long ago. "The only reason why we fought John the way we did in 1949 was that it seemed to us he was trying to take away our summer home

—and he was. It is typical of his lack of sensitivity, too, that he would assume we would have to be 'bought off.' John, of course, had some very strange theories about money. He thought that the only way to get what you want was with money, and that people never did anything for other people unless there was money in it for them. We Hales were not like that. I suppose that is why we baffled him."

In the meantime, the *Saturday Evening Post* was in a much more expansive financial mood than the motion picture companies. No sooner had the film sale of *Wickford Point* fallen through than the *Post* came up with an enticing offer. Everyone knew that John and Adelaide had been having their difficulties, that John had been begging for a divorce against her stubborn refusal, and Stuart Rose at the *Post* had recalled how, when John had been having similar troubles with Christina, the *Post* had sent Marquand on a trip to the Far East to gather new Mr. Moto material—with profitable results. Rose's idea was: Why not another Mr. Moto serial? The sibilant-tongued little agent had become a part of the American vernacular, and a new serial about him would surely sell magazines. Why not another Far East trip for its author? Rose offered Marquand $75,000, sight unseen, for the book, plus $5,000 cash expenses for an Orient trip in advance. Little, Brown would publish the result in hard cover after the *Post's* serialization. It was to be written with an eye to a movie sale. Marquand was delighted, and presently—in June, 1955—he and his oldest son, Johnny, were off from Boston to San Francisco, Honolulu, Tokyo, Hong Kong, Singapore, Bangkok, with a two-day side trip to Angkor Wat, then to Colombo, Beirut, and Cairo—first class all the way. From Cairo, John would fly on alone to Milan, where he would meet Carol at Marcia Davenport's villa on Lake Como. From there the two would go to Paris and to Versailles, where they had first met. There they would be joined by Carol's son, Carl, Jr., and there John would begin dictating to Carol the Mr. Moto yarn, working much the way they had worked years ago, under the mulberry tree at Maule. They would go on—for more work, more dictating—to London. It was going to be a glorious and busy summer, with a chance for John to get reacquainted with his son, who was already a promising author and who had written a novel of his own, which Harper had published, *The Second Happiest Day.*

By the time father and son had circled nearly the entire circumference of the globe—they left Boston on June 25 and arrived in Cairo at the end of July—there had been at least one mishap, or misunderstanding, and when John joined Carol at Lake Como he was still bristling about it. The argument was over an Oriental rickshaw boy to whom John had given an order; when the boy had not obeyed speedily enough, John had shouted at him harshly. His son had taken the attitude that this was not the way to speak to another human being, to which John had answered, "Who knows the Far East better— you or I?" He explained that rickshaw boys expected to be shouted at, that this was the only way to get them to do what they were supposed to do. One of the stories John loved to tell was of how, on another trip to the Orient with his friend Walter Bosshard, their car had become stuck in the mud in Mongolia, and Bosshard—who knew the Orient even better than Marquand—had ordered some Chinese peasants to push the car out of the mud. When the peasants had balked, Bosshard had said to John, "Hit them!" And John, after at first demurring, found himself whacking peasants in the stomach to get them to do as they were told, and they eventually did. He had even made the anecdote a part of one of his Tuesday Night Club papers in Newburyport. But John, Jr., was still unconvinced of the propriety of such treatment of peasants and menials and said so, and the argument became heated and bitter. Son accused father of being autocratic and arrogant, and father accused son of being romantic and naïve. John— as he always did when he was certain that he was in the right— kept going back to it again and again, and it was still with him when he got to Europe. For days he could talk of almost nothing else.

As soon as they got to Versailles and settled at the Trianon Palace Hotel, John started dictating to Carol. Of these happy summer days, Carol Brandt recalls, "It was a perfect example of how Carl, John, and I worked together as a team and as a family. Back home in New York, Carl had set up all the arrangements, worked out all the business details. John was doing what he liked to do best of all, writing, and I was there with him in a pleasant place, helping him get his book down on paper. Carl junior was with us, with this or that young girl friend of the moment, and the young people provided John and me with pleasant company at dinner—John loved talking with young people. It wasn't just a civilized arrangement. It was *wonderful*."

By August 23 Carl Brandt in New York was able to report to Stuart Rose at the *Post*:

> I've heard from Versailles and the report is that John is at work. He goes out with Button [their nickname for Carl, Jr.] for an hour's walk and commences work at 10. Then luncheon and a walk. It doesn't sound like much but Button says they are run ragged. If it kills them off, they'll get Junior [their nickname for John, Sr.] to do that hour of work in the afternoon.
>
> As of last Friday, he seemed to have been on the beam with it. There's a block to cut out and he's maybe not as far along as his 45 pages lead him to think. But he is adroit and a pro and they find it fun to watch the wheels work. He asked me to tell you not to worry—John has a good story, subtle and adult as well as strong and deadly, timely and knowledgeable. It will be laid in Tokyo and Cambodia. That's the end of my news.

And, a week later, Carl wrote to John: "I'm delighted and so is Stu Rose (I saw him yesterday afternoon) with the progress you have made on MOTO. I'm also pleased at the reports your typist gives me of your mastery of your medium! When you get that lady enthusiastic you really have got something! Keep up the good work. To say that I am burning up with curiosity is to put it mildly."

The little party moved on, at the end of August, to London and ensconced itself at Claridge's, where the work went on. Carol Brandt recalls, "Everything that John wrote he wrote with enormous joy—that was to me one of the special things about his writing, that he never wrote about anything he disliked—but this Mr. Moto book was a special joy for him because it was returning to an old character he had always loved, and applying to it all the skills and subtleties he had

The Ending 269

acquired since the last Moto. The book just zipped along, with John loving every minute of it. You could tell how much John enjoyed what he was doing by watching the expression on his face. As he dictated, his upper lip and mustache would curl with pleasure. It was wonderful to watch a man get such a kick out of his own words and sentences."

There were pleasant diversions, other than work, in London. John had been complaining, off and on, about the amount of American income tax he had had to pay and reiterating his belief that writers were taxed unfairly; a piece of work might take several years to complete, but its earnings were all taxed within the calendar year of its publication. But one afternoon John's blue eyes had lighted up, and he said that he suddenly felt like doing something completely extravagant, "like buying a solid gold chamber pot." Taking young Carl Brandt with him, he marched out into St. James's Street in search of such a purchase. The two had often gone duck-shooting together at Kent's Island, and when they passed the window of an elegant gunshop John took Carl by the arm and led him inside. The first thing John looked at was an antique Purdey shotgun, which was priced at a thousand guineas, or about $3,000. Murmuring that he didn't think he wanted *that* much of a solid gold chamber pot, he settled on a fine old Atkins, for $1,700 and promptly presented it to the young man. "How is the gold chamber pot working?" he would always ask Carl, later on.

It was in London that summer that John received word of the death of his old friend, Gardi Fiske. Gardi had suffered so long with the strangling torture of emphysema that his death was, in a real sense, a release from terrible pain—and a release for Conney too.

Still, Gardi's death put John in a dark mood. The day the news came marked the first and only time he raised his voice against Carol Brandt in anger. John hated to have to handle money, and whenever he traveled someone else—a secretary, a companion—was always delegated to take care of John's finances. On this trip, it was young Carl whose job it became to hire cars, pay bills, deal with taxis and waiters and bus boys and concierges. Now John had written his letter to Conney

Fiske and all at once found himself in the lobby of the London hotel with no stamp with which to mail it. He could, of course, simply have handed the letter to the room clerk, who would have stamped it, mailed it, and put the charge for the stamp on the bill. But this did not occur to John, and he flew into a rage because no one had thought to provide him with postage stamps. Carol and young Carl were upstairs having breakfast in the suite they all shared when the telephone rang. It was John, from below, shouting and cursing. "The fact that he didn't have a stamp suddenly became very much our fault and nobody else's fault," Carol recalled later. "He was shouting at me so over the telephone that there was no way to answer him, no way to reason with him. Finally I took the phone away from my ear and just let the receiver dangle by the cord until it stopped making those terrible noises. Then I picked it up and said, 'And darling, what time shall we meet, and what shall we do today?'"

The first draft of John's Mr. Moto yarn was finished in slightly over six weeks' time—431 triple-spaced pages. But the editors of the *Saturday Evening Post* were not entirely happy with the results of that summer's hard work when they received the manuscript, which John had titled *Stopover: Tokyo*, that fall. The ending, the editors contended, was too downbeat. Couldn't John lift it a little and close the story on a brighter note? After all, mystery and spy-story tradition practically demands that a book end with all villains either dead or fittingly punished, and heroes rewarded and ready to live happily ever after. In *Stopover: Tokyo* John had had the nerve to kill off a "good guy" or, in this particular case, girl. John, however, felt that this unusual ending was important to the over-all honesty of his book and refused to change it. Furthermore, he was in a position, if the *Post* would not publish the tale as written, to refund the magazine its money. Reluctantly, the *Post* capitulated.

Even so, the whole *Post* episode nettled John considerably. It would not have happened, he told Carl and Carol Brandt, in the good old days of George Horace Lorimer. John was not the sort of writer, he insisted, who could turn out machine-made fiction to order, according to an editor's preconceived plot idea or plan, with a guaranteed happy ending every time. Some writers might do that, but not he. Besides, the *Post*'s attitude had made him feel as though they regarded him as simply another *Post* employee, a journalist on assignment. (In the *Post*'s behalf, it should be noted that, by accepting the generous expense account, John had put himself somewhat in that position.) For all the diversion the trip and writing the book had provided, he told the Brandts that he wished to be involved in no further writing tasks of this sort.

Carol's first big piece of business for the Brandt office (which she had joined a few months earlier to help her ailing husband) was to sell *Stopover: Tokyo* to Twentieth Century-Fox for $65,000, plus a number of attractive escalator clauses, to be made into a film starring Robert Wagner and Joan Collins. This news, along with the well-known fact that John had written the spy thriller on a commission from the *Saturday Evening Post*, caused book reviewers—who often seem to be of the theory, Sedgwickian in its feeling, that only trash makes money—to be waiting for *Stopover: Tokyo* with freshly sharpened knives when it was published in 1957. They leapt on the book with glad little cries and wrote enthusiastically unfavorable reviews.

Orville Prescott, retired daily book reviewer of the *New York Times* and a Marquand admirer, has said that he considers the book "an embarrassing potboiler." But Mr. Prescott missed the point. *Stopover: Tokyo* was written partly for fun and partly out of a sense of nostalgia, to find out if perhaps you *can* go home again, back to the old days with Christina and pounding out those precision-smooth spy stories for the *Saturday Evening Post*, days when life was simpler, people were kinder, and editors knew what they wanted—or seemed to. John had plenty to keep his pot boiling, and the pot was made of gold.

Chapter Twenty-nine

*D*uring one of the bad periods of Carl Brandt's drinking, a number of their friends, including Carl's psychiatrist, had urged Carol to divorce her husband. She had told him this. Because he always felt that he expressed himself better on paper than orally, he wrote to her one of his characteristic letters, in pencil, on sheets of yellow legal paper:

> The important thing is what you said tonight—that it's almost all worthwhile just to find out that what we have kept of our closeness is not synthetic but an inviolate welding. I have felt it all along but, being so woefully in the wrong, I could not call the piper's tune. I had to trust in the end result. I did and have.
>
> I shall not—in fact I cannot—do anything to try and crack that weld. The weld, like the scar of a wound, is always stronger than the adjacent uncut surfaces. I may be a giddy goat, having a hell of a time hopping from crag to crag, trying to believe you are still with me. It may be change of life. I dunno, but I do know I love you most, have more fun with you, trust you utterly (no matter what crags *you* leap lightly and gracefully between), admire you beyond all women (with good cause)

and am proud of you beyond the power of words to say and tongue to tell. . . .

I fear for myself should you, in fate's hands, become Blithe Spirit. Not for you—you'd reorganize and dust out all the corners of hell (I trust you'd have no interest in heaven?) And you'd find a reason to justify and dignify bad luck. I, very simply, would not know how to envision life without you. That I fear, of that I'm so truly terrified that it physically hurts—it's the whole truth, lady. . . .

Make up your mind what you want most. You are the arch priestess of that religion. I'll help you get it when you're sure. I love you that much, no matter what it does to me. Count me out of your figuring—that is, what it'll *do* to me. I'll be strong enough, I reckon.

But remember there's this to be said, that few people could love you as I do or want you as consistently. I know you better than anyone else. We've had more together than can be jettisoned with a "skip it." There's a hell of a lot no one can ever touch, particularly what you have suffered for and from me.

But I love you—and want and need you—now and always.

Carl

Think hard, lady!

And she did think hard, and in the end she decided that too much had been spent and invested in her marriage in terms of time and caring to let it all go. She could not let it go.

The last decade of Carl Brandt's life were years of triumph. Not only did he prosper in a business sense but he also conquered the alcoholism that at one point had threatened to undo him altogether. He did this with the help of a psychiatrist who suggested a new approach. Always before, after one of his prolonged drinking bouts, Carl had been placed in the luxury of Doctors' Hospital or Connecticut's Silver Hill, an expensive sanitarium that seems not to be one and is run along the lines of a comfortable country inn. The New York doctor proposed that Carl be placed, just once, under lock and key in a West Side "snake pit" for alcoholics. After his last bout he was committed to such a place, and during three days there he saw many aspects of himself that he had never seen before. He never had another drink and was sober for the last eight years of his life. But the drinking years had taken their toll on his health, and, like Gardi Fiske, he developed that most frightening of diseases—one must struggle for every breath—emphysema.

Then it was discovered that he had cancer. Early in October, 1957, Carl Brandt was taken to Roosevelt Hospital where, from pain and from the drugs prescribed to control the pain, he soon became delirious. John Marquand came down from Newburyport to join Carol for the ordeal of waiting for the end, which came at last on October 13. He was sixty-eight years old.

Carl's and Carol's had been a strong marriage, though not without its share of anguish. Not a perfect marriage, and never a conventional one, it nonetheless had represented two people bound together by powerful ties of respect and love, a respect and love shared by their two children, Carl and Vicki. Perhaps because John Marquand had come into that marriage at an early stage he had, in joining it, in a sense strengthened it. It was as though each point in the triangular relationship had served to strengthen the other two. As John's relative Buckminster Fuller has often pointed out, the triangle is the strongest geometric form in nature.

As for John and Adelaide, there were long separations and reconciliations of sorts, vituperative letters and telephone calls followed by extended silences, pleas for the freedom of a divorce, but still the marriage dragged on, bearing with it the heavy burden of two unhappy people, with Adelaide stubbornly refusing to quit her role as Mrs. John P. Marquand. At one point, Adelaide announced that she was taking her children on an extended trip to Egypt, and John's lawyers had to threaten her with a restraining order to keep her from taking the children out of school. To their friends, watching them together had become an experience that was ghastly—John, with his skill at sarcasm and ability to make his wife look foolish, and Adelaide, who had let herself become fat and yet who still insisted on bedecking her heavy body in bizarre costumes. There were repeated meetings between Adelaide's and John's lawyers in which they attempted to get her to sign the separation agreement necessary to proceed to the divorce, and after one of these sessions, Brooks Potter's secretary put in a memo to John: "If anyone wants my opinion of Mrs. M, I think she is a candidate for McLean. . . . She seems to have an aversion to telling the truth."

But at last, in 1957, not long after Carl Brandt's death, John's lawyers did seem to be wearing down Adelaide's resistance, and it looked as though she would sign the necessary documents. John was advised that he could go to Reno to wait out the customary residence requirement. He checked in at the Riverside Hotel, using an assumed name so that Adelaide could not reach him. But Adelaide, in the process of going over the papers John's lawyers wanted her to sign, discovered his whereabouts and alias and flew to Reno, where she appeared in the lobby of the Riverside, demanding to see him. He refused to let her come up to his room but did go down to the lobby and told her, "If it takes me a divorce in every state of the Union to do this, and if it takes me the whole year to live out the period of time necessary in Nevada, I will do all of these things, and this divorce is going through."

Adelaide's trip to Nevada was ill-advised for another reason. By physically setting foot within the boundary of the state where John was pressing his divorce action, she made herself subject to being served. Discovering that she could be served, she submitted to the jurisdiction of the Nevada courts, and it was then possible for the divorce proceedings to go ahead, and for John's residence to be limited to just six weeks. "The minute she came to Reno, we nailed her," Brooks Potter says.

She flew back to Boston and telephoned Carol. "She asked me if I would intercede with John," Carol remembers. "She asked me to say, 'Please don't do this, it's not good for anybody.' But as far as I could see, at that point, it could do nobody any good to live in this atmosphere of terrible hate and bitterness—not for the children, certainly not for John's work, not for anything. John hated her so much at that point —I've never witnessed such hatred in a man."

John also hated Reno. Topographically it reminded him of Aspen, which he had also grown to hate. He hated, he advised Carol, the entire West—hated it, in all probability, simply because Adelaide liked it. His letters from Reno grew increasingly irascible, the longer he was required to stay. He referred to Reno as "this Sodom and Gomorrah" and complained bitterly that nobody but Carol gave him any news of home. He fidgeted during the days, drank too much in the evenings, and tried to busy himself with Book-of-the-Month Club reading. He moved from the Riverside Hotel to a guest ranch near Carson City whose letterhead depicted a bucking bronco, and he amused himself by doodling generally vulgar details in pencil here and there about the horse's body. He complained that he couldn't understand what his lawyers were telling him. At one point, they told him he could probably leave Nevada in ten days to two weeks, and at another he was told that he might have to take up permanent residence in the state—a thought that appalled him. The whole proceedings, he told Carol, seemed to him humiliating in the extreme and was destroying his faith in American jurisprudence, his manhood, and the human race.

He could not sleep at night without a Nembutal, but his doctor, Dana Atchley in New York, would not prescribe them for him, and so Carol was required to bootleg them to him in Nevada. Also, Carol had heard that some of John's neighbors in Newburyport had been critical of her occasional presence at his house there, and she told him that she felt she ought not to go to Newburyport again. John begged her to reconsider, blaming the trouble on small-town gossips. He complained that he felt exhausted, sick, and old. His hair seemed to be falling out faster than ever. In the mirror he was shocked by the face he saw. A photograph of himself in the *Herald-Tribune* made him look terrible. He felt, he said, ready for a wheel chair. Meanwhile, the divorce inched its way through the courts.

There were few bright moments in Reno. One divorce-bound lady to whom John had taken a particular dislike had been taking riding lessons at a nearby guest ranch, and one afternoon John had the pleasure of seeing her horse throw her and land her very softly in a large pile of horse manure. He told Conney Fiske that another woman had said to him, "Do you know you look quite a lot like John Marquand, the novelist?" He had replied, "It's curious you should mention it because several people have told me that and you're right, there is a resemblance." He bought some boots called Wadis and "frontier pants—made in the West, for the West, and worn proudly by Westerners" in order to identify himself a little more with his environment. But dark thoughts continued to assail him. He worried that Reno's altitude might give him another coronary, and of his three children by Adelaide he said, "I feel that in a week or so all the kids will be so brainwashed that it will be kinder to them if I see little or nothing of any of them in the future."

In a few more weeks' time, however, Adelaide had made the necessary legal moves, John's case had come to court, and his divorce was granted. The marriage had lasted just over twenty-one years. John was free to leave Nevada and flew to San Francisco, where he was met by Carol. It was autumn, San Francisco's best time, and the two spent several days celebrating John's release from matrimony. They flew home together to New York.

Meanwhile, John had asked young Carl Brandt—who was finishing up his studies at Harvard—to go down to the house at Kent's Island and be there when Adelaide arrived to pack up her personal possessions. It was John's lawyer's suggestion, to be sure that Adelaide took away from the house only those articles that had been agreed upon under the separation agreement. Young Carl arrived with books to study and a paper to write and settled himself at a table in the living room. Presently Adelaide Marquand appeared, waved distantly to him, and proceeded with her packing, moving in and out of rooms, up and down stairs. In the years since John had bought his first tiny place, Kent's Island had grown to a house of considerable size with a big wing added on either end.

Presently, Adelaide strode into the living room, stared hard at Carl Brandt, and said, "You do know, don't you, that you are presiding over the dissolution of an empire?" She turned and strode out again.

As soon as his divorce was final, John asked Carol to marry him. Before his death Carl had said to her, "When I die, and if you should want to marry John, I think I should tell you that I think you will find him a very cruel and selfish man."

But this was not why Carol said no—and kept saying no, repeatedly, in the months that followed. With Carl's death, Carol, assisted by her son, had taken over the management of Brandt & Brandt and its many clients, an occupation she thoroughly enjoyed and wanted to continue to enjoy. It was lifeblood to her. Once, at John's house in Pinehurst—it was during the closing of the movie sale of *Stopover: Tokyo,* and calls were going back and forth between Carol and the West Coast as details of the deal were being settled—John's housekeeper, Julia, had asked, bemused, "Mrs. Brandt—who *are* you?" Carol had smiled and said, "Just a woman who has always worked for a living." She was and still is that.

Carol treasured her work, and John did not want a wife who worked. He wanted a wife who would keep house and entertain for him in Newburyport, Massachusetts, and in Pinehurst, North Carolina. Carol knew that she could not endure the role John wanted to cast her in, in either of the places he had in mind. He said he would not marry her unless she gave up the agency. She said she would not marry him unless she could be permitted to keep it. And that was that.

"I could tolerate the kind of life he liked to lead for short periods," Carol Brandt says. "But if I'd had to live it with him—the Somerset Club, the Myopia Hunt, Pinehurst and the golf—I'd have been climbing up the walls in two weeks. And John didn't really approve of the kind of life *I* liked. I like writers, and working with them and talking to them. But John didn't like many other writers. After Carl died, John and I began giving little dinner parties together at my apartment, and there would always be writers there—either clients or friends. And after the guests had left, John would turn to me and say, 'My *God!* How can you stand those people?' Those people were my life.

"And Carl was right. John could be selfish, and he could be cruel. But he could never be cruel to me because he had no claim on me. If he tried to be, I could simply have walked out on him. If I had married him, God knows what it would have been like. As it was, I was the bearer of the lantern. He was the flame, I was the keeper. I could do more for him than any other woman could, or wanted to, in terms of making him comfortable, making it easier for him to write. I loved his dependence on me. If a man is dependent on you, he is closer to you than to any other woman. With John, I had a marriage without a marriage. With Carl, I had a union without a union. It has always seemed to me that with both those men I had the best of both possible worlds."

Perhaps there was still another reason why they did not marry. In every relationship there comes a moment when the opportunity to move forward into another area, onto another level, must be seized or let go. The crucial moment rarely if ever returns. Also, it may have been the strains and pressures of their respective marriages that held John Marquand and Carol Brandt together, but their affair may also have helped both marriages to last as long as they had. Now that they were both free, the affair seemed somehow less important. The crucial moment had passed.

John was deeply saddened by Carl Brandt's death. It struck him as bitterly ironic that now he was free, and had sufficient money to be able to enjoy life—to play a bit and not work quite so hard—the playmates he would have most enjoyed, the old friends, were departing, one by one, leaving him stranded and alone. He felt this way even about Pinehurst where, in the beginning, he had had so many good times at the Pinehurst Country Club, the Tin Whistle, and the Wolves. "Just think," he said once, "I've spent all my life working so I can meet and have fun on their own level with people like the people at Pinehurst, and now all the best ones are dead or dying. And all the rest are nothing but God damned fools."

Chapter Thirty

*T*hey were legally divorced, but still Adelaide would not let go of John. John had even had her name removed from the copyright assignments of the four jointly copyrighted novels, *H. M. Pulham, Esquire, B. F.'s Daughter, Repent in Haste,* and *Melville Goodwin, U.S.A.* Still she tried to remain a part of his life. John was back at Kent's Island working quietly and steadily on a new novel, pouring himself into this book with more gusto, perhaps, than he had done with any previous book. The telephone would ring, sometimes late at night, sometimes early in the morning, and it would be Adelaide, and she would begin one of her long harangues. At times she would scream and scold. At others she would weep. If Carol happened to be at the house when these calls came through, John would hand the telephone receiver to her, saying, "Listen to this—you won't believe what is happening." Carol recalls, "Those calls were perfectly appalling. One really did get the impression of a madwoman on the other end of the line. It did no good to hang up on her, for then she just called back again. If you didn't answer, she would let the phone ring and ring. The only way John could handle these calls was

to let her continue until she was finished or too exhausted to
go on. He would plead with her, saying 'Please, please . . . just
leave me alone.' He never liked to use four-letter words, either
in his fiction or his conversation. But other than use profanity
with her he was as firm as he possibly could be—but it did
no good."

There was a terrible moment when John learned that
Adelaide had communicated with the Boston *Social Register*
to have his name removed from its listings. John cared about
such things as being in the *Social Register,* and it infuriated
him to think that Adelaide could have his name dropped from
it because of the divorce. He flew into a dreadful rage and
could talk of nothing else for days. Actually, in fairness to
Adelaide, her intention may have been to advise the *Social
Register* that John no longer resided at 1 Reservoir Street, as
the 1958 edition of the little book had it, but John refused to
look at it that way and insisted that she had acted out of
malice and spite. In any case, he saw to it that his name was
back in the 1960 edition, with his address given as Pinehurst,
North Carolina.

But aside from these interruptive episodes, the pace of John's
life had eased and his friends commented that he looked
happier and healthier than he had in years. There were fewer
of those explosive moments when his normally pink skin became poppy red, reminding those who knew him, uneasily, of
his previous heart attack. A few months before undergoing the
divorce proceedings, he had published a small book called
Life at Happy Knoll, which was a collection of pieces about
the goings-on at a fictitious country club, all of which had been
originally written for *Sports Illustrated.* The idea had come
from an encounter John had had with Time, Inc., publisher
Roy Larsen several years earlier at a meeting of the Harvard
Board of Overseers, of which John had been made a member.
Larsen's idea had been for John to write a series of letters
such as might come from a member of a country club to the
president of the club or the chairman of the house committee,
and these letters would comprise, as Larsen put it, "a rather
satirical taking off of the things that are funny and annoying
about all country clubs."

It was a frankly frivolous undertaking, but John had been amused by the idea. His protestations to the Brandts to the contrary, John was easily tempted back to his old medium, the magazines. Working with Richard Johnston and Sidney James at *Sports Illustrated*, he had dashed off a number of Happy Knoll pieces. They were fun to write, were intended to be fun to read, and John had had considerable background as a clubman—particularly as a member of the Pinehurst Club and the Myopia Hunt Club outside Boston—to draw on for material. *Sports Illustrated* paid him $2,000 for each piece, plus an expense allowance, and John, with his shrewd New Englander's feelings about money, had even worked out an arrangement whereby the magazine paid his Myopia Club dues and golf charges. In submitting his Myopia bills to the magazine, John was careful to instruct that they be paid to him, direct, so that he could then pay the club out of his own account—lest any member of the club get the notion that he was using members as models for his little Happy Knoll sketches. He was, of course, doing just that, and there had already been some grumbling in corners at both of John's golfing places, and complaints to the effect that he was exploiting his relationship with members and club officers in the process of putting private clubs into commercial fiction. One can imagine with what consternation the Myopia Hunt Club's treasurer would view John's golf bill paid by a check from *Sports Illustrated*.

Now a gathering of the pieces was between hard covers, and the book, with humorous drawings by John Morris, was selling well. Critics were quick to point out the book's slightness. The reviews ranged from the *Dallas Morning News,* which said, "This is Marquand in a lightsome, unimportant mood. But even at pot-boiling John P. remains one of the best of our writers," to *Harper's Magazine,* which called the book "moderately entertaining." There are indeed some amusing moments. One of the most successful letters is an elaborate rationalization of why the golf pro is a genius and must be kept on in the club's employ at any cost, despite the glaring fact that he has never in a single instance been known to improve a member's game by a single stroke. Another reveals how an aging Negro bartender at the club, long past any point of competence at his job, uses information gathered from members when they are in their cups to blackmail the club into keeping him on its payroll. To readers who wanted a chuckle at the vagaries of country club life, the book seemed worth its modest price of $3.75. And John himself, clutching his forehead in mock anguish at the demonstrated stupidity of all reviewers, cried, "It is fun and games, the book was written as fun and games! Can't they understand that? Must everything I write be so bloody serious? Aren't I entitled to some fun and games at my age?" He was sixty-three.

Meanwhile, though Carol continued gently to put off his proposals of marriage, she took up the tasks of substitute wife to help him put his new bachelor's life in order. An extremely organized person herself, she also had a well-trained office staff to call on, and after John's divorce the Brandt & Brandt letterhead not only contained matters of literary business and contracts—including a nice $71,000 advance extracted from *Ladies' Home Journal* for the Marquand novel-in-process—but also shopping advice, household management suggestions, as well as confirmations of hotel and airplane reservations as John continued his restless travels from one part of the globe to another. It was a far cry from Adelaide's disheveled housekeeping as Carol—writing to John, who was redecorating and furnishing his Pinehurst house—helped cut through domestic red tape:

> There has been sent to Miss Pleasants a set of three glass pitchers, two of which will do for martinis—one for a larger party, one for just two or three people—and a third as a water pitcher. The set of three cost under $9. But I think they're useful and rather pretty. You undoubtedly have a long slender-handled spoon which will serve as a mixer.
>
> I've bought you a dozen finger-bowls with matching glass plates—white, of course. The matching plates will serve as dessert plates or else with a doily will serve to terminate a luncheon meal when you are not serving fruit or anything else.
>
> I've also, of course, bought very plain, useful lace finger-bowl doilies.

I've bought bathroom wastebaskets, Kleenex boxes and waste-baskets that will do for all the bedrooms and the library. They couldn't be plainer or cheaper.

I've also bought a number of ashtrays. I couldn't remember what you had in the house or what you may need. One always needs more of them.

All of these things have gone from Altman's, and I trust in due course Miss Pleasants will take the time to acknowledge that they have arrived. I enclose a copy of my letter to her.

Adelaide had trouble catching trains and was forever making John late for appointments, but Carol kept John on schedule:

Your Pan American flight is due in at 11:15 from Rome. I came in by jet from London on Sunday and it was right on the button. What I shall do is find out if your flight is to be on time and if so will meet you with Paul Reilly or one of his chauffeurs. If it's late, I'll simply have the car meet you.

Should I be asleep by any hideous chance upon your arrival, pound loudly on the door and we'll have a bottle of champagne.

Miss Pleasants, handling the details of the house from the Pinehurst end, was no match for Carol's efficiency and thoroughness. Carol wrote to her:

Now that the time for John Marquand's arrival is close at hand, I want to make doubly sure that the large carton of sheets and pillow cases addressed to him in your care arrived safely from Gimbel Brothers in New York.

I had hoped there would be word from you on my desk upon my return from a month's trip to Europe.

Thank you for an early reply. . . .

In addition to a new novel, John was working on another, very personal project. It was to be a complete rewriting of a biography John had written in 1925 called *Lord Timothy Dexter of Newburyport, Mass.*, and which Minton, Balch had published (before John's final and permanent alliance with Little, Brown). Lord Timothy Dexter—he conferred the title on himself—was a rags-to-riches New England eccentric who started life as a tanner and ended up in an implausible mansion surrounded by statuary in the center of town, and who even employed his own poet laureate. Dexter's extravagant career had always fascinated John, who enjoyed the grotesque—the wild contrast, for example, of Dexter's flamboyant life and house in the middle of staid, quiet, and conservative Newburyport—but John's earlier treatment of this character had been a noticeable publishing failure, perhaps because readers found Dexter's outlandish antics simply impossible to credit. There are some creatures, after all, who are too grotesque to stomach. John was rewriting the biography for a number of reasons. First, he had reason to suppose that one reason for the first book's failure to reach a wide audience was that its author in those days was relatively unknown. In 1925 there was no ready-made readership for John P. Marquand's books and, in a way, the rewritten Dexter would be a test of that readership's loyalty. Also, he assumed that thirty-five years later he was a better writer and could therefore give Dexter a better portrayal. But woven into both of these reasons like threads in the tapestry of everything he was doing was John's wish, once more, to return to the past, to go back to the old streets of Newburyport of his youth and to see, in the process, what had happened since.

Little, Brown was not at all happy about the Timothy Dexter project—it seemed a rehashing of a tired subject that had perhaps been not much good to begin with—and his editor, Alexander Williams, who had succeeded Stanley Salmen, told John so as gently as possible. But John was Little, Brown's favorite author, and since they had to indulge his whims they agreed to publish it. Even more dubious about the Timothy Dexter book was Carol Brandt. She considered it an utter waste of time and told John so frankly and firmly. At one point, John told Williams, "I'm thinking of dedicating the Dexter to Carol, simply because she says it's no damn good." He did not do this, but he forged stubbornly ahead with the book.

He had begun to complain that the Book-of-the-Month Club was working him too hard, giving him too many books to read and review and requiring him to attend too many meetings. He had, after all, been with the club for nearly fifteen years, and much of the freshness and stimulation of the judges' meetings had worn off. Specifically, he asked to be excused from the January, February, and March meetings—

these were his Pinehurst months—unless his attendance was considered "urgent"; otherwise, he would handle the details of these meetings by telephone. This would leave him with six meetings a year, and he also wanted to be free to travel abroad in this period, keeping in touch with the club and keeping up on his reading by mail, telephone, or cable. In addition, he asked that he be given no more than eight books a month to read and that he be asked to do no reviews for the club *News* unless he felt genuinely enthusiastic about the book in question and volunteered to do so. In the process of airing his grievances, John added that he felt Book-of-the-Month Club meetings too often stressed the commercial possibilities of the books in question, and not the judges' opinions. Finally, he complained that Harry Scherman, the late chairman of the Book-of-the-Month Club, took too active a part in the meetings of the judges, and tried to influence the selections. In return for a lightened work load, John agreed to accept a cut in salary and, naturally, Carol was delegated to meet with Scherman and Meredith Wood, the club's president, and state John's position. Carol did so, tactfully not stressing John's waning interest in the club and mentioning instead his heart condition. Both men were happy to give John whatever he wanted. And of course there would be no reduction in his salary.

When John's new novel, *Women and Thomas Harrow*, was published in 1958—first serially in *Ladies' Home Journal* and then in hard cover by Little, Brown—it struck many people that the book represented something of a departure. Bruce and Beatrice Gould, then editors of the *Journal*, commented that it was the first Marquand novel they could remember in which John appeared truly in sympathy with his hero. Though the book is set again in John's fictional town of Clyde, Tom Harrow is certainly a far more sympathetic individual than the previous resident of that city whom John had dealt with, the obnoxious Willis Wayde. Harrow is also older—John Marquand heroes tend to age with their author—and, at fifty-four, is a playwright of the generation just previous to Tennessee Williams and Arthur Miller. He is at a crisis point in his life—financially, in his career, and in his marriage to Emily, an overtalkative nag who enjoys reminding Tom, just as Adelaide reminded John, that all he has done has been to repeat himself for the last five years. Once again, time is the villain and the thief. New and younger and more vigorous playwrights are coming into the theater, the theater is changing, and Tom Harrow, despite his eminence and his success, sees that his own work is becoming old-fashioned, that his best work is behind him, he is past his prime. But it is too late to change course, and he cannot go back. Tom Harrow is of course John Marquand, and his doubts and fears are dark dreams are John's.

Long ago, in Tom Harrow's past, there was the beautiful Rhoda Browne, one of John Marquand's most subtly delineated female characters. Rhoda Browne's father not only had a lower-class job—as an automobile dealer—but he was successful at that, while Rhoda's mother had great social ambitions for her daughter. Tom Harrow's early success in the theater gives him the money with which to marry Rhoda. But theater money is like a novelist's money, ephemeral. It comes and goes; it is never sure; a writer is rich one minute and poor the next. It is not like inherited money that is safe and secure, doled out by banks and clipped by coupon. And so, after a few giddy years as the wife of the famous playwright, Rhoda leaves Tom to marry Presley Brake, old-rich and so highly bred that he comments that gin is "a charwoman's drink." It is almost as though John had come to blame his loss of Christina on the lack of security afforded by a writer's livelihood, and of course that was a part of it—a small part. After Rhoda, Tom married briefly and unhappily a successful actress with whom he had had an affair. Then came the garrulous and bossy Emily, who likes to do over old Federalist houses. And so here we have John Marquand the misogynist, with "women" singled out as the cause of all his woes. "Women and Thomas Harrow" was John's choice for a title—against such others as "Script by Thomas Harrow" and "Lines by Thomas Harrow"—because, as he said to his publisher, "it tells what the book is about."

Women and Thomas Harrow received, on the whole, good reviews. William James Smith in *Commonweal* wrote, "In his latest success, *Women and Thomas Harrow,* Mr. Marquand cites an aphorism of the theater—a 'bit' that goes over big once will go over big twice; after that you're pushing your luck.

Mr. Marquand is proof that this does not hold in the world of the novel. He has done his big bit at least half a dozen times and it is still going over great. It is another respect in which he is uniquely successful." And, to John's surprise and ill-concealed delight, *The New Yorker,* whose views in those days probably carried the greatest cachet of any magazine and which had always high-hatted John Marquand novels in its *nil admirari* fashion, gave the book a rave, saying, "Rarely is there a novel as fine as this one." And Arthur Mizener wrote a long and enthusiastic letter, saying:

> Marquand does not, I guess, any more than Thomas Harrow, need to worry that he is slipping. This is certainly as competent and finished a job as he has done in other novels, much better that way than Willis Wayde. . . . I think Marquand has never done so well—or indeed developed so fully—the loved Marquand wife as he has in Rhoda; the nearest thing is Charley Gray's wife, but Rhoda manages to have the defects or limitations more clearly and yet be more charming. . . . If the book hasn't anything like the narrative hold of POINT OF NO RETURN or B. F.'S DAUGHTER or MELVILLE GOODWIN, because it has almost no narrative in the direct sense, still it has a couple of characters from whom a lot of onion skins are peeled during the course of the book, and Marquand does that kind of peeling well enough for any man.

Mizener is right about the lack of narrative, or suspense, in the book, aside from the suspense of character being slowly revealed. And in the process of peeling off skins from his onion, John was so firmly in control of his material that he could pause for a leisurely paragraph or two simply to describe a room, or a table setting, or a flower bed, and the reader does not feel unduly irked. At the same time, in this novel, John had developed his celebrated flashback technique to such an extreme that almost nothing of importance happens in the present. It is all in the past. Though the reader is reminded, periodically, that the characters' lives are going on in the present, it is the long-ago story of Tom and Rhoda that holds the book together.

Perhaps these are two reasons why, from a sales standpoint, the book was a disappointment. Books are always sold by publishers to booksellers on a returnable basis, and in the case of *Women and Thomas Harrow* Little, Brown sadly overestimated the book's market. In the months following publication, over 17,000 unsold books were returned from bookstores, leaving the "hard" sales figure under 50,000.

And—another possible reason for the book's failure to sell well—there is a pervading sadness throughout the book, a sense of mortality and a sense of doom. The usual satiric and comic Marquand touches are scarce here. From the earliest pages to the final half-unconscious attempt at suicide, Tom Harrow broods not only on the past but on death, the fact that his life is more than half over, that all that was best is gone. The nostalgia is carried to such a degree that the tone becomes one of aching, almost unbearable despair. "In the end, no matter how many were in the car, you always drove alone." Perhaps readers simply had difficulty accepting such a pessimistic book, such dark foreboding.

And yet, since this is John's most autobiographical book, it is in many ways his most interesting. It is as though he had decided, through the medium of his art, to say: This is all I can, or rather all I *choose*, to tell you about myself, and my craft, and my feelings about my work and what it has been like to be successful at it and yet, in a sense, to have failed. And this is all I can—or rather all I wish to—tell you about those people I have loved and lost. As Tom Harrow says:

> He was on his way toward that bourne they wrote about and that one fact, after birth, that was completely unescapable. These were obvious facts, but now there was an urgent reminder . . . he too was a part of the big parade. The younger generation, the younger writers . . . were waiting for him to pass the stand in review. Time was gently nudging so that he would make room for someone else. The show was never over, but pregnancy was continuing, drums were beating, and you had to march along.

And in *Women and Thomas Harrow* John Marquand seems to be saying: This is my literary last will and testament. There will be no more novels now. This is the last. And so it was.

The hero of *Women and Thomas Harrow* discovers, at the beginning of the book, that he is about to be wiped out financially. But John was in no such serious straits. He had,

however, mistakenly thought that he did not need to pay
United States income tax on his British royalties. The Internal
Revenue Service discovered this oversight and advised John
that he still owed the government $27,000 for previous tax
years. It was a blow, of course, but not as stunning a one as
John first made it out to be. He talked gloomily of the necessity
of selling his beloved Kent's Island, but his Boston lawyers
went to work on the problem. John had begun talking of
making some sort of substantial gift to Harvard and had considered giving his share of Curzon's Mill. An arrangement was
worked out, however, whereby John gave the stage, film, and
television rights to *Women and Thomas Harrow* to Harvard,
a gift on which an estimate was placed of $150,000. Ironically,
the stage, film, or television rights to the novel have never
been bought, and so Harvard is no richer from the gift. But it
was a large gesture, and the gift deduction in John's 1958
income tax helped ease the pain of the $27,000 owed.

John spent the winter of 1958–59 in Pinehurst. Carol and
her son Carl visited him there, and there were the pleasant
little dinners at Conney Fiske's. Intellectually, she charmed
him more than any other woman. Though he continued to
boast of how lucky he was to be rid of Adelaide, John was a
man who had always needed a woman's company, and he
wanted to marry again. He had proposed several times to
Conney Fiske, but she had also turned him down, though for
reasons different from Carol's. Conney was a New Englander
by birth and by choice and would have gone with John to
live in Newburyport without a moment's hesitation. But she
had been through the agonizing years of Gardi Fiske's illness.
John had a heart condition, and Conney, fond as she was of
John, simply did not want to take the chance of finding herself
having to nurse another invalid husband. John that winter was
lonely and restless, even though there was golf and plenty of
parties to go to. There was the companionship of his secretary,
Marjorie Davis, but that was not enough. He worked, in a
desultory way, on a new novel.

It was to be about a family named Pettengill, and it was to
be, he promised, a "gayer" book than his previous ones—a
return, in other words, to the fun of *Wickford Point* and *H. M.*

Pulham, Esquire. He was going to write his way out of his doldrums. He gave Conney Fiske seventy-odd pages of the manuscript to read. She doesn't recall that it was a particularly memorable opening, but after all it was just a fragment, just a beginning. In the meantime, John was busily planning a photographic safari to Africa for the coming summer. He would go with George Shearwood, a friend from Pinehurst who ran a travel agency, and he would take Marjorie Davis with him. They would visit the three largest game parks in Kenya and then go into a restricted military district to visit a tribe called the Karamojo which was still completely undisturbed by civilization. Best of all, *Sports Illustrated* wanted six pieces from the trip—the idea would be a Happy Knoll member writing home of his adventures in Africa—and this meant that the expense of the trip, for both John and Miss Davis, would be completely tax deductible.

The African trip was a great success. They stayed at Treetops and watched the wild animals feeding under simulated moonlight, and John promptly perfected a vivid imitation of a wading hippopotamus. They visited a tiny village called Kitale, at the foot of Mount Elgon, and stayed at a local plantation. On the farm, John, with his customary curiosity, wanted to see everything—the coffee and the maize fields and the shambas. He even said that if he were younger he would like to buy a farm like it, recalling that he had once been offered a temple in Mongolia for $100. In the evening he was at his genial and storytelling best, swinging his glass in his hand, telling of how on a trip to the Near and Middle East he had come into Persia and had been asked if he had any alcoholic beverages to declare. "Five beers," he said and, asked where they were, he replied, "Right inside me." He had to pay duty anyway. Later, leaping and jumping to a tom-tom's beat, he demonstrated a dance he had learned from visiting an American Ojibway tribe.

Everywhere the little group went in Africa they were treated as celebrities, and the Famous American Novelist was forever being stopped by reporters who wanted interviews, which John enjoyed, and who asked him literary questions, which he usually tried to dodge. But once, in Kenya, a reporter asked him what he thought of James Joyce's *Ulysses,* and he flung his hands heavenward and rolled his eyes in horror, crying, "Hopeless! Absolutely hopeless!"

The group returned in autumn, to Pinehurst again, as Little, Brown was putting the finishing touches on *Timothy Dexter, Revisited.* The book was published without much fanfare in the spring of 1960 and, as Little, Brown had warned, with only a small sale. But the biography of the Newburyport nonconformist was also an echo of the theme of the last novel, as John wrote of his favorite seaport: "No past can ever return. There is no use weeping over things that are gone. They can never be retrieved in their ancient combinations." Newburyport was a finer place then than it has become, and "its inhabitants were more skilled in more crafts and more diligent in their work and worship." Of *The Unspeakable Gentleman,* he had once explained that in those days he had been "in love with candle light and old ships." He had not really lost that love.

And "worship"? Had he also wistfully begun to miss the religiosity of his Unitarian ancestors? He used to speak to Carol of "the hereafter—the place you don't believe in."

By late spring, 1960, John was back in Newburyport, and on July 14 he came down for the July Book-of-the-Month Club meeting. He was in his usual anecdotal form for that Thursday luncheon and meeting, amusing his fellow judges —John Mason Brown, Basil Davenport, Gilbert Highet, and Clifton Fadiman—with stories of Africa, including the hippopotamus imitation. He shared a taxi with Brown on the long trip uptown from Hudson Street to the Knickerbocker Club where John was staying. John got out of the cab, waved a cheery good-by, and Brown continued uptown.

By Friday, John was back at Kent's Island. Conney Fiske was also back in Boston, and John had asked her for dinner that night, and to stay on at the house overnight or for the week end if she wished. Conney had to decline because of a previous commitment. She was very sorry. She had dined with him about a week before, and it had been very pleasant, but suddenly in the middle of dinner John did a strange thing. He rose from his chair and went to a cabinet and fetched a Chinese cricket cage that he had bought, years before, on one of his trips to the Orient, and he presented the cricket cage to Conney, saying, "May the crickets always sing for you." The words curiously moved and touched her.

And so, that Friday night, John dined alone with his youngest son, Lonnie, who was seventeen. During dinner John complained that at his age he couldn't eat a thing. A few minutes later he said gloomily that he felt as though he was going to have another heart attack. But Lonnie, familiar with his father's dark moods and his habit of exaggeration, paid little attention when his father talked like this. "It's probably just nerves," Lonnie said. John then said that he was going straight to bed. He patted Lonnie affectionately on the head and said good night.

In the morning, Floyd Ray, the houseman-chauffeur whose wife Julia served as John's cook and housekeeper, went up at the regular hour with John's breakfast tray. Floyd opened the bedroom curtains and, with the tray in his hands, turned to waken his master. There was a crash that woke Lonnie, and he ran from his room down the hall to his father's room. Floyd was standing there by the breakfast tray that had crashed to the floor. Floyd said, "Your father won't wake up!"

Nor did he. He had died in his sleep early that morning, and his death had a kind of completeness one feels at the end of an interesting book. It was over too soon—sixty-six years is not a long life for a man. And yet John had seen *Timothy Dexter, Revisited* published, that intensely personal project that everyone had assured him would not be successful, but which he had done simply because he had wanted to do it. He was probably "written out" and probably knew it. He had got rid of Adelaide, who had become worse than a thorn in the flesh to him. He had made his peace with Harvard. And he had died in the house he had built for himself, in his beloved New England which he himself had helped to create. And so it was over, and his death was another example of fêng-shui, the fitness of things, and a reminder that in the end you always die alone.

*A*ftermatter

*A*ll lives do not end as neatly as well-made novels. Some
have loose ends. Some never stop ending. Some, it almost
seems, go on too long. Adelaide . . .

Adelaide insisted on coming up to Newburyport for John's
funeral, even though all his friends begged her not to, knowing
that he would not have wished her there. But she came, and
even as Eddie Goodwin at Curzon's Mill was clearing the
underbrush on Sawyer Hill, traditional burying place of Marquands and Hales, Adelaide was trying to take over arrangements. Finally, someone had to remind her, "You are not the
legal widow." Brooks Potter, meanwhile, had earlier received
humorous but nonetheless serious and specific instructions from
John requesting that a certain Newburyport undertaker, whom
John considered a "parvenu," not be used, and that his grave
on the Hill be placed "as far as possible" from the Hales'.

There was a big crowd at the church, and John's old friend
Ed Streeter remembers that as he looked around the church
it seemed decidedly familiar to him, even though he knew he
had never been inside it before. Then he remembered: He had
been in that church before in *Point of No Return*.

Afterward, everyone went back to Kent's Island and gathered there, and drinks were served. At first everyone was solemn and sympathetic, but soon there was laughter and, Ed Streeter recalls, people were saying, "I say, this is a jolly good party, isn't it?" and thinking that John would have approved.

Most shattered of all, perhaps, by the news of John's death was secretary Marjorie Davis, who had told friends that she expected to become the third Mrs. John P. Marquand before long. An autumn "honeymoon" cruise in the Aegean had even been booked and planned. There are several of John's friends, however, who think that something would have prevented him from taking the young woman who had occupied an apartment over his garage into his house. The Greek Island cruise, these friends point out, was to be taken with another couple, and John had traveled with Marjorie Davis before in an unmarried state. Still, John and Brooks Potter, who had married a woman several years his junior and who had become John's close friend during and after the divorce, often talked late into the night of the problems and the rewards of marrying a younger woman.

Carol Brandt received the news of John's death on July 16 in England, when her son telephoned her there. She had gone to England to be married—at her friend Enid Bagnold's house—to a widowed New York lawyer, and her wedding date was just twelve days away. She was to be married to a man of whom John approved, indeed they were friends, and though she was deeply saddened by the news she did not change the date. It struck many people as uncannily coincidental that John should have died just a few days before Carol was due to embark on a new life of her own. It added one more of those odd fictive notes to John's life. The year 1960, though it marked the beginning of a happy new marriage, was also a year of loss for Carol. That Thanksgiving, her daughter Vicki was killed in a plane piloted by her husband, a French aviator. It crashed while they were bound for the Bahamas and a holiday.

John's will, when it was read, seemed a rather harsh one. After certain specific bequests to servants and secretaries, three quarters of the residue of the estate went to his daughter Christina and one fourth to John, Jr., with the will saying that the "unequal division was not intended in any way to reflect a difference in my affection for them," but "my daughter is and always will be in greater need of assistance than my son John." No money at all went to his children by Adelaide, though they were bequeathed the house at Kent's Island. Adelaide's money, after all, had helped turn Kent's Island into the showplace it had become.

Adelaide continued to live at 1 Reservoir Street and at a New York apartment. In New York she gave little parties at which she tried to gather together groups of John's old friends, as though she felt it her duty to keep John's memory alive. She invited Philip Hamburger, who had written the *New Yorker* profile, to one, and he remembers her sad and disheveled appearance.

In Cambridge, she continued to indulge her interest in music, toiling as best she could for various musical causes. The house at 1 Reservoir Street grew stranger as Adelaide added Benjamin West paintings, all of Mozart's musical scores framed and hung on the wall, and two stuffed leather pigs in front of the fireplace. She had a Nova Scotian couple working for her, but they weren't, she complained, very good, and she ended up doing most of the housework herself. To ward off loneliness, she invited Harvard and Radcliffe music students to come and live at her house. They were supposed to do chores —cut the grass, shovel the walks—in return for their board and keep, but the students did little work, raided her larder and liquor closet, and otherwise took advantage of her.

She tried to control her drinking and would have extended periods of relative sobriety. She and Anne Pusey, the wife of the then president of Harvard, ran an exercise class on the third floor of Adelaide's house where they and several other ladies tried to lose weight. But once, when drunk, she fell through a low plate-glass window and slashed her abdomen. Such friends as she had were deeply worried.

Two of these friends were Peggy and Roy Lamson, she a novelist and he a professor at M.I.T. Roy Lamson, an excellent amateur clarinetist, had once played in Paul Whiteman's orchestra, and a shared interest in music had brought them together. Roy had borrowed a book from Adelaide—Matthiessen's book on the New England renaissance—and one autumn evening in Cambridge the Lamsons ran into Adelaide at a cocktail party at the Puseys', and Adelaide mentioned that she would like the book back. After the party—since their houses were only a few short blocks apart—Roy Lamson strolled over to Adelaide's house with the book.

The door to Adelaide's house was standing ajar, but the house seemed dark and empty. There was no response to the bell, and the Nova Scotian couple were nowhere in evidence. Roy Lamson became concerned. The Lamsons had found her passed out in her house once before and had carried her into bed, and so, after calling several times, he went into the house. There was a light in the upstairs hall and, as he mounted the stairs, a light from under the bathroom door. He knocked, several times, then opened the door. He entered the room with the huge sunken marble tub and the steps leading down, and there floated Adelaide in the tub, naked, face down. Lamson pulled her with difficulty—she was a heavy woman and it was a dead and slippery weight—out of the tub and covered her body with his coat. Then he called the police. The scene of that discovery still returns to him in nightmares. The coroner's verdict was not suicide. She had been preparing for her bath and perhaps had slipped or passed out. There was excessive alcohol in her blood stream. She died leaving $3,000,000 to her children.

Other lives go on.

Conney Fiske still lives outside Boston in her house with its pretty pool and private jumping course, and goes south to Southern Pines in the winter with her horses, where she rides in the hunt—sidesaddle, as always. She is rather glad she could not dine with John that last Friday night, for if she had been in the house at the time of his death there would have been unpleasant publicity for both herself and her old friend. She continues to treasure the memory of John's longest and closest friendship, and the recollections of those evenings with just the three of them, John, herself, and Gardi. Like Carol, Conney was away from Boston at the time of the funeral and could not attend. "Were you in love with him?" Conney Fiske was asked not long ago. She thought for a moment and then said, "I don't know. There were people in Boston, of course, who thought I might marry John after he divorced Christina, even though that would have meant divorcing Gardi." Carol Brandt, happily married, lives in New York and runs Brandt & Brandt with her son. John's children, all married and in one case remarried, are scattered here and there.

Sedgwick House still stands in Stockbridge, an imposing residence. John's children by Adelaide still go back to Kent's Island now and then. His children by Christina still summer at Curzon's Mill with the Hale cousins in a state of uneasy truce.

After John's death, "Nandina Cottage" in Pinehurst, where he had enjoyed his final winters, was sold to a Mr. and Mrs. Curtis Gary. The house has not been changed much, with the exception of a black rubber doormat which has been placed outside the front door, and which reads, in large white capital letters:

THE GARY'S

If the dead do spin, even slightly, in their graves over the follies committed by the living upon the things the dead once loved, then surely John must have winced—in amusement, in mock dismay—just winced, or turned a little, beneath the soft soil of Sawyer Hill, at this last touch that had been applied to his old house. It is not so much what he would have had to say about the use of "personalized" doormats. But to John, such a stickler for proper punctuation and such a foe of the overuse of it, the misused apostrophe on this particular doormat would have struck him as the final comic capstone of his life. He would certainly have used it in a story.

A John P. Marquand Check List[*]

Symbols: N, novel; SN, serial novel; SS, short story; NF, non-fiction; MP, motion picture; P, play. The titles of the major published books are given in capital letters; their titles as magazine serials, if different, follow in parentheses.

1915

PRINCE AND BOATSWAIN. SEA TALES FROM THE RECOLLECTION OF REAR-ADMIRAL CHARLES E. CLARK. As related to James Morris Morgan and John Phillips Marquand, NF.

1921

"The Right That Failed," *Saturday Evening Post*, July 23, SS.

[*] It has not been possible to include, in this list of Marquand's published work, the many articles, stories, and humorous pieces he wrote as a *Harvard Lampoon* staffer and editor, or pieces written as a reporter and feature writer for the *Boston Transcript* and the *New York Herald,* or the various "fugitive" pieces he produced during his early writing years. Also not included are the many reviews he wrote as a judge for the Book-of-the-Month Club *News.* Check list is based on the John P. Marquand bibliographies prepared by William White.

1922

"The Unspeakable Gentleman," *Ladies' Home Journal*, February, March, May, SN.

THE UNSPEAKABLE GENTLEMAN, N.

"Only a Few of Us Left," *Saturday Evening Post*, January
14, 21, SN.

"Eight Million Bubbles," *Saturday Evening Post*, January
28, SS.

"Different from Other Girls," *Ladies' Home Journal*, July, SS.

"How Willie Came Across," *Saturday Evening Post*, July 8, SS.

"The Land of Bunk," *Saturday Evening Post*, September 16, SS.

"Captain of His Soul," *Saturday Evening Post*, November 4,
SS.

1923

FOUR OF A KIND ("The Right That Failed," "Different from
Other Girls," "Eight Million Bubbles," "Only a Few of Us
Left"), SS collection.

"The Ship," *Scribner's Magazine*, January, SS.

"The Sunbeam," *Saturday Evening Post*, January 20, SS.

"By the Board," *Saturday Evening Post*, March 17, SS.

1924

"The Jervis Furniture," *Saturday Evening Post*, April 26, SS.

"The Black Cargo," *Saturday Evening Post*, September 20
through October 18, SN.

"'Pozzi of Perugia,'" *Saturday Evening Post*, November 8
through 22, SN.

"A Friend of the Family," *Saturday Evening Post*, December
13, SS.

1925

THE BLACK CARGO, N.

LORD TIMOTHY DEXTER OF NEWBURYPORT, MASS.,
NF.

"The Educated Money," *Saturday Evening Post*, February 14,
SS.

"The Big Guys," *Saturday Evening Post*, February 21, SS.

"The Foot of the Class," *Saturday Evening Post*, March 21, SS.
"Much Too Clever," *Saturday Evening Post*, April 25, SS.
"The Old Man," *Saturday Evening Post*, June 6, SS.
"The Jamaica Road," *Saturday Evening Post*, July 4, SS.
"The Last of the Hoopwells," *Saturday Evening Post*, December 5, SS.

1926
"Fun and Neighbors," *Saturday Evening Post*, February 20, SS.
"A Thousand in the Bank," *Saturday Evening Post*, May 1, SS.
"The Tea Leaves," *Saturday Evening Post*, May 8, SS.
"The Blame of Youth," *Saturday Evening Post*, May 29, SS.
"The Spitting Cat," *Saturday Evening Post*, July 3, SS.
"Good Morning, Major," *Saturday Evening Post*, December 11, SS.

1927
"The Artistic Touch," *Saturday Evening Post*, February 19, SS.
"The Cinderella Motif," *Saturday Evening Post*, March 5, SS.
"Once and Always," *Saturday Evening Post*, April 9, SS.
"Lord Chesterfield," *Saturday Evening Post*, June 18, SS.
"The Unknown Hero," *Saturday Evening Post*, July 30, SS.
"The Harvard Square Student," *Saturday Evening Post*, December 10, SS.

1928
"The Last of the Tories," *Saturday Evening Post*, March 24, SS.
"As the Case May Be," *Saturday Evening Post*, June 16, SS.
"Do Tell Me, Doctor Johnson," *Saturday Evening Post*, July 14, SS.
"Three Rousing Cheers," *Cosmopolitan*, August, SS.
"Aye, in the Catalogue," *Saturday Evening Post*, August 11, SS.
"The Good Black Sheep," *Saturday Evening Post*, August 25, SS.

1929
"Warning Hill," *Saturday Evening Post*, March 23 through April 20, SN.

"End of the Story," *Collier's*, April 6, SS.
"Oh, Major, Major," *Saturday Evening Post*, April 27, SS.
"Mr. Goof," *Saturday Evening Post*, May 4, SS.
"Rain of Right," *Saturday Evening Post*, May 11, SS.
"And Another Redskin—," *Saturday Evening Post*, May 18, SS.
"Darkest Horse," *Saturday Evening Post*, May 25, SS.
"The Powaw's Head," *Saturday Evening Post*, July 20, SS.

1930
WARNING HILL, N.
"Bobby Shaftoe," *Saturday Evening Post*, February 8, SS.
"Leave Her, Johnny—Leave Her," *Saturday Evening Post*, March 15, SS.
"Simon Pure," *Collier's*, July 5, SS.
"The Same Things," *Saturday Evening Post*, August 2, SS.
"The Master of the House," *Saturday Evening Post*, September 27, SS.
"There is a Destiny," *Saturday Evening Post*, November 8, SS.
"Rainbows," *Saturday Evening Post*, December 20, SS.

1931
"Golden Lads," *Saturday Evening Post*, February 14, SS.
"All Play," *Woman's Home Companion*, April, SS.
"Upstairs," *Saturday Evening Post*, August 8, SS.
"Tolerance," *Saturday Evening Post*, October 17, SS.
"Gentlemen Ride," *Saturday Evening Post*, November 7, SS.
"Call Me Joe," *Saturday Evening Post*, November 28, SS.

1932
"Ask Him," *Saturday Evening Post*, January 23, SS.
"The Music," *Saturday Evening Post*, February 6, SS.
"Deep Water," *Saturday Evening Post*, February 20, SS.
"Sold South," *Saturday Evening Post*, March 12, SS.
"Jine the Cavalry," *Saturday Evening Post*, April 16, SS.
"Jack Still," *Saturday Evening Post*, June 11, SS.
"Far Away," *Saturday Evening Post*, August 13, SS.
"High Tide," *Saturday Evening Post*, October 8, SS.
"Dispatch Box No. 3," *Saturday Evening Post*, November 5, SS.
"Fourth Down," *Saturday Evening Post*, November 19, SS.

1933

HAVEN'S END, N.

"Number One Good Girl," *Saturday Evening Post,* October 14, SS.

1934

" 'Winner Take All,' " *Saturday Evening Post,* January 20 through February 17, SN.

"Davy Jones," *Saturday Evening Post,* March 3, SS.

"Blockade," *Saturday Evening Post,* March 24, SS.

"Step Easy, Stranger," *Saturday Evening Post,* April 14, SS.

"Lord and Master," *Collier's,* April 21, SS.

"Time for Us to Go," *Saturday Evening Post,* April 28, SS.

"Take the Man Away," *Saturday Evening Post,* May 12, SS.

"Back Pay," *American Magazine,* August, SS.

"Ming Yellow," *Saturday Evening Post,* December 8 through January 12, 1935. SN

1935

MING YELLOW, N.

"Mr. Moto Takes a Hand," *Saturday Evening Post,* March 30 through May 4, SN.

NO HERO ("Mr. Moto Takes a Hand"), N.

"Sea Change," *Saturday Evening Post,* May 25, SS.

"A Flutter in Continentals," *Saturday Evening Post,* June 8, SS.

"You Can't Do That," *Saturday Evening Post,* June 22, SS.

"What's It Get You?" *Saturday Evening Post,* July 13, SS.

"Yankee Notion," *Saturday Evening Post,* November 2, SS.

1936

"Thank You, Mr. Moto," *Saturday Evening Post,* February 8 through March 14, SN.

THANK YOU, MR. MOTO, N.

"Hang It on the Horn," *Saturday Evening Post,* March 21, SS.

"No One Ever Would," *Saturday Evening Post,* April 7, SS.

"A Young Man of Great Promise," *Liberty,* June 13, SS.

"Put Those Things Away," *Saturday Evening Post,* June 20, SS.

"The Road Turns Back: The Author in Search of Earthly Paradise," *Forum,* September, NF.

"Think Fast, Mr. Moto," *Saturday Evening Post*, September 12
through October 17, SN.

"Don't You Cry for Me," *Saturday Evening Post*, November
21, SS.

"Troy Weight," *Saturday Evening Post*, December 5, SS.

"The Late George Apley," *Saturday Evening Post*, November
28 through January 9, 1937, SN.

1937

THE LATE GEORGE APLEY, N.

THINK FAST, MR. MOTO, N.

"The Marches Always Pay," *Saturday Evening Post*, January
30, SS.

"The Maharajah's Flower," *Saturday Evening Post*, March
27, SS.

" '3-3-8,' " *Saturday Evening Post*, April 10 through May
15, SN.

"Just Break the News," *Saturday Evening Post*, July 3, SS.

"Pull, Pull Together," *Saturday Evening Post*, July 24, SS.

"Think Fast, Mr. Moto," screenplay by Howard Ellis and
Norman Foster, August, MP.

"Everything Is Fine," *Collier's*, October 9, SS.

"Thank You, Mr. Moto," screenplay by Willis Cooper and
Norman Foster, December, MP.

1938

" 'Castle Sinister,' " *Collier's*, February 12 through March
26, SN.

"Mr. Moto's Gamble," screenplay by Charles Belden and
Jerry Cady, March, MP.

"Shirt Giver," *Saturday Evening Post*, April 30, SS.

"Mr. Moto Takes a Chance," screenplay by Lou Breslow and
John Patrick, June, MP.

"Mr. Moto Is So Sorry," *Saturday Evening Post*, July 2 through
August 13, SN.

"Mysterious Mr. Moto," screenplay by Philip MacDonald and
Norman Foster, October, MP.

MR. MOTO IS SO SORRY, N.

1939
"Wickford Point," *Saturday Evening Post*, January 28 through March 11, SN.

"Mr. Moto's Last Warning," screenplay by Philip MacDonald and Norman Foster, January, MP.

"Mr. Moto in Danger Island," screenplay by Philip Milne, April, MP.

"Beginning Now—," *Saturday Evening Post*, April 8, SS.

"Do You Know the Brills?" *Saturday Review of Literature*, April 29, NF (humor).

"Mr. Moto Takes a Vacation," screenplay by Philip MacDonald and Norman Foster, July, MP.

"Don't Ask Questions," *Saturday Evening Post*, September 30 through November 11, SN.

WICKFORD POINT, N.

1940
"Gone Tomorrow," *McCall's*, September through January, 1941, SN.

"Come On, Prince," *McCall's*, March, SS.

"March On, He Said," *Saturday Evening Post*, June 29, SS.

"Children's Page," *Saturday Evening Post*, August 31, SS.

1941
H. M. PULHAM, ESQUIRE ("Gone Tomorrow"), N.

"My Boston: A Note on the City by Its Best Critic," *Life*, March 24, NF.

"These Are People Like Ourselves," *Asia*, July, NF.

"Mercator Island," *Collier's*, September 6 through October 25, SN.

"H. M. Pulham, Esquire," screenplay by Elizabeth Hill, December, MP.

1942
LAST LAUGH, MR. MOTO ("Mercator Island"), N.

"Merry Christmas, All," *Cosmopolitan*, January, SS.

"Doctor's Orders," *Collier's*, May 9, SS.

"Taxi Dance," *Good Housekeeping*, May, SS.

"Good Soldiers Can't Be Introverts," *Harper's Bazaar*, June, NF.

"It's Loaded, Mr. Bauer," *Collier's*, June 13 through August 1, SN.

1943
SO LITTLE TIME, N.
"The Island," *Good Housekeeping*, September, SS.
"I Heard an Old Man Say," *Good Housekeeping*, October, SS.

1944
"The Late George Apley," with George S. Kaufman, P.
"The End Game," *Good Housekeeping*, March, SS.

1945
"Iwo Jima Before H-Hour," *Harper's Magazine*, May, NF.
"Lunch at Honolulu," *Harper's Magazine*, August, SS.
"Repent in Haste," *Harper's Magazine*, October, November, SN.
REPENT IN HASTE, N.

1946
B. F.'S DAUGHTER, N.

1947
"The Late George Apley," screenplay by Philip Dunne, April, MP.
"Why the Navy Needs Aspirin," *Harper's Magazine*, August, NF.
"Close to Home," *Good Housekeeping*, November, SS.
"Banking Is an Art," *Atlantic Monthly*, November through January, 1948, SN.

1948
"B. F.'s Daughter," screenplay by Luther Davis, March, MP.
"Point of No Return," *Ladies' Home Journal*, December through April 1949, SN.

1949
POINT OF NO RETURN (incorporating "Banking Is an Art"), N.

"Return Trip to the Stone Age," *Atlantic Monthly*, April, NF.
"Fitzgerald: 'This Side of Paradise.'" *Saturday Review of Literature*, August 6, NF (book review).

1950
"Sun, Sea, and Sand," *Cosmopolitan*, May SS.
"The Gargle Case," *Flair*, August (reprinted from the *Harvard Lampoon*, 1914), NF (humor).

1951
"Melville Goodwin, U.S.A.," *Ladies' Home Journal*, May through December, SN.
MELVILLE GOODWIN, U.S.A., N.

1952
"Point of No Return," by Paul Osborn, P.
"Inquiry into the Military Mind," *New York Times Magazine*, March 30, NF.
"Two's Company," *McCall's*, November, SS.

1953
"Boston," *Holiday*, November, NF.

1954
THIRTY YEARS, collection of short fiction and nonfiction.
"Sincerely, Willis Wayde," *Ladies' Home Journal*, November through March, 1955, SN.

1955
"'Happy Knoll' Series," *Sports Illustrated*, June through November, SS.
SINCERELY, WILLIS WAYDE, N.

1956
"'Happy Knoll' Series," *Sports Illustrated*, February, May, July, August, SS.
NORTH OF GRAND CENTRAL: THREE NOVELS OF NEW ENGLAND ("The Late George Apley," "Wickford Point," "H. M. Pulham, Esquire").

"Apley, Wickford Point, and Pulham: My Early Struggles,"
Atlantic Monthly, September, NF.

"Top Secret Affair" ("Melville Goodwin, U.S.A."), screenplay
by Roland Kibbe and Allan Scott, MP.

"Rendezvous in Tokyo," *Saturday Evening Post,* November 24
through January 12, 1957, SN.

1957

LIFE AT HAPPY KNOLL, SS collected from *Sports Illustrated.*

STOPOVER: TOKYO ("Rendezvous in Tokyo"), N.

"Stopover: Tokyo," screenplay by Richard L. Breen and Walter
Reisch, MP.

1958

"Women and Thomas Harrow," *Ladies' Home Journal,* July
through November, SN.

WOMEN AND THOMAS HARROW, N.

1960

TIMOTHY DEXTER, REVISITED, NF.

*I*ndex